LEARNING SERVICE

DEDICATION

We dedicate this book to our beloved co-author Zahara Heckscher (1964-2018) who died only days after we submitted the final manuscript for publication. She had been battling cancer for nearly a decade. Zahara was a social justice activist to the core—campaigning against racism as a student, fighting against apartheid in the eighties, and in recent years risking arrest by standing up to big pharma to keep cancer medications accessible. Zahara was a role model for the path we advocate for in this book; she lived by her values and was committed to lifelong learning.

PRAISE FROM...

Noam Chomsky: *Philosopher, historian, social critic, author and activist*
"This is an extraordinary contribution to the conversation on what effective volunteer service looks like, and how a learning service approach enriches volunteers and communities in equal measure. This book brings together theory, practice, and the wisdom of experience to map the landscape of challenges and opportunities you'll face before you leave, when you arrive, and after you return home. A manifesto for doing good well, this is an indispensable book for anyone volunteering overseas."

Elizabeth Becker: *Author of* Overbooked: The Exploding Business of Travel and Tourism
"Learning Service is a must read for anyone considering volunteer tourism. Whether you are a would-be volunteer or an organization sending volunteer tourists abroad, this wise book gives clear warnings about the manifold and serious mistakes being made through insensitivity to outright corruption. The authors use their own years of trial and error, as well as a deep understanding of current research, to guide us to a humane and deeply-satisfying approach to helping ourselves learn through service."

Philip Goodwin: *CEO of Voluntary Service Overseas (VSO)*
"Over the last few decades, international volunteering has grown in popularity, accessibility, and complexity. Learning Service explores the challenges for the sector, tackling the ethics and impact of international volunteering while simultaneously offering one simple message: if you want to help, you have to be willing to learn. It is packed with real-life stories that are in turn engaging and entertaining, as well as giving pause for thought. Learning Service's core message seamlessly aligns with VSO's People First theory of change, developed through six decades of experience in this field. This is recommended reading for all those considering volunteering in a developing country."

Steve Gwenin: CEO of Global Vision International (GVI)

"Learning Service is a great tool for anyone who wishes to help others, whether that be through international development, volunteering or simply helping friends or family. It has a simple message in its core, if you wish to really help, you must learning how to do it, and how not to do it! The book is accessible, and often humorous, whilst reflecting current global community learning and best practice in a complex field ethics and full of potentially unforeseen outcomes (both good and bad). It should be essential reading for all people looking to volunteer and I will be strongly recommending every volunteer's journey starts with this book!"

Rishi Bhandari: Volunteer Host and Educational Travel Guide

"Growing up in Nepal I witnessed the upsurge of volunteer tourism, noticing the mismatch between what the volunteers thought they were doing and the actual impact of their actions. I had always wished that there was a way to call them out on this and help volunteers understand the complexity of the issues they were engaging in, and also transform what they were doing for the better. Reading this book I saw my wish had come true. I hope it lands into the hands of every single person who wants to do 'service' to the world, as it will have a profound impact on the way they choose to do it."

Costas Christ: Editor-at-Large and Senior Advisor, National Geographic Travel

"If you are among the growing number of today's travelers eager to give back in a positive way to the people and places you visit, then read this book now. The authors provide a profound understanding of what it takes to have a meaningful volunteer experience abroad with important insights that will also help guide you on a lifelong journey to make the world a better place."

Frances Moore Lappé: Author of 19 books including Diet for a Small Planet, and Co-Founder of Food First: Institute for Food and Development Policy

"Volunteering overseas is life changing, and getting and giving the most from it requires an experienced partner. Learning Service is that partner, as the authors offer their combined lifetimes of accumulated knowledge. Gain insight and confidence for an adventure more rewarding than you'd ever imagined."

Ayelet Waldman: Bestselling author of Bad Mother: A Chronicle of Maternal Crimes, Minor Calamities, and Occasional Moments of Grace

"An illuminating approach to international volunteering, this book will help you change lives for the better, including your own. Seasoned travelers as well as first-time volunteers will find the stories presented here fascinating and thought-provoking, timely and awe-inspiring. More than just a guide to volunteering, this is a tribute to activism in all its forms."

Ben Keene: Founder of Tribewanted and Co-Lead of Escape the City's Escape School

"The idea of helping out people less well-off than you in an exotic land is an intoxicating force. It's never been easier to 'volunteer abroad'. But only if matching good intention and wanderlust would simply guarantee sustainable development and a better, fairer world. Unfortunately it's not that simple. Thank goodness for the guidance of Learning Service to help us navigate the potential and pitfalls of this brave new world."

Daniela Kon: Founder of Social Impact Media Awards (SIMA)

"Everyone who has ever intended to make a change, or is in the midst of doing it should read this book, re-trace their steps, and go out re-fueled to do it better. Learning Service is both the journal and ammunition to participate in building a better world. It's the Art of War for responsible and impactful travel."

Kristin Lamoureux Visiting Professor of Hospitality and Tourism, Virginia Tech University

"Learning Service fills a critical gap in the volunteering abroad literature. The authors pool their vast experience in service learning, international volunteering and tourism, together to create an essential tool for those seeking to do go while traveling. Educators and students embarking on an international volunteer experiences or study abroad need to read this book. Understanding how volunteering helps, but can also do terrible harm is the responsibility of each and every person seeking to volunteer. The authors lead the reader through the important process of preparing yourself, reviewing your options, understanding the skills you need to be successful and then the important process of pre, during and post trip preparation and processing. Too many well-intentioned volunteer experiences either have little impact or far worse, actually cause harm to the people and place the volunteer was seeking to help. Learning Service is a must-read for those seeking to help, not harm."

Rithy Thul: Founder of SmallWorld Cambodia and Frequent Volunteer Host

"Volunteering is a good thing that we do for the world and for ourselves. It's especially for ourselves. One must learn how to serve, to volunteer, to help, to support. In Cambodia, we have seen a lot of wrongdoing from those who want to make profit out of volunteers' money, while at the same time also taking money from the people who the volunteers intended to serve and help. Learning Service will help volunteers identify good organizations. Most importantly, this book will help people be better volunteers and good ambassadors for the future volunteers who come after them."

Cho Choch: Founder of Local Trail Adventures and experienced volunteer host

"As someone who has hosted many volunteers in my home country, I think Learning Service's approach is the best guideline for those who seek to volunteer responsibly abroad and aim to have a positive and long lasting impact. This book helps volunteers to ask the rights questions, contact the right projects or organizations, and prepare themselves to contribute and learn. Through growing up and living in Cambodia, I've seen lots of unskilled volunteers who come into my country with the idea of "saving Cambodia" or "changing Cambodia". I have found the language used and actions taken to be patronizing and if anything, disempowering. Often volunteers have come and not asked what's needed, but assumed what's needed. For example, wells have been built, without asking why a well, just a metre away, is broken and remains unfixed. This is why a book such as this is so needed, inspiring learning before serving."

Reed Harwood: Executive Director of Where There Be Dragons
"If you seek meaningful and impactful travel experiences, this book is a must read. The pedagogy of Learning Service is foundational to responsible travel, and has become a cornerstone principle for Where There Be Dragons' cross-cultural engagement."

Tara Winkler: Founder of Cambodian's Children's Trust, author of How Not to Start an Orphanage (By a Woman Who Did)
"The desire to help others is one of the most remarkable traits human beings possess, but the truth is, our good intentions are not enough. Well-meaning help can lead to devastating, unintended consequences. The stories within these pages taught me valuable lessons and played a vital role in changing the trajectory of my life and work in Cambodia. This book is mandatory reading for anyone interested in helping others by volunteering overseas. It should be in every school, every library and every institution of higher learning as it encourages us all to not only become responsible global citizens, but to help in the right way, with eyes wide open."

Lily Lapenna: Social Impact Coach and Founder of MyBnk
"The book I wish had accompanied me years ago as I set out on my volunteering adventures. If you are volunteering abroad and want to redefine the 'doing good' status quo, this book is for you. With vivid stories of what worked and what didn't, this book will nurture your desire to be open, to question, to learn and to 'do good' better."

Tom Scott: Founder of Nantucket Nectars and The Nantucket Project
"This book has spirit, passion and clarity aplenty. Learning Service encourages us to put listening first—something we all could do more of. This book is a very practical guide for anyone considering international volunteerism, but it also uses real stories from the field that everyone can (and should) learn from."

Thavry Thon: Author of A Proper Woman
"Cambodia is one of the most targeted countries for volunteering. People who have good hearts but not much expertise in the thing they are going to do for their volunteer work could cause more harm than good. I have seen volunteers who have the aim to "save Cambodia" yet they are helping local families building

vegetable gardens while they don't even know how to plant the seeds. Often times, most of the work is done by the local people, but when the volunteers leave, they put their name on the project so that they feel good about it and can show their work to everyone back home. This is not right. Learning Service could be a very powerful tool to help millions of those who are going to do such volunteers projects in emerging markets."

Eric Glustrom: CEO and Founder of Watson Institute
"Learning Service provides anyone looking to make the world a better place — whether a first time volunteer or experienced veteran in the field — a set of frameworks, stories, and a philosophy behind how we can all best serve in a complex, global context."

Emily Braucher: CEO of ReFresh Communication
"Had I read this book before I left for the Peace Corps 20 years ago, I might have had the courage to be really honest with the question: who is really getting the most out of this experience? I thought that my youthful energy and eagerness to help would be enough to make me an effective volunteer. I soon found myself in a mess of politics, new faces, a foreign language and utter discouragement. The framework of "learning service" would have humbled my eagerness and prompted me to think more critically about the impact I was having in this new culture. I am now a professional in the field of intercultural competence due to all the mistakes and fumbles I made during my time abroad, but this book gives you the opportunity to shortcut many novice fumbles and sets you up to hit the ground running. The book emphasizes something that took me years to learn: when we want to help others, we need to start by understanding ourselves. The stories will guide you away from classic volunteerism traps and teach you how to navigate this massive industry with true intelligence. It is a must for anyone who is looking to be an effective volunteer and looking to have a profound international experience they can feel proud of."

Lindsay Morris: Director of The Nantucket Project Academy
"Part thought-provoking expose, part how-to guide, Learning Service is a timely resource for prospective volunteers and anyone interested in international development. As the problem

of misguided and damaging social volunteerism continues to worsen, this book has the power to turn volunteers into learners and developing communities into teachers."

Conor Grennan: Author of Little Princes: One Man's Promise to Bring Home the Lost Children of Nepal
"Learning Service should be required reading for anyone looking to volunteer abroad. The stories in this book illustrate the obstacles and pitfalls that everyone will face at one time or another, and is chock full of lessons from experienced volunteers on how to avoid them. If you are going to invest your time and resources in volunteering, you need to read this book."

Claire Diaz-Ortiz: Author of 8 books including Twitter for Good
"This is the book I wish I'd had before my first trip abroad. It's an essential guide for helping navigate the complex learning that comes with international travel and the self-reflection that is necessary to understand hidden power dynamics. Thank you for this resource!"

Beathe Øgård: President of SAIH and Radi-Aid
"Volunteering programs are expanding rapidly. Before we even decide to go, we should start by questioning our intentions: Why volunteer abroad? Is it for ourselves or do we really want to make a difference? I would definitely check out this book before traveling. It's a very concrete, critical and useful guide to how we can do it better. Even though we are equipped with good intentions and harm is not intended, many volunteers and travelers end up playing the role of the white savior and reinforce stereotypes about poverty. When you travel to work as a volunteer you have a chance to provide nuanced information, talk about the complexities and tell something different than the one-sided story about poverty and pity. Put this book in your bag, learn from the practical advice, and you'll be on the right track!"

THE ESSENTIAL GUIDE
TO VOLUNTEERING ABROAD

CLAIRE BENNETT   JOSEPH COLLINS
ZAHARA HECKSCHER   DANIELA PAPI-THORNTON

red press

Red Press Ltd.
Learning Service: The Essential Guide to Volunteering Abroad
Claire Bennett, Joseph Collins, Zahara Heckscher, Daniela
Papi-Thornton

Cover design by Leah McDowell, ELEMdesign
Band-Aid graphic (page 70) by DEEDA Productions
Printed in England by TJ International (Cornwall)
Typeset in Poppins

Published by Red Press Ltd.
ISBN 978 1 912157 068 (Paperback)
ISBN 978 1 912157 075 (Ebook)

A catalogue record for this book is available from the British Library

Red Press Ltd. Registered Offices:
6 Courtenay Close, Wareham, Dorset, BH20 4ED, England

www.redpress.co.uk
@redpresspub

TABLE OF CONTENTS

GETTING STARTED

Perspective: A Tumultuous Relationship With Volunteer Travel
By Daniela

Volunteer travel and I have had a tumultuous relationship. We never officially got divorced, but we've certainly had our moments of true love and, at other times, calls for a separation. Currently, I'd put our relationship status as 'it's complicated.'

I fell in love with volunteering while mixing my first bag of cement in Nepal, helping a woman build a new house. I can close my eyes and still see her in her sari, shoveling cement, and I can still remember the songs I learned to sing on our hike through the foothills of the Himalayas: *Resham phiriri, resham phiriri...*

On that first trip to Nepal, I viewed volunteer travel as a way to do good in the world while exploring it, and I was thrilled to think that I was making a tangible difference in someone's life. The visit ended with tearful goodbyes and talk of returning. By the time I got on the plane, I was already dreaming of my next volunteer trip. Over the next decade, I volunteered all over the world: helping to build homes in Papua New Guinea, clear debris in post-tsunami Sri Lanka, paint a school in Thailand, and interview entrepreneurs for a microfinance project in Honduras. Inspired by these trips, I founded PEPY Tours, a travel company in

Cambodia, to help other people experience the positive effects of volunteering abroad and to support education projects in rural areas.

It was in Cambodia that my relationship with volunteer travel became strained. The PEPY Tours team and I led groups of volunteers from all over the world on trips in an effort to help local nonprofit organizations and rural schools. We painted murals, awarded bikes to graduating students, filled libraries with books, and brought visiting foreigners into schools to teach classes for a few days. At first, I ended these trips proud that travelers were contributing to education in rural Cambodia and, at the same time, reporting that they had "the best week of their life." Cambodia, however, was the first place I stuck around after the rest of the volunteers left and the excitement of volunteering faded away into real life. Once the travelers had moved on and the 'Thank You' banners had been taken down, I discovered that real life was less glamorous than volunteering; in fact, real life was sometimes depressing. Improving education in rural Cambodia was complicated, and my experiences over time were not as rosy as those I recalled from my first volunteer trips.

I started to realize that we were investing in English classes when most students still hadn't learned to read and write in Khmer, that giving away bikes threatened to put the local bicycle shops out of business, and that bringing volunteers into a classroom for a few days was a lot of fun but might not do much more than gain us some Facebook 'likes.' Later we recognized that by promoting interactions with adults who were not properly screened, we could be putting children at risk of harm. I began to understand that not all volunteer projects were created equal. In fact, it slowly became clear to me that some volunteer trips were actually doing damage. I didn't want to believe it at first, but, as I watched increasing numbers of volunteers come through Cambodia on trips organized by PEPY Tours and other travel companies, I saw that even those of us with the best of intentions were fueling a system gone awry.

Money can put a strain on any relationship. With the surge of money into international volunteering in Cambodia, more and more problems developed. Volunteers' wishes were prioritized over local project needs, as these 'clients' began demanding the feel-good experiences they felt they had paid for. Over the years, I witnessed the opening of increasing numbers of organizations funded primarily through the fees paid by volunteer travelers. Shrewd entrepreneurs disguised their organizations as nonprofits—a misnomer, as some were not only making significant profits but were also lacking any concrete or measurable social mission.

One of the most disturbing trends I saw was the growing number of so-called orphanages, run like businesses, which welcomed an endless stream of volunteers to play with vulnerable children and then squeezed the volunteers for donations. The number of visitors to Cambodia increased from about 750,000 per year when I first visited in 2002, to more than 3 million per year when I moved out of Cambodia a decade later. According to a study commissioned by the United Nations and the Cambodian government, within this time, the number of actual orphans in Cambodia decreased, yet the number of children in orphanage care nearly doubled. More than three-quarters of the children living in these institutions are believed to have one or both living parents. I started to realize that the rising number of fake orphans was linked to the rising numbers of tourists, and that volunteer travel was part of the problem rather than the solution.

I realized that in many cases, these orphanages had an incentive to keep the children under their care in dire conditions, because visiting volunteers often stated a desire to give their time and money to the places that looked like they had the greatest need. It was almost as if orphanages were in competition to keep their children in the poorest conditions in order to attract foreign support. Volunteers lent their time, fundraising efforts, and an air of international legitimacy to these orphanages while at the same time, the orphanage owners sometimes pressured or even paid parents to give up their children with false promises of better care thanks to the presence of foreigners. In effect, the good intentions of volunteers were fueling corrupt institutions to break up families. Unnecessarily separating children from their parents led to an array of devastating problems for children, ranging from emotional damage to physical abuse—the exact opposite of most volunteers' intentions. Even after I stopped taking volunteers to orphanages on my own trips, I felt complicit as I watched more and more well-meaning volunteers and donors buy into this harmful treatment of vulnerable children.

Over time, I have learned that this problem is not unique to Cambodia. In many countries around the world, children in orphanages are exploited to attract volunteers and generate income. Despite the growing movement to publicize these abuses, orphanage volunteering remains one of the top-five most-searched volunteer program types.

Unfortunately, exploitative orphanages were not the only volunteer travel problem I encountered. I used to think of volunteer travel as the most responsible form of travel, but while working in Cambodia, I came to understand that it was in fact part of a wider system of international development. As I learned more about best practices in development, I began to suspect that volunteer travel was the least sustainable intervention on the development spectrum. In my head I replayed the movie of my relationship with volunteer travel, and all those weeks I had once seen as "the best weeks of my life" started to look more like scenes from a horror movie, or at least a really bad soap opera.

Then an actual movie came out: a documentary with footage from the founding years of PEPY, "Changing the World on Vacation." I realized I had learned a lot about how volunteer travel could be improved in the intervening years, because the film showed me making all of the old mistakes! Watching it, I had to cover my eyes in embarrassment at images of our volunteer groups playing blaring music and dancing with kids who should have been in school. At screenings of the film, I found myself trying to explain why others should not try to emulate what we had done, and I started questioning why I had gotten into this relationship with volunteer travel in the first place.

But there were other scenes in that movie, and in my day-to-day life, that reminded me why I had originally fallen in love with this work. I had met people who demonstrated what living life through their values looked like. Cho, a trip leader at PEPY Tours, decided to align his daily life with his goals for environmental protection and inspired people around the world by taking one action every day to improve the environment. Mickey awed our trip participants with his innovative agricultural and health inventions and his commitment to promoting culturally-appropriate development practices. A group of middle school students from rural Chanleas Dai, after seeing so many foreign volunteers come through their school, took the development of their community into their own hands and created an award-winning organization with the help of some exceptional local teachers. The list goes on.

I believed in parts of the work we were doing, but felt that the model for how we were approaching international volunteering was inherently flawed. I eventually realized that our service trip model was focused too much on serving and not enough on learning. We needed to shift not only the impact that volunteers were having on the communities we were 'serving,' but also the impact on the travelers themselves. We had been telling international volunteers they could hop off the plane and immediately help in a country that wasn't their own, with a culture and language they didn't understand. We had been teaching them that they could solve problems *we* defined—we who were also outsiders to the place and issues. My belief that I had an obligation, or at least a right, to bestow my benevolence on others, and my narrow view that volunteer travel was the way to do it, had trickled down into our programs and was fueling an unhealthy sense of superiority among the volunteers. It was as if we saw ourselves as heroes, coming in to save the day, with local people as simply recipients of our good work.

So at PEPY Tours, we began to shift how we framed and operated our programs, from learning as a byproduct of serving others to learning from others as a primary goal of service. This meant a focus on learning about the context of the problems we perceived and whether our 'service' was wanted or needed at all. And if it was, we needed to learn how it might best be offered and about the spectrum of ways in which we might be of help. We started to emphasize personal development and an understanding of the historical and cultural context of Cambodia. Thus, through trials, error, and self-reflection – and informed by colleagues from Cambodia and around the world – the concept of *learning service* was born. Instead of offering volunteer trips where travelers tried to improve the world during a few weeks abroad, we stopped offering service projects and began focusing on providing learning trips that would enable our students to have a *lifelong* impact.

In this near break-up with volunteer travel, I decided I needed to try to stop others from making the same mistakes I had made. I became a vocal critic of mainstream volunteer travel, writing articles about the topic for media outlets such as the BBC and *The Huffington Post*, doing TEDx talks, and generally getting the word out about the unintended negative consequences I had witnessed while living in Cambodia. I also teamed up with some experienced childcare experts and social workers to help them create a website that exposed the problems with orphanage tourism.

When Zahara Heckscher and Joe Collins approached me about working together to write a book about volunteering abroad, I realized that, rather than continue to complain about the problems I had seen in volunteer travel, I could have a broader and more positive impact by being part of a team spreading messages about how to improve it. Claire Bennett had already been an integral part of creating the learning service model, serving as a trainer, trip instructor, and co-author of the Learning Service Toolkit that PEPY Tours had published online. We felt that, as a team, we had the experience to help shed light on the problems we had seen with volunteer travel while providing practical tools to honor, but refocus, the desire to do good in the world.

The original plan was to publish an updated version of Joe and Zahara's previous book, *How to Live Your Dream of Volunteering Overseas*. However, since its publication in 2002, the field of international volunteering has undergone rapid changes, fueled by the growth the internet, a seemingly unending stream of new volunteer programs, and the rise of short-term 'voluntourism.' What was needed was not just an update but an entirely new book—a book that would both delve deeper into the challenges associated with overseas volunteering and promote a fresh way of framing volunteer work. And that's the book you hold in your hands.

Through the process of capturing and sharing these lessons, I have patched up bits of my relationship with volunteer travel. I have become more hopeful about the positive impact that thoughtful, self-reflective, and humble international travelers can have on the world and on themselves, if they approach other people and cultures with a learning mindset. I have come to believe that shared experiences across cultures, by travelers and local hosts, can contribute to the achievement of our common desires for peace and sustainable prosperity. What it will take to get there, though, is people like you, who are willing to learn before taking action. I know that if I had read this book and learned more about the criticism, as well as the positive potential, of volunteer travel before I jumped in, I could have avoided many of the mistakes I made. I'm grateful you decided to pick up this book. I hope it will serve you well in your ongoing quest to leave the world a better place than you found it.

The Explosion of Volunteer Travel

International volunteer travel is going mainstream at an astounding rate. It's all over the internet: ads on social media, targeted e-marketing, and search-engine results seem limitless. Magazines, from teenage fashion to retiree lifestyle, feature glossy advertisements of happy volunteers and smiling children. Companies offer it as a professional development opportunity or as part of their corporate social responsibility policy. Schools increasingly encourage their students to take it up, sometimes as a way to fulfill graduation requirements. Parents worry that unless their children can list it on their application, they won't be strong candidates for top colleges.

You no longer need to offer up two years of your life to be part of an international service corps. An emerging trend, dubbed 'voluntourism,' consists of short-term volunteer opportunities, sometimes for as little as a few hours, often wrapped into travel packages. It seems that no upstanding global travel company can resist getting on the volunteering bandwagon, both to attract more clients and to ensure its brand is seen as responsible. One study found that 55 percent of US travelers did some form of philanthropy on their trip. This figure is significantly higher in younger age groups, and among millennials who engaged in philanthropic travel, a whopping 81 percent volunteered, for an average of double the length of older age groups. In short, volunteer travel is an increasingly accessible option for anyone seeking to 'give back.'

There is also a lot of money in the volunteer travel business. As many as 10 million volunteers a year are spending up to $2 billion to volunteer abroad. There are hundreds of organizations matching people with volunteer experiences, with dozens of new groups popping up every year. This rapid expansion of volunteer travel has been accompanied by increased attention from the media, academics, and individual commentators. Volunteer tourism companies have attracted criticism for being profit driven, and for failing to benefit – and sometimes harming – the communities they purport to be helping. Many issues are attracting scrutiny: the lack of sustainability and long-term impact of many volunteering projects, insufficient engagement with host communities, poor or even non-existent monitoring of projects, disruption of local markets, risks posed to vulnerable children, and the patronizing approach embodied in some volunteer tourism marketing.

Discussions on the topic of volunteer travel are heated, and controversial articles can go viral. Claire's article in *The Guardian*, discouraging inexperienced volunteers in Nepal after the 2015 earthquake, was shared 150,000 times. Criticisms have seeped so deeply into public consciousness that they have even worked their way into comic parody. 'Gap yah' entered popular lexicon in the UK (as a twist on 'gap year') after a mock video of a student talking on the phone about his enlightening experiences of vomiting abroad attracted nearly 6 million YouTube views. A spoof of "Who Wants to Be a Millionaire?" offered contestants the chance to 'Save Africa!' in the mock game show "Who Wants to Be a Volunteer?" J.K. Rowling, of *Harry Potter* fame, set Twitter on fire with a series of tweets that described voluntourism as treating "poor children as opportunities to enhance Westerners' CVs." All these parodies and critiques are based on a truth: while some international volunteering organizations and projects have a positive impact, a worrying number of them do not.

Navigating the diversity of options while avoiding the pitfalls of volunteer travel is a daunting task. That is where this book comes in. It provides practical advice as well as a new way of thinking about international volunteering: it's an exposé of the problems, a manifesto for what is possible, and a guide for how to get there.

Perspective: Balancing Learning and Action
By Claire

"It's a *vajra*," he said, as he pointed out the metal object in the hand of the statue. "It's an ancient symbol and ritual object used by both Buddhists and Hindus."

(A vajra)

I was speaking with a Tibetan scholar near my home in Nepal, where I have lived for much of the past decade. I had seen these objects before: a metal bar with identical loops at either side, almost like an infinity symbol. Over the years, I had learned about Hindu and Buddhist traditions and heard many stories about the vajra's power, yet I still didn't have a clear grasp of what it represented.

"And its meaning?" I asked.

"There are many. But one way to look at it is as a representation of the balance between wisdom and skillful action," the scholar said. "Too much in one direction upsets the balance. It is said that: *action without learning is ignorance. Learning without action is selfishness.*"

When I brought this aphorism to the *Learning Service* team, they agreed with me that it was the perfect summary of our book. The concept the vajra represents, balancing thoughtful action and self-reflective learning, mirrors the balance we are striving to offer in the learning service model.

We have used this mantra as the framework for this book. The book is written in a linear format, with half of the book focusing on *learning* and half on action in the form of *service*. Of course, the

START

9

real relationship between the two is more like the symbol of the vajra, neither part coming first or last but rather a balance that forms an infinite loop where each part depends on the other.

What is 'Learning Service'?

The balance between learning and action can apply to almost every aspect of life. In this book, we will focus on how it applies to international volunteer travel. We call this *learning service*. Learning service is an approach to international volunteering where:

- Learning is embraced as a primary purpose of a trip abroad, rather than a byproduct. Learning comes first and continues throughout the experience: before, during, and after volunteering overseas.
- Service consists of humble and thoughtful action, designed to 'do no harm.' This service includes the work volunteers do overseas, the unofficial daily interactions they have with people while abroad, and the long-term actions that are inspired by their experience.
- Learning and service interact in an ongoing cycle, with each depending on the other. This loop is fueled by self-reflection – taking the time between activities to think critically about motivations, accomplishments, and challenges – and applying learning to future action.

Learning service is an inversion of the term *service learning* that, in some settings and parts of the world, is used in place of the word *volunteering*. Service learning was coined to acknowledge the learning goals that are part of many volunteer projects. However, in this framing, 'learning' appears to be secondary. With 'learning service,' we have flipped the term to put learning front and center: it is the emphasis of our approach and a key to mitigating the sometimes negative impacts of international service.

Fundamental to learning service is the idea is that 'we have to learn before we can help.' This means that before volunteering, you need to learn about the potential pitfalls of international volunteering, examine your motivations and options thoroughly, understand the context and culture of communities overseas, and ask how to put your skills and experience to use. The action you take should aim to tackle root causes, be done with openness and humility, and may also mean adjusting your lifestyle and priorities at home.

Learning service in practice

We can illustrate the need for the learning service approach by imagining a volunteer hopping off a plane in a foreign country and exclaiming: *Hi! I'm here to help you!*

Although the traveler might learn something along the way, the emphasis of this approach is on 'taking action' first, which can be problematic. Imagine a typical volunteer, a student who arrives in Nairobi, Kenya to 'help' by teaching children in an orphanage, but does not speak Swahili, has no experience as a teacher, and is not trained in how to deal professionally with the emotional problems of vulnerable children. This could also apply to a skilled doctor who arrives in Bhutan to work in a rural clinic, but is not accustomed to working without the technology he has at home, lacks the cultural knowledge to make patients feel comfortable talking with him about their sensitive medical problems, and has no background in the relationship between traditional healers and Western medicine in the Himalayas.

Clearly, taking action before learning in these cases would be ineffective at best, and possibly even harmful. And yet, this is the model that most potential volunteers have been taught to expect—a model repeated thousands of times each day as international volunteers arrive overseas expecting to get right to work and immediately be able to help.

Now imagine a second traveler who follows the learning service approach. This would look more like getting off the plane and saying: *Hi! I'm here to learn from you about how I might be of help, now or in the future.*

The traveler's role flips from 'helping' right away to 'learning,' which re-frames their whole experience. This shift creates different power dynamics and different ways to measure success. In the learning service approach, we don't assume that the people hopping off the plane have the answers. Instead, they have a chance to learn how they can offer effective help by learning

START

from the only people who deeply understand the situation—the individuals who are affected by it. These individuals are the real experts on their true needs, and are the ones best placed to work for lasting change in their own community. Volunteers can join local people as effective advocates and allies, but only once they have put in the work to understand where and how their skills best fit.

In this second scenario, 'taking action' is just as important, but what that looks like has not been fixed in advance. The second traveler doesn't jump off the plane and start to take action in a place where the language, history, relationships, culture, and framing of the problems are all foreign to her. Instead, she acknowledges a need to start by learning, rather than teaching. She learns about herself, in order to understand her motivations and assumptions. She learns about the culture, the language, and the skills needed on her assignment—before she leaves home. Once she arrives, she looks to the local communities for knowledge on how and when she might be able to add value, and she is open to learning from them—including ways in which she can improve herself and her own corner of the world. She lets her learning inform her actions and realizes that the process of 'serving' might take a lot longer than her trip abroad. She then integrates that learning throughout her life, staying open to self-reflection as she takes actions to do good in the world.

This learning service approach is better for both volunteers and hosts. The commitment to learning first and throughout makes for an engaging volunteer journey, as well as making the impact of the service more effective and sustainable. In this book, we'll assist you in applying the learning service approach to your own experiences—enabling you to take effective, responsible, self-reflective action, now and in the future.

What to Expect from this Book

Practical guidance and tools
This book will help you answer your questions about volunteer travel, from how to evaluate a potential volunteer opportunity to how to be effective while abroad. We offer strategies for dealing with common problems and provide practical tools for

everything from staying safe and healthy to dealing with reverse culture shock when you arrive back home.

Support in making the right choices for you

Volunteer travel is complex, and the best option for one person may not be suitable for another. The goal of this book is neither to encourage nor to prevent you from volunteering abroad, but rather to give you the means to make the best decision for you. This book will help you find and evaluate the options that align with your values and priorities. We made a conscious decision not to provide a list of volunteer programs we recommend or suggest you avoid. The field is changing so rapidly that a categorical list of programs would be out of date before this book landed in the bookstore. In addition, a specific volunteer option might be a great fit for one potential volunteer and not for another. Rather than listing recommended programs, we point out effective and harmful practices and strategies to help you ask the right questions and gather information yourself. This way, the advice in this book will be helpful for you regardless of your age, skill level, or interests.

A range of first-person perspectives and insights

You will find provocative first-person vignettes throughout the book—sections that we call 'Perspectives.' These come from us as co-authors and from other experts in the field, providing stories and reflections on some of the challenging issues of international volunteer travel. There are quotes and insights from volunteer travelers around the world—people who participated in programs ranging from agriculture in rural Mexico to education in urban China. We also include the voices and perspectives of overseas volunteer hosts who share stories of the sometimes positive, sometimes ugly impact of volunteers on their communities.

A user-friendly synthesis of current ideas and research

We combined our own original research with that of other practitioners and analysts. We started with dozens of on-the-ground interviews with volunteers and their hosts that Joe and Zahara had gathered for their earlier book—spanning more than 20 countries in Africa, Latin America, Asia, and the Middle East. We then conducted new interviews and surveys of hundreds of volunteer travelers, travel companies, and host organizations. In addition, we had access to studies by top researchers in the field, including Erin Barnhart's PhD research—a comprehensive study of the perspectives of organizations that have hosted international volunteers. (Erin's host perspectives were all collected anonymously. In other cases, where possible, we have attached names to quotes, although some of those we spoke with asked to remain anonymous, especially when sharing critical perspectives.) We read books, scoured scholarly articles, visited volunteer blogs, talked to experts, and watched YouTube videos. We compiled this sometimes-disjointed information into coherent themes and research-based practical tips for volunteers. Thus we were able to compare trends across time and share stories and advice to help you navigate the current state of the volunteer travel sector.

A new way of thinking about volunteer travel

This book sets out a fresh new framework, *learning service*, which radically changes the assumptions and practices of international volunteering. We explore why this new form of travel is needed, exposing the deep and shocking problems with current practices, as well as the benefits of this new approach. Learning service puts learning at the forefront, arguing that before we can effectively 'serve,' first we must learn—about ourselves, our options, and the wider context in which our action takes place. It is this learning-first approach that we set out in this book, both explaining why it is needed, and helping you put it into practice.

Defining our Terms

Throughout the book, boxes like this offer an explanation for how we use controversial words in order to create a shared understanding.

Volunteer travel

'Volunteer travel' covers a broad field, and we use it interchangeably with 'international volunteering,' 'volunteering abroad/overseas,' 'voluntary service' and 'overseas service.' We like the term 'volunteer travel' best because it reminds us that volunteers working abroad are on a journey and need to approach their experiences with as much cultural sensitivity as responsible travelers anywhere. We consider volunteer travel to include work that:

1. Takes place in a country other than the volunteer's own
2. Is designed to do good in the world
3. Is not a paid employment role (though we recognize that some volunteer programs offer stipends that can be higher than the average local income).

The time commitment and other details of volunteer travel vary widely. For the purpose of this book, we include anything from an afternoon clearing non-native plant species in a park in Costa Rica to three years advising public health campaigns in Madagascar.

Overseas, abroad

Many different terms are used to describe the areas where most international volunteer service takes place: 'developing countries,' 'the Third World,' 'poor countries,' 'emerging markets,' 'the Global South,' and many more. Each of these labels is riddled with contradictions, inaccuracies, or stereotypes. We do our best to avoid this problem by referring to specific regions or countries where applicable, and by using more neutral terms such as 'abroad,' 'overseas,' and simply 'other countries.' Our examples tend to come from Africa, Asia and Latin America, but most of the concepts covered in this book will apply no matter where you volunteer, including North America, Australia, the Middle East, or Europe.

ON LEARNING

"The whole of life, from the moment you are born, to the moment you die, is a process of learning."

-Jiddu Krishnamurti

In learning service, learning is embraced as a primary purpose of a trip abroad, to help channel your desire to do good into positive outcomes for yourself and those around you. Learning comes *first*, and this part of the book guides you through the learning you need to do before volunteering overseas. Start with a learning mindset, and challenge your assumptions. Then explore the motivations that drive you in order to work out if, where, and how you might best fit into the puzzle of international volunteering. Don't forget to explore the wider context and the history of volunteer travel; the challenges, mistakes and successes of volunteers that have gone before you. Then explore and weigh up the many options for volunteering so that you can make a decision that is right for you and others.

As you move through the first few parts of this book, we ask you to keep the image of the vajra in mind as you read: learning and action interacting in a never-ending loop. In order for action to be effective it is essential to learn, and learning requires active engagement. Central to this process of learning and acting, what could be referred to as the middle point of the vajra, can be summarized by the command: 'Know thyself!' And that is where we will start.

PART ONE:

LEARNING ABOUT YOURSELF

"The most positive thing about my volunteer experience was getting to know myself and my limits. It made me more aware of who I am and what my good and bad characteristics are. Volunteering also helped me to see what my assets are, where I can contribute in helping others, and how to develop the skills I need to contribute effectively."

–A volunteer who spent over three months in India

When we say *learn first*, many people assume we mean learning about different volunteering opportunities, or the details of a particular country. While that type of learning is also vital, and will be covered in later chapters, learning service starts with looking inwards. In fact, we believe that self-awareness is the single most important quality someone must possess in order to successfully learn about and contribute to the world.

Taking the time to build your own self-awareness might seem like a waste of time when there are real needs in the world that demand immediate action. But when you know yourself well, you will be able to make better decisions about whether or not volunteering overseas is right for you, and, if you do volunteer, what type of role you would be best suited for. By understanding your own motivations and capacity, and critically exploring your assumptions, you will be:

- More open to the new cultures in which you find yourself
- More likely to reflect critically on your actions and improve them, or to change course completely should you realize you are on the wrong path
- A more effective volunteer, who is less likely to make harmful mistakes
- Much better positioned to make a positive contribution to the world—both during and after your volunteer trip.

1.
EMBRACING A LEARNING MINDSET

Perspective: I Needed to Learn Before I Could Teach
By a volunteer who spent two years in West Africa

I was extremely excited when I got my assignment to volunteer in Mali. After spending most of my life up until then as a student and then paper-pusher, I thought I would finally be able to do something useful. My role would be teaching people in rural villages about how to protect their wells from dangerous pathogens, which caused simple-to-prevent but deadly infections among children.

When I arrived in Mali, armed with lots of enthusiasm and a degree in government, I quickly realized that I needed to embrace quite a bit of learning before I could teach anything. Luckily, the volunteer program was set up with a three month training component. I dove into learning the Bambara language, with the help of my host family. I learned about wells, and that chirping frogs were a sign of healthy well water. I learned what to do when a chicken fell into the well—how to disinfect a well. It had never occurred to me that chickens might wander into wells before.

Then I realized my learning needed to go deeper. As I faced some health problems, I had to learn to be honest with myself and others about my physical challenges. I also had to prioritize taking care of myself in order to be of service to others. When I was reassigned to another country in the region, I had to learn how to function in a bureaucracy. And, of course, I had to learn culturally appropriate techniques such as not suggesting anyone use their left hand to pick up a spoon or the shared water cup.

My first experience in Africa ended up with me learning more than I could possibly teach. And almost all of my learning was not from a book or computer, but from the people around me. I learned to listen deeper; to my host family, to the five year-olds, as well as the elders. It wasn't quite what I expected. But that learning was what launched me into a lifelong, rewarding career in international development, continuing to pursue my dream of doing something useful... and continuing to learn!

What is a Learning Mindset?

"I have learned from my experience and encourage everyone else to do the same, but instead of learning afterwards, learn before you go. I cannot express how important it is to challenge your own preconceived ideas, ambitions and motivations and to open yourself up to opposing ideas and lessons before you embark on a life-changing experience. It is okay to be wrong sometimes."
   -Hayley Blythe, who volunteered in Ghana for five weeks

The process of building self-awareness starts with a learning mindset. With a learning mindset, you see every task, difficulty, and encounter as a learning opportunity. You are willing to challenge your own assumptions and stereotypes, and you are committed to being open to new ideas and ways of doing things. Embracing a learning mindset is a cornerstone of learning service.

A learning mindset is important not only for the young. The learning process only gets richer as you gather more experience to inform your judgment and beliefs. Sometimes it is younger volunteers who feel certain that they know all the answers, while more mature volunteers know from experience that they do not. Volunteers of all ages seem to do less harm and more good when they start by welcoming learning instead of starting with what they want to teach.

Getting into a learning mindset is not a one-time action but a way of being that requires ongoing work. Cultivating an awareness of the opportunities for learning and growth starts with self-reflection, but the learning mindset applies to every step of volunteering and therefore every other section of the book. Here are some tips to help you get started:

Re-frame the way you think about learning
See learning not as a mammoth task that looms ahead, or as a dreary chore, but as an opportunity to come alive, achieve your goals, and engage with the world around you. For example, your previous experience of language learning may have been sitting in a classroom trying to memorize verb conjugations for an exam. However, the process of learning a language in the country where you are living can enrich your cultural understanding, build friendships, and add humor to your experience. Instead of sitting in a classroom, you may find that your best language lessons come while buying eggs in the market or helping your homestay family wash the dishes.

Be willing to change your mind
We encourage you to think of changing your mind as an empowering process: a sign that you're growing and developing, rather than a show of weakness. We even suggest rephrasing it to something less loaded: instead of 'changing your mind,' we prefer 'forming new opinions based on new information.' For example, a volunteer we interviewed told us that after a month in Japan, she altered her perspective on how to deal with difficult personalities: "I learned that there is good in almost everyone, so it makes it easier for me to accept people as they are." Zahara had a realization after volunteering in a rural area of Zambia, "I used to think people who lacked formal education were unintelligent, but through my experience I realized that some people who don't know how to read and write have smarts

LEARN

I never even thought about—like knowing how to build a whole house with only a machete, a tree, and mud." Several people told us that what they learned through their experience abroad made them completely change their opinions of volunteer travel, so be open to forming new opinions as you learn!

Ask "why, why, why"

A volunteer who worked in the Philippines, Costa Rica, and Peru told us, "My mindset has focused upon asking why, and trying to discover root causes for these social problems to see what I can do about them." You can practice this "why, why, why" thought exercise with anything to try to gain a more nuanced understanding. It's also a helpful decision-making tool. Asking why can help you to probe the reality of a belief, assumption, or inference and to understand how the root causes of issues are interlinked. For example, if you see children living in an orphanage, you might ask yourself, "Why are they living here?" You might find out that some of the children are not orphans, so the next question could be, "Why did their parents decide to leave them here?" and then "Why did the parents think their children would be better off in an orphanage?" As you peel back the reasons parents might have left them there, and consider the political, social, economic, and cultural factors that influenced them, your 'whys' will lead you closer to the root causes of the situation. You will begin to uncover areas where you need to learn more in order to answer the question or to test your own assumptions about 'why' something happens.

Another great example comes from Mark Watson from the charity Tourism Concern. He talked to a girl who volunteered to build a school in Tanzania. "She told me the volunteers always gossiped about how lazy the locals were because they slept for most of the morning. It was only at the end of the placement that they discovered that every day, after they finished building a wall, the locals had to come and rebuild it again properly." If the volunteers had been more open to asking why from the outset, their morning gossip would have certainly looked different.

You can also use this thought exercise to probe your own ideas about volunteer travel. For example, you could ask, "Why am I attracted to volunteering abroad?" or "Why do I feel this is an effective way for me to create positive change?" Each time you answer, ask yourself *why* you have reached that conclusion, and where you got your supporting information. This will help you to gain a deeper understanding of your assumptions and thought processes.

Root cause

The underlying reason for a problem or issue. Root causes of social problems are often extremely complex and multi-layered. For example, the root cause of a high child mortality rate may be a combination of inadequate education for parents, lack of access to healthcare, prevalence of preventable diseases, and food scarcity. A project that is addressing the root cause tries to create a sustainable solution for one or more of the problems. By contrast, a one-off health camp with western doctors and donated fancy equipment, may look impressive, but will have little long-term impact if it is not addressing the root causes.

Be willing to live with gray zones

When the lack of certainty about an issue feels uncomfortable, many of us tend to seek black-and-white answers. For example, when you see a police officer taking bribes from farmers at an unofficial road checkpoint, you might think the officer is doing something 100 percent wrong. If you dig deeper, however, you might find that he is not paid a living wage, or that he is expected to take bribes and give a cut to his superiors in order to keep his job. The unequivocal sense of blame you initially felt might then become less clear-cut. Seeking out this nuance and being open to the complexity of social issues is essential in order to be able to see how you might contribute to ameliorating them.

Keep a journal

Document your reflections about yourself, your goals for volunteer travel, your learning goals, and observations along the journey. Consider starting this journal now, as you explore your assumptions about volunteering, rather than waiting until you decide to volunteer or until you're on the plane. Whether you keep a record of one sentence a day or a longer journal tracking your daily experiences and inner thoughts, you'll find that writing

LEARN

down your lessons and observations helps you build upon them and grow as you reflect.

Challenging Your Assumptions

"I knew I wanted to go to 'Africa' to volunteer with children. My naivety, as well as a hearty dose of media-fueled stereotyping, meant that to me Africa was one place—full to the brim of need and helpless suffering, which I, as a privileged and caring Westerner, wanted to do something to stop. I wholeheartedly bought into the idea that Africans needed help from Westerners and that this help was indeed something that everyone could quite easily provide in an effective capacity. My intentions were right (as are those of most volunteers), but my comprehension of the situation was basic—I had no clue what African country I would like to visit, nor did I think to research the countries in any detail to learn more about them and counteract my ignorance. All I knew was that I wanted to volunteer in Africa and I figured, although rather subconsciously, that the experience would be the same no matter where I went."

– Ruth Taylor, who volunteered three times in Ghana

When thinking about volunteering in another country, no one starts with a blank slate. From an early age, most of us are bombarded with stories of international volunteers—from media stories about a local church group going to build houses in Puerto Rico for Christmas, to fundraising appeals from friends wanting our support to volunteer with kids in townships in South Africa. These images mix with lessons we have absorbed from our faith traditions, the history textbooks we read as children, and shocking photojournalism from war-torn countries.

Your understanding of the situation in other countries, and the role of outsiders in 'developing' them, has probably been shaped by charity fundraising campaigns or over-simplified news reports. The media tends to glamorize international volunteering and to characterize volunteers as selfless or heroic, often sidelining or not even mentioning the role of local actors.

A representative of a volunteer hosting organization highlighted the need for volunteers to *unlearn* some of these assumptions about volunteers being the stars of the show, saying "People want to come and feel like they 'make a difference,' like it is all about them... We would benefit if volunteers arrived understanding that actually they are the ones who will learn from this experience, and they are the ones who will gain."

Cultivating a learning mindset first requires unlearning— recognizing that things you thought were facts are really just assumptions, cultural viewpoints, or interpretations derived from your own world view. Mary Helen Richter, who volunteered in Vietnam, told us, "Volunteers should either have a really open worldview or a willingness to have their worldview opened. Don't be afraid to acknowledge your prejudices. If you think that you do not have any, then you are pretty naïve."

"It's my responsibility to help poor people overseas," "A college degree is the most important thing needed to have a successful life," and "Everyone appreciates the chance to receive direct feedback," are all opinions disguised as facts. A common assumption in the volunteering world is that 'something is better than nothing.' Someone who makes this assumption might argue that an untrained foreign volunteer teacher is better than no teacher at all—without any evidence that there would be no teacher if the volunteer were not there, and without considering the sustainability of an education system that relies on a stream of short-term volunteers.

Once you recognize that your culture and experiences shape your knowledge, many things you had previously thought were true come into question. You might realize that you were being ethnocentric—that your opinions were formed by your cultural context, your race, your social status, your religious background, or global stereotypes perpetuated by marketing campaigns. As Karin, who volunteered in Nepal for over a year, said, "No matter how well-traveled we are and how big we think our worldview is, our Western lenses definitely impact how we think and how we interact with the rest of the world."

Unlearning can be an uncomfortable process. However, by analyzing your own background and influences and identifying the limitations or biases of the sources of information you have

LEARN

had access to, you will better understand other people's varied perspectives and appreciate that they, too, have developed their beliefs and opinions through their own unique life experiences.

Here are some questions to get you going on your journey of unlearning and learning, starting with your assumptions about volunteer travel:

- How did you hear about volunteer travel? What do you know about it? What opinions do you have about it?
- Where has this information come from? What are the limits of your sources?
- How and why might the media present biased views about international volunteering? Who are the people usually portrayed as heroes in media stories? How have fundraising campaigns influenced your thinking, and what angle do they usually take when portraying foreign countries?
- What do you assume about your own potential role as a volunteer?
- What do you assume about the people you will be working with and 'helping'?

Flipping the Volunteer Travel Perspective

"The most positive aspect of my experience was seeing my own culture through a different lens. Being a part of Nicaraguans' lives really gave me a concrete experience to compare my own white, American privilege. Seeing a community that valued family above all else was the first time I was able to ask, 'Is America really the greatest country in the world?' Maybe America doesn't have it right."

—Volunteer who spent over a month in Nicaragua

One way to try to unpack your assumptions about volunteer travel is to flip the traditional idea of international service on its head. Instead of imagining yourself going abroad to volunteer, consider what it would be like to have foreign volunteers visit your hometown. Think about the area where you grew up, and try to identify a few problems within your community that you would like to change. Now imagine that a group of passionate but inexperienced volunteers from another country – for example, Mongolia – turn up in your hometown offering to help. Maybe they can't speak the same language as you, and they certainly don't know the nuances of your community and your life. They say they are planning to 'help' you for the next month and that they want to 'make a real difference.' Think of practical tasks that you could give them that would contribute to the changes you identified.

- What logistical support would you need to provide (such as accommodation, transport, and meals)?
- What resources would you need to be able to channel the volunteers' positive energy into real impact?
- Could there be any long-term benefits of their help?
- What are the limitations or possible negative consequences?
- Would the activities you planned be in line with the main problems you want to solve, or would you have to create tasks that fit their skills and limitations?
- Would there be more effective ways to solve the problems you identified without these volunteers?
- If an article were written about the volunteers who have shown up to help you, what might it say? How might the representation of the volunteers in the media in their country be different to that in the media in yours? Why? To what extent would each of these media stories be a fair representation of the situation, and what might be inaccurate?

LEARN

Ethnocentrism

The conscious or subconscious belief that the way something is done in your own culture is the way it is, or should be, done everywhere. Volunteers can be ethnocentric when they assume that they understand a problem in another country without learning from local people first.

You can use your thoughts from this exercise to reflect on your own plans and perspectives on volunteer travel, asking questions such as:

- What parallels and lessons can you draw that relate to your own travel or volunteer plans?
- If volunteering could be more truly *inter-national* and people from the countries you volunteer in would have a chance to, in turn, come to your community to help, would you support it?
- While attending a poverty-alleviation conference that Daniela was at, a Ghanaian director of a nonprofit stood up to say, "We don't send people over to the US to help with the emotional poverty we see in the US: with unhappy people, broken family units, and dependence on material wealth. So, why do you send people over to 'help' us with our financial poverty?" How would you respond?

Developing a learning mindset is the first and most important step towards being an effective international volunteer. Starting to cultivate this mindset now will give you a strong foundation for the rest of this book and for any action that you choose to take, at home or abroad. There will be plenty of opportunities to practice this mindset in the coming sections. We'll begin with a chapter that aims to help you examine your own motivations and goals for international volunteering.

2.
EXPLORING YOUR MOTIVATIONS & GOALS

Perspective: Blind to the Downside of my Can-Do Spirit
By Zahara

I was 22 when I volunteered in Zambia. I had no experience in farming and no prior travel in Africa, but I had an almost pathological desire to fix other people's problems. At home, I had directed that energy toward a boyfriend with a drinking problem. Now, without realizing it, I wanted to focus that energy on the people of Africa. I arrived in Zambia with my head full of media images of the help that African people needed: help learning how to intercrop, help learning about proper nutrition, help learning how to meet the needs of poor and hungry children.

My initial experiences in Zambia reinforced the idea of Africa as a place of poverty and deprivation. A Zambian co-worker told me he only had one set of clothes. I saw children out of school because their parents could not afford school fees. And I learned there was no medical clinic nearby to provide even the most basic care.

That's when my 'fix-it' desire went into high gear. This desire was fueled by a dangerous mix of my individual temperament and an American cultural 'can-do' spirit so ingrained in me I didn't even see it; I was an American fish and the 'can-do' spirit was the water I was raised in.

So I set out on a mission to build a medical clinic at the Munsakamba Frontline Youth Center where I was working as an agricultural volunteer—never mind that I would only be there for three months and had no experience providing medical treatment. I created a budget for the cement required, talked to my Zambian co-workers about their health needs, and wrote a petition asking the project's directors to create the clinic. I then proceeded to ask my Zambian co-workers to sign the petition. They gave me some strange looks, but, perhaps eager to please me, most of them signed.

To my frustration and dismay, when I presented the petition to the project's directors, they immediately turned down the idea. In retrospect, I can see their logic: there were no doctors or nurses on site and no funds to pay them or buy medicine. They knew a clinic would need more than a little cement house in the bush. But as I hadn't considered the full implications of my proposal, I was angry and disappointed. I was also embarrassed that I had raised expectations among my co-workers for an unrealistic project, and I realized belatedly that I had put them in an awkward position by asking them to sign a petition addressed to the very people who had the power to hire or fire them.

To the best of my knowledge, I did not get anyone fired, but I did disrupt the delicate dynamics of the organization in a way that may have generated negative effects long after I left. And I definitely diverted energy into a dubious side project—energy that might have been more productive if channeled elsewhere. I will never know the exact effects of my actions, but I think it is quite likely, no matter how good my intentions were, that this effort created more harm than good.

When I look back now, I wish I had learned more before taking action—more about the Zambian economy, history, agriculture, culture, and language, and more about the typical problems international volunteers face. But most of all, I wish I had taken the time to learn more about myself. What were my internalized assumptions about the needs of African farmers? Where did those assumptions come from? Why was I blind to the strengths of these farmers? What were my own practical strengths and weaknesses, personally and professionally? Why was I so fixated on solving other people's problems? What was I really hoping to accomplish as a volunteer? If I had known myself a little better, I think I would have been a much more effective (and less dangerous) volunteer.

Why Do You Want to Volunteer Abroad?

"When I first said I'd come out to Ghana I was thinking mostly about myself: what I would gain from it, how employers would look at it, what the food would be like. But partly I decided to go to Ghana because I wanted to do some good in the world."

-Roman Christoforou, who volunteered
in Ghana for six weeks

"Why do you want to volunteer abroad?" We've asked this question of ourselves and hundreds of others as we wrote this book. Most people can identify a series of interlocking reasons. In the quote above, Roman touches on a big motivating question for many volunteers, one that you may also be asking yourself, "How can I do good in the world?" Volunteer travel is marketed as a fun and seemingly simple answer to that question. But once you take a critical look, it may not be the easy answer that it seems.

In this chapter, we'll share strategies to help you think through your broad motivations, including beliefs and values that inspire you to volunteer, as well as specific goals, such as things you want to learn and changes you hope to make to yourself and the world.

Personal growth or global development?

Our research shows that the main reasons most people think about volunteering abroad relate to either *personal growth* (fulfilling their desire to expand their horizons, develop new skills, and challenge themselves) or to *global development* (helping to make a positive change in the world). These two categories of reasons are sometimes referred to as 'selfish' or 'altruistic' reasons to volunteer, but as we will discuss, we don't think these motivations are necessarily in opposition. Nor do we think the global development motivations are more valid or relevant than the personal growth motivations.

Many volunteer travel experiences are marketed as if they are designed to achieve results such as improving education, protecting the environment, and increasing the incomes of local people. In reality, however, volunteer experiences are often designed to prioritize the volunteers' needs and goals. Most travel companies are not set up to facilitate meaningful international development interventions, but their marketing pitches are fashioned around what sells best to travelers; in this case, travelers' desire to feel that they can have an impact on an international development issue.

International/Global Development

"A developed country is not a place where the poor have cars. It's where the rich use public transportation."
    -Bogotá Mayor Gustavo Francisco Petro Urrego

'Development' is a highly-contentious term that is much debated and could use a book in itself to define. The quote above is useful as it demonstrates that the meaning of the word depends on your own perspective on the goals and meaning of the process. Because of this, this widely-used concept has been discredited, as it is misleading and implies that all countries are naturally headed in one direction—that is, in the direction of already 'developed' nations, such as the United States. We, and the Mayor of Bogotá it seems, are concerned by this connotation. As this term is still used widely, we use it here and define it broadly as 'action taken that helps improve the quality of life of the majority.' We also use 'international development' to signify both the organizations that do that work – ranging from international nonprofit organizations and government aid agencies to grassroots community-led projects – and the actions taken by these organizations and individuals.

We have also met volunteer travelers who prioritize their own personal growth. These are the volunteers that critics can be quick to label 'selfish.' On the contrary, we believe that those who can recognize the personal benefits of their experiences abroad are probably the ones thinking most clearly about their decisions. We are joined in this perspective by many volunteer hosts. Adama Bah, from the Institute of Travel and Tourism in The Gambia said, "If you know it, can do it, and want to share and learn with us—you are our volunteer. If you know it, can do it, but want to impose on us because we are 'less fortunate'—keep it to yourself!" There is, of course, a difference between the personal motivation to take selfies while volunteering and the personal motivation to improve your knowledge about global issues—we will focus on the latter to point out that personal motivations are not necessarily inferior to supposedly more altruistic motivations.

In reality, the difference between the two approaches, *global* or *personal*, is not clear-cut. Many returned volunteers we spoke with noted that they had started out assuming that their motivations were entirely focused on global development, and it wasn't until they were deep into their volunteer trip that they realized the importance of developing themselves. Often they wished they had done more personal development beforehand as it would have made them a more effective volunteer. A volunteer who worked in India gave this advice: "One tip for future volunteers is to focus not only on what you can do for others during your experience but also on what you can gain for yourself. That really can help you make yourself a better person or become more aware of who you are." Another volunteer reflected that his two years spent in Mongolia "allowed me the space and time to figure out who I really wanted to be and how I wanted to change the world." Taking responsibility for improving the lives of others goes hand in hand with taking responsibility for improving yourself— for increasing knowledge about the problems you want to tackle, practicing empathy, improving your listening skills, and ensuring you are always willing to learn. All of this points towards 'learning to serve' rather than just 'serving to learn'—the essence of the learning mindset!

LEARN

Our answer to the question about whether personal growth or global development is more important is therefore: both. Just as with the vajra, and the constant interplay between action and learning, personal and global development are intimately interconnected. As you consider your own motivations in depth, be sure to take the time to unravel the many overlapping layers. If you are honest and thorough with this exercise, you will find that some of the answers surprise you.

Imagine a young volunteer interested in helping a shelter for victims of human trafficking in Mexico. When considering her motivations, the volunteer might identify that she cares about the issue and wants to help trafficked people in any possible way. On further reflection, however, she might realize that she would be disappointed if she was offered a placement where she didn't get to interact directly with the people staying in the shelter. She is a budding journalist and was hoping to interview some of them. She had chosen Mexico because she speaks fluent Spanish. She is bored by her current job, and has been considering further study, so she hopes this experience could get her into a good school. She has just come out of a relationship and wants some time away from home. If she was told that the best way she could support trafficking victims was through a desk job in the Mexico office, or through volunteering at the organization's shelter in Senegal, or through staying in her home town to work on advocacy, not all of her goals would be met, and accepting any of those placement offers may be a disappointment for all parties involved.

Belinda Forbes, who previously worked for the Committee for Health Rights in the Americas in Nicaragua, advises volunteers to write down their goals. "Don't say, 'I don't have expectations, I am open to anything.' It's better to try to dig out what your expectations are, articulate them—and then realize that they might not be met."

Questions to Ask Yourself

"International volunteers have certain expectations— invariably different to our own and often high. They want to 'make a difference,' and it is hard to convince them that big changes come from small efforts."
                                        -Volunteer Hosting Organization

The following questions are intended to help you dig deeper into your motivations for considering volunteer travel. Ask yourself the questions that seem the most challenging. If you find it easy to identify ways you want to improve the world, also reflect on how the world could improve you. The most successful volunteers, even those who are extremely experienced, view their time volunteering as reciprocal, acknowledging that the support they receive in their placements and the skills and experience they gain through the process is at least equal to what they can offer in return. On the other hand, if the initial motivations you identified are all about personal growth, you might want to reflect on how you can transition that experience into longer-term positive impact for others. Remember the message of the vajra, "Action without learning is ignorance. Learning without action is selfishness."

What kind of personal growth opportunities do I seek?
Do you want to go overseas for the experience of living and working in another culture? To stretch your comfort zone by putting yourself in new and challenging situations, and practice qualities such as patience, gratitude, or flexibility? Start by asking questions like: how do I want this experience to change me?

What are my core skills?
Consider which of your skills could make a contribution in a situation abroad. Think about what you have studied, your work history, your technical know-how, and what tasks you find easy. Do you have a practical degree or specific skills that might be useful in other contexts, such as skills in health or veterinary care, education, or counseling? Do you have management or business skills such as accounting, fundraising, sales or marketing? Do

LEARN

you have experience training others in your area of expertise so you can transfer skills in a sustainable way? Even if you are less experienced, you may have some skills (such as editing, organizing or computer skills) that would be valuable to an organization overseas.

What skills and experience do you currently lack but would need in order to be more useful in a placement abroad? As you consider your options, you will probably recognize some gaps in your knowledge or skills (for example, that you don't speak Chinese or that you have never taught in a classroom before). Consider what you might want to learn before you go abroad. For example, before signing up for a volunteer teaching placement in Jordan, even if you are fluent in Arabic, you might need to learn some teaching techniques and classroom management skills. To fill the gaps, you can seek out appropriate training, books, videos, degrees, volunteering opportunities close to home, experts to talk with, or learning trips you can take before volunteering.

What are my learning goals?

Your learning goals for international volunteering could be anything from brushing up on language skills or making new friends, to returning to the country from which you were adopted to learn more about your heritage. Your goals might include learning practical skills, such as permaculture techniques, or gaining experiences that you can build on in the future, like learning about responses to global health issues. Karin, who volunteered in Nepal for over a year, said, "Right now, I am here as a language and culture learner. I am allowing the culture and the people to impact *me* before I attempt to impact them."

Is there a specific topic that you want to learn about—for example, child rights? Are there specific skills you want to learn or experience in action—such as fundraising tactics, or monitoring and evaluation practices?

What are my passions?

These days, there is a trend of people trying to secure jobs they feel passionate about. Rather than simply supporting a family or making a comfortable standard of living, many people are looking for jobs with a purpose—work that has a positive impact on the world. This trend towards social impact careers has led to many TED talks, books, and courses about 'finding your passion.' Yet the idea that everyone should have a passion can also be paralyzing. In a presentation recorded at Stanford University, the Silicon Valley entrepreneur Randy Komisar talks about how he has found it more helpful to consider a 'portfolio of passions' in life, rather than a constant search for the holy grail of one main passion.

If you are looking to identify a cause that fits into your portfolio of passions, think about the topics you learned about during your studies, the books and articles you always choose to read, and the conversations that you find most stimulating. You might want to ask yourself these types of questions: What do I love doing? When do I feel most engaged, connected, and alive? When were the times in my life that I have been really enraged about an issue or motivated about a change I'd like to see in the world? Which opportunities would help me learn enough about issues to become passionate about them? How can I use my passion to positively influence the world?

Every passion – dancing, programming, good practice in management, campaigning to reduce the amount of plastic in the ocean – can be enhanced and channeled into supporting a good cause. One of our favorite quotes is from Howard Thurman, who said, "Don't ask what the world needs. Ask what makes you come alive, and then go and do that, as what the world needs is people who have come alive."

What are my values?
Certain values may fit in with, or go against, plans to volunteer abroad. For example, if family is important to you, will an extended period away from home be too challenging? Or does it mean that you would like to be immersed in a culture that mirrors your strong family values? If you value honesty or transparency, look for these qualities in a potential volunteer placement—for example, honest marketing and transparent financials. Also ensure you are being honest and transparent with yourself about your motivations and goals. Once you have a solid grasp of your

LEARN

own values, it will be easier to evaluate opportunities against those values.

How does a sense of responsibility or guilt play into my decision?

Many people we interviewed talked about 'responsibility' when they discussed their motivations to volunteer abroad. Most commonly, due to their own relatively privileged backgrounds, volunteers felt a responsibility to share that with others. Some referenced 'guilt'—a feeling that they needed to repay the world for the good fortune, advantages, or excess of their own lives.

Many volunteers can trace their motivations back to what we refer to as 'guilt offsetting.' Feelings of guilt about certain lifestyle choices, such as choosing convenience over sustainability by using a car instead of public transport, a sense of extravagance in daily life, from overflowing closets to wasted food, or feeling too busy to support needy people in their local communities, can all lead to wanting to 'give something back.' Peter Buffet, son of the famous investor and philanthropist Warren Buffett, wrote in the *New York Times* about a similar phenomenon he calls 'conscience laundering.' Instead of taking action to address root causes, individuals can "feel better about accumulating more than any one person could possibly need to live on by sprinkling a little around as an act of charity, [while] keeping the existing structure of inequality in place." Volunteer travel can seem like a fun and adventurous way to 'offset' guilt-inducing behaviors, but it is a false solution. The only way to solve those original problems is to change the original behavior.

As you consider your motivations, think about how they relate to what you feel you 'should' do, and what you feel is your 'responsibility,' and analyze where these ideas come from. Your perception of your responsibility may shift over time as you learn more about the complex root causes of poverty and inequality, as well as the interplay between personal and global development. Often volunteers end a placement realizing that their main responsibility was to learn.

What impact do I want to have on the world?

Volunteer travel is often marketed as a way to tackle the injustice, inequality, poverty, or environmental destruction in the world. But the impact of volunteering is often not as profound as it is portrayed, at least in the short term. Therefore, we encourage you to think about how an experience abroad might affect your ability to make long-term changes, looking beyond the immediate effects of your trip overseas. Will you learn skills, such as movement-building or effective fundraising, which will enable you to continue to contribute to this cause in the future? If you haven't figured out a cause that inspires you, volunteering can be a place to explore the issues and possible impact you want to have, getting you closer to clarifying your mission.

You might already have a clear idea of the issue you care most about, and even how you might like to contribute to the cause. If there is a change you would like to see, or an injustice you would like to challenge, and you are considering volunteer travel as a way to make a difference in that area, ask yourself: What do I already know about the issue? How did I get this knowledge—from personal experience, other people's stories, or media and fundraising campaigns? Whose voices are missing? What else is there to know about the issue, and how can I find it out? For example, if you are a huge advocate of organic farming and have plenty of technical skills from experience in your own country, it is crucial to find out how organic farming is seen in the country you want to travel to. How much understanding is there in the local community of the benefits? Is there an existing market for it? Are local farmers requesting it? What impacts might introducing it have on people's livelihoods?

How does this fit into the 'big picture' of my career path or life goals?

If you already have an idea about what you want to do in the future, even if your specific plans are not fully formed, think about how and why volunteer travel could – or could not – fit into these plans and take you one step closer. If you have no distinct plans for the future (that's okay too!), start by thinking about the various paths that volunteer travel could open up for you and if there are alternate ways to walk down those paths. Even if you have a clear idea of where you are heading, remember to stay open to how your plans might change, especially when you throw an extended period abroad into the mix! We have known

LEARN

high-powered executives to return from a volunteer experience and drop everything to retrain as teachers, and students who have spent years preparing for a career in development to abandon their plans after just a few months of volunteering with a nonprofit.

Again, we advise you to not view your time overseas as a complete action in itself but rather as part of a process that will continue throughout your life.

Motivations: Red Flags

As you analyzed your motivations, you may have found that there are some that, if you were really honest with yourself, do not fit well with plans to volunteer abroad. Trying to deceive yourself about your motivations now can have magnified consequences overseas, as you will depart with misaligned expectations. There are a few warning signs that suggest that volunteer travel will not deliver what you want or expect. Here are some indications that you may want to reconsider or postpone your plans:

Seeking a geographic solution to an emotional problem
Going abroad for an extended period might seem like just the fresh start you need to get over an emotional or health issue like depression, an eating disorder, or an addiction. We don't recommend looking at volunteer travel as an escape. Traveling overseas, especially if you plan to undertake volunteer work, can be unsettling and stressful. Far from providing the clean break you are looking for, it could instead exacerbate the problem and create a situation dangerous for both yourself and others. Remember that if you do not work through these issues, they are unlikely to stay at home when you leave and will instead follow you. Resolve to work through these challenges before departing overseas.

Looking to convert others to your faith
Religious beliefs can be deep-rooted and form part of both personal and community identities. Therefore becoming aware of how your perspectives are influenced by your religious beliefs can be important as you make decisions. Be honest with yourself

if converting others is a motivation for you, and spend some time exploring the assumptions that underlie this goal. Although a strong faith may have inspired your wish to do good in the world, the desire to convert others to your religion can mean you think you have the answer to other people's problems. This can limit you from humbly learning about others' personal goals and supporting them in achieving their own desired paths towards those changes. Consider how your faith can be used to positively motivate your work, without becoming an imposition on the values and beliefs of others, and think about ways you can live out your religious beliefs by showing compassion and working for justice.

If your religious beliefs are important to you, consider what the challenges and benefits might be in living and working in a community of a different faith. Simply learning about another set of beliefs and sharing what you learn with those at home can be extremely important, as it can help bridge the knowledge gaps that often fuel religious conflict. All volunteers, of any religion or none, can identify potential blind spots in their own worldview in order to be more open and flexible, and to respect diverse perspectives.

Simply needing something that looks good on a résumé

You may find that the main reason you are interested in volunteer travel is to build experience for your college application, to have something on your résumé that will impress employers, or even just to have some interesting anecdotes to tell at a party. If these motivations dwarf others, and especially if you otherwise don't have much interest in the day-to-day hard work that volunteering and personal development entails, you should reconsider. Gabriela Corbera, who volunteered in Cambodia for over three months, told us, "In Cambodia, I saw a lot of people using volunteering as a CV line. I hope to try and educate my peers and friends that volunteering is not just the fact of doing it, but the complexities of what you learn from service."

There are plenty of other things you can do to build your experience that do not require such a large investment of energy and money, or have such a high risk of backfiring. Effective volunteering requires drive, passion, and a commitment to

LEARN

monitoring your impact, and if this all seems like a chore to be ticked off on a lifelong to-do list, you are in danger of having a negative impact on both yourself and others.

Wanting to rescue poor people and 'lift them out of poverty'

If your reasons for wanting to volunteer primarily come down to wanting to save people, or solve their problems, then we need to warn you that these lofty ambitions will never be achieved through a volunteer trip abroad. In the words of one volunteer who spent three months in Nepal, "If you think you are going to change the world and lives of millions of 'poor children,' this will not happen!" In fact, we have seen how this attitude can have detrimental effects, with volunteers who were so busy trying to fix the problems they saw that they were not open to learning. And, no matter how long you volunteer abroad, we don't think you can ever lift people out of poverty—they do that themselves. Instead, you can learn to help remove the barriers preventing them from doing so, especially those rooted in your own country's policies and economy.

Caring about others in the world is admirable, and there are a great many things that you can do over the course of your life to put your compassion into action. Volunteering overseas may be one way of channeling your compassion, but is just one small part of the picture. So let go of any expectation that you are going to be the savior of other people, and avoid becoming frustrated further down the line. Instead, open yourself up to the long-term commitment, sensitive engagement, and continual learning needed for the slow process of both personal and global development.

Seeking to practice beyond your skillset

Examine your motivations carefully if you are drawn to volunteer travel as a way to do work that you are not qualified to do at home. It's easy to get sucked into the hero narrative of volunteers with no background in health delivering babies in an understaffed hospital, or volunteers who have never planted anything introducing a new system of rice planting to a food insecure community. Such expectations are not only unrealistic but they can potentially be dangerous for the people you work with, and ultimately could end with frustration and disappointment on both sides. Meredith Thornton, the manager of International Marine Volunteers in South Africa, told us this story: "A volunteer once arrived with no relevant work experience yet expected to be doing the work of a marine biologist. However, when he was given research assistantship opportunities he dropped them very quickly due to lack of interest. He was unwilling to muck in with his teammates and ended up being of minimal assistance to the project and, while staff continued to treat him with respect, his teammates ended up alienating him."

Needing a vacation

If your main motivations are that you are tired, want a break, are looking forward to relaxing, want to drink copious amounts of alcohol in a tropical location, can't wait to meet and hang out with other like-minded travelers, or need time to make sure the important sights are ticked off the bucket list, then find yourself a fitting vacation package and leave the volunteering for another time! There's no shame in just taking a break. You might choose to volunteer in the future when you have the energy, mindset, and motivation it demands.

What if my Motivation is Just to 'Feel Good?'

Fantastic! Doing good in the world, learning, and helping other people can make you feel good; it's an addictive feeling that we're happy you're hooked on! We disagree with the view that all development work should be hard or that volunteering is only of value when it's tough and not fun.

If your motivations are to give to the world in a way that makes you feel proud, valued, or that you have contributed, then your first step is to make sure you invest time in researching and identifying a project that is really worth being proud of. To make responsible choices, it's important to understand the context of volunteering, the pitfalls to avoid, and the power of its positive potential.

LEARN

PART TWO:

LEARNING ABOUT VOLUNTEERING

"If we just go overseas and start doing things without understanding the complete picture, then even with our good intentions, we can err."
   -Martin Jacks, who volunteered in Ghana for over a year

The next stage of learning service is to take a step back and look at the wider context of international volunteering. Although your choice to volunteer in another country might seem entirely personal, the reality is that you are not volunteering in a vacuum—you are part of a wider process. Thousands of volunteer travelers before you have learned important lessons that can help you understand how to make a positive impact through a choice to volunteer and beyond. A crucial part of learning service is becoming aware of this context—how the current situation of a country has been shaped by what has come before.

This part looks at what we know about volunteer travel. We start with the history and context, examining why and how volunteering became such a popular trend, and offer the backdrop of international development to help explain its rise in popularity. We then to explore some of the current problems and pitfalls of the way volunteer travel is currently practiced, to help you avoid making the same mistakes. Finally we explore how volunteering has been, and could be, a force for good, and how learning service can help you be part of transforming the way volunteering is practiced. But first, let's look at what has gone before.

3.
PUTTING IT INTO CONTEXT

Perspective: Cheese Sandwiches, Rotten Tomatoes and Yanquis
By Joe

As a boy in suburban Cincinnati in the early 1960s, I biked a newspaper route that included the regional headquarters of the Maryknoll Fathers—US priests who worked overseas. In social studies class at my Catholic school, we read copies of *Maryknoll Magazine*, something like *National Geographic* with an American-Catholics-help-the-poor spin. What caught my attention were stories and photos of priests doing cool things: helping Quechua farmers on the shores of Lake Titicaca start credit unions, or facilitating a meeting of women in Hong Kong who hoped to start a neighborhood noodle factory.

It was with such pictures in mind that one afternoon I asked Father Dan, as I handed him his morning paper, whether I could spend the next summer's vacation helping out on one of the foreign missions. To my surprise, he was encouraging. A couple weeks later he told me he had contacted a priest in a parish in Chile, and that, yes, if I could get myself there, I could stay at the parish house and help out. I was excited. As soon as I finished my last exam of the school year, I rushed to the airport and flew south.

The parish served a *población*, or shantytown, on the periphery of Santiago. Though I was there for three months, I can hardly recall what 'work' I really did. After all, what could a 16-year-old from Cincinnati – who showed up not even knowing Spanish – contribute? But I tried to make myself useful. I could help with some filing at the credit union. I could drive into town for supplies (which would be good for my Spanish learning, the *padre* assured me). And I could answer the door. Throughout the day, people poorer than any I had ever seen before, but – I will never forget – looking dignified, came and rang the doorbell seeking food. The most powerful earthquake ever recorded had hit Chile the year before, making the lives of many impoverished people even worse, forcing them to live on handouts. What I had to give them was cheese sandwiches; so I opened can after can of processed cheddar, part of the US food aid program.

All summer long – winter in the Southern hemisphere – I tried to be useful. And to a certain extent I was. But without my presence, not much would have been different other than the lack of amusement of Chileans hearing me try to learn Spanish. I was greatly affected, however, more than I realized at the time. Keep in mind that this was the beginning of the 1960s. Not long before, angry crowds had hurled eggs and tomatoes at Vice President Nixon's limo at virtually every stop on his 'goodwill' tour of Latin America. When I volunteered in Chile, millions of people all over Latin America were protesting US interventions. I quickly learned that many Chileans believed the *yanqui* copper companies were robbing countless millions of dollars of Chilean resources—and that while most Chileans were poor, Chile was very rich. I also heard that my government and its CIA were carrying out covert operations in Chile to boost politicians there who would let the copper companies continue to have their way. At first, I resisted what so many Chileans told me. However, with my reading and talks with the priests, I soon started to see the US as experienced by many people in its 'backyard.'

One night dramatized for me the connection between my country and the impoverishment of so many Chileans. On the edge of the parish was a *latifundio*, an extremely large farm,

LEARN

thousands of acres. Like many of these *latifundios* in Chile, most of the land went uncultivated. With the earthquake in the south the year before, hundreds of families had moved into the already-cramped homes of their relatives in our *población*. Many people expressed anger about all this vacant land being fenced off while so many families lacked even the smallest plot of land to use. The same politicians that supported the US copper companies had opposed any land redistribution. Growing up in conservative Cincinnati, I had been taught that private property was sacrosanct. But, to my surprise, the priests agreed with the people that they had a right to land and to housing. That evening, at dusk, several hundred people carrying torches and banners marched toward the fence. Some of the banners proclaimed that the copper belonged to all Chileans and that the *yanqui* companies should go home. Many of the men and boys were carrying rough-hewn wooden planks, hammers, and nails. The first ones to get to the fence cut the barbed wire. They started putting up shacks, more or less finishing by dawn. And, despite my upbringing, I felt that what they were doing was the right thing. That night, I realized that being in Chile was changing the way I viewed my own country and its impact around the world.

The most important thing I learned on my first stint of volunteering overseas was that the big picture matters. I had been handing out cheese sandwiches without questioning why these people, in a land so rich in natural resources, had nothing. My view was cracked wide open, and as a result it shifted the trajectory of the rest of my life. I now realize that volunteering and international development work are closely interlinked, and how important it is to learn about both before forming opinions on the best ways to help.

Seeing the Big Picture

"If there is no awareness of the context, communication and problem-solving will be very difficult for outsiders or foreigners. They mean well, but they'd end up coming across like people from another planet."

–Charbel, a volunteer host in Lebanon

As a traveler arriving in another country, you are not the first foreigner to set foot in that land. Depending on where you volunteer, you might follow centuries of soldiers, missionaries, colonizers, businesspeople, diplomats, humanitarian workers, or other travelers. And no matter what their actions were, it is likely that most of them were convinced – and told the local community – that they were there to help. A brochure for International House in 1979 wryly stated, "Once we used to send gunboats and diplomats abroad; now we are sending English teachers." International interactions in the present day are just as multi-layered and complicated. They can come in the shape of military campaigns, where statements of humanitarian goals can be associated with an invading or occupying force, or large corporations drawn to a country by abundant natural resources and access to a cheap labor force. Fleets of aid-workers may be sent to oversee multi-million-dollar interventions, some of which fail to benefit local communities, or thousands of tourists may choose to stay in luxury hotels on segregated beaches. The varied aims and impacts of these international movements of people all influence how foreigners are seen by local people.

It is beyond the scope of this book to include a comprehensive history of colonialism, global commerce, and international aid, which form the backdrop of most volunteer travel experiences. However, we'll offer you some background, point you in the direction of additional reading, and encourage you to learn the specific history of those who have come before you.

A History of Help

The colonial era: Explorers and missionaries (1492–1898)

> "I gave them a thousand handsome good things, which I had brought, in order that they might conceive affection for us and, more than that, might become Christians and be inclined to the love and service of Your Highnesses and of the whole Castilian nation, and strive to collect and give us of the things which they have in abundance and which are necessary to us."
> -Christopher Columbus, in a letter to King Ferdinand, 1493

To understand the context of international volunteering, we can start by looking back at Columbus's journey of 1492. From the very first moment he set foot in the Americas, his language of 'helping' by converting the so-called Indians was mixed up with goals of finding gold and capturing slaves. Missionaries and businessmen followed in the next round of ships to the Americas, continuing to weave together trade in souls and goods with fancy words about helping the local population, whom they thought needed saving.

During the Spanish conquest, the harm most certainly outweighed the help. Disease, starvation, and violence devastated the native communities of the Caribbean Islands, with the Taino population of Hispaniola declining by up to 85 percent in just one generation after Columbus landed. Bartolomé de las Casas, an early Spanish settler, may be seen as the spiritual grandfather of today's international volunteers. After witnessing many atrocities, he worked hard to end Spanish human right abuses in the Americas, he tried to improve the welfare of the indigenous population, and he argued in the Spanish court against those who claimed that the Indians were less than fully human. However, his mixed legacy also included promoting immigration of farmers from Spain, who took over land from the local peoples.

The patterns of Spanish colonialism in Latin America were repeated throughout the next few centuries during European expansion into the Americas, Africa and Asia. These efforts were often bound up with altruistic ideas about helping the indigenous populations, with many expressing their belief that colonialism was a force of good. For example, Sir Joseph Banks, writing about British-governed Bengal, in 1787 said, "The latest posterity... will wonder how their ancestors were able to exist without them and will revere the names of their British conquerors to whom they will be indebted for the abolition of famine." Sadly, the Europeans more often reduced the self-sufficiency of local communities than improved it.

Over the next few centuries, missionaries continued to play the double role of las Casas, with altruistic enthusiasm that mirrors that of some of today's volunteers. On the one hand, they often documented the excesses of colonialism and spoke out for the humanity of colonized people. But they also inadvertently caused hardship and suffering when they suppressed indigenous cultural practices, contributed to environmental degradation, or unwittingly spread disease. Note that the 'help' being offered was almost always decided on by the missionaries, without input from the intended beneficiaries—the colonized peoples.

The roots of volunteer travel: Thomasites in the Philippines and workcamps in Europe (1901–1945)

The modern concept of international volunteering can be traced to the Thomasites, a group of over a thousand teachers sent to the Philippines by the US Government starting in 1901, shortly after the US replaced Spain as the colonial power. A Filipino uprising had sparked the growth of the anti-imperialist movement in the US. In the face of this growing domestic opposition, the US government was eager to put a positive spin on its involvement in Asia. Sending educators abroad also seemed like a good strategy to reduce Filipino support for the resistance to the US occupation and to create a group of English-speaking Filipinos who were loyal to the US forces.

We know from their journals and books that the Thomasites were mostly motivated by altruism sprinkled with a desire for adventure. Named for the US Army Ship Thomas, which carried some of the first teachers, these men and women traveled to remote villages where they taught English using the pedagogy of the time—mostly rote memorization from readers that used examples from the US. The Thomasite program lasted until the 1930s. The influence of the American teachers was so pervasive over time that English became one of the national languages in the Philippines. According to some analysts, the positive legacy of the Thomasites includes a high rate of literacy in the country. Unfortunately, the Thomasites were also used as a sort of 'smiley face propaganda' to mask some of the worst abuses of US domination. The Thomasites left their mark on the American idea of international service, opening the door for the Peace Corps and other volunteer programs to follow.

In Europe, another trend was also helping to shape the global volunteer sector as we know it. Starting in 1920, peace-loving people in Europe created 'international workcamps' designed to repair towns physically damaged in World War I and by natural

LEARN

disasters, as well as healing relationships between people from countries previously in combat. Pierre Ceresole and the other founders of the workcamp movement were aligned with the principles of what we now call learning service: they placed a high value on inter-cultural learning, solidarity, mutual respect, and lifelong service. Young people full of idealism traveled to these camps in the hope that people-to-people connections would prevent future conflicts between countries. World War II proved that the power of volunteering was not strong enough to prevent a catastrophic war.

The rise of international volunteer sending organizations (1945–2000)

As Europe emerged from the rubble of World War II, several factors combined to feed a growing interest in international service. The success of the Marshall Plan (US aid that helped rebuild Europe) led to an optimistic perspective on the benefits of outside intervention in poorer nations, and the concept of 'international development' was born. As former colonies in Africa and Asia fought for and gained independence, western powers sought ways to compete with the perceived threat of the Soviet Union and communist ideas. Because of the domestic upheavals of the 1950s and 1960s in the US and Europe, governments were eager to channel the spirit of youthful rebellion into idealism that they could control. Increased prosperity around the world meant that more people could consider international travel.

These trends formed the backdrop to President Kennedy's creation of the Peace Corps in 1960. The mission of the Peace Corps was to "promote world peace and friendship" in three ways: providing skilled volunteers to promote development efforts, helping Americans better understand other countries, and helping the rest of the world better understand Americans. From the earliest days, the Peace Corps' own evaluations found that its programs fell short in recruiting highly-skilled volunteers and in having any tangible impact on development efforts, but did provide for many learning experiences for volunteers and the people where they served.

In the UK at around the same time, Voluntary Service Overseas (VSO) was founded. It began with 16 volunteer English teachers who went to Borneo in 1958, in response to a request from a British bishop. Initially, the program recruited male high school graduates, although by the early sixties the requirements had changed to recruit only university graduates, with females also accepted. Australian Volunteers International (AVI), another national volunteer program with similar aims, was launched in 1963.

The rapid increase of government volunteer programs in the 1960s coincided with the expansion of the US military presence in Vietnam, which spurred an increase in critical scrutiny of the role of the US and Europe in the developing world—and outspoken criticism of international intervention. This deep skepticism about the real goals of foreign policy also led to critical assessments of the role of international volunteer programs. One of the most outspoken critics was the radical Catholic priest Ivan Illich, who gave a powerful speech in 1968 to a group of young US volunteers in Cuernavaca Mexico, where he lived. "Today, the existence of organizations like yours is offensive to Mexico," he said to the crowd. "A group like this could not have developed unless a mood in the United States had supported it—the belief that any true American must share God's blessings with his poorer fellow men. The idea that every American has something to give, and at all times may, can and should give it, explains why it occurred to students that they could help Mexican peasants 'develop' by spending a few months in their villages." His words are still circulated today, and still provide relevant critiques of some current service offerings.

Although many others joined Illich in sharing critical perspectives on volunteering, mainstream media coverage of the 1960s and 70s focused on the positive narrative—the headline of young, idealistic people 'making a difference' overseas. This narrative was reinforced in many ways—from photographs in hometown newspapers of young men and women going off to small villages in India, to a Norman Rockwell painting of Peace Corps volunteers in Ethiopia teaching an old farmer how to plow. Never mind that the Rockwell painting was staged and the volunteers depicted actually did not know how to plow—these images played a major role in popularizing a romantic vision of

LEARN

international volunteering, and the mainly government-funded programs through which people could volunteer.

All these early volunteer programs followed a similar model— they were large, they did not charge placement fees or run for profit, they sent volunteers abroad for lengthy periods, and they had several application restrictions. These programs ruled out or rejected tens of thousands of eager potential volunteers, who began to look for other ways to volunteer internationally. In the 1980s and 1990s, dozens of other volunteer sending organizations were founded to meet this demand for alternatives. These included faith-based, secular, high school, university, spring break, summer, and corporate employee programs. While they varied in mission and effectiveness, most volunteer sending organizations offered a range of services including identifying and preparing volunteer placement sites, and screening, training and orienting volunteers. They also arranged logistics such as travel, room and board, and troubleshooting in case of illness or problems with the match between volunteer and host. For these services, they charged fees ranging from hundreds to thousands of dollars.

By this time, the government programs began to diverge in structure and programmatic priorities. In line with its mission of "bringing people together to fight poverty," by the early eighties, VSO had evolved to focus on recruiting only highly-skilled volunteers. In contrast, the Peace Corps continued to recruit mostly recent college graduates with less than five years' work experience. Because of its reliance on government funding, the Peace Corps was subject to political pressure—for example, expanding volunteer programs in Central America during the Contra war, then pivoting to more Eastern European and Asian programs after the fall of the Soviet Union. Unlike the Peace Corps, VSO is not an official government agency; perhaps for that reason it has been less influenced by political goals than the Peace Corps.

Proliferation and diversification of international volunteerism (2000–present)

The new millennium marked another phase in the history of international volunteerism, as the internet transformed connectivity and communication around the world. Volunteer sending organizations could engage in targeted marketing to find potential volunteers, and volunteers could much more easily find out about opportunities that matched their interests, skills, and timeline. The internet also led to an increase in independent volunteers: people who found their placements directly through an overseas organization's website, or through web portals that list various international volunteer opportunities. Even tiny schools and organizations overseas could now post openings for volunteers without the middleman of a volunteer sending organization.

In some senses, the changes fostered by the internet were positive: they democratized the system, allowing organizations of varying sizes and resources to make their causes and needs known. Instead of a few dozen possibilities, there were now thousands of options, some with minimal or no placement fees, and volunteers had them at their fingertips—all types of experiences, lengths of placement, and areas of the world were just a click away.

However, there were also downsides to the ease of advertising and abundance of information. With the internet, volunteers no longer needed to have an extensive series of interactions with a volunteer sending organization before booking a flight. They could now just 'buy' a volunteer experience in one click, but with so many options to choose from, it was difficult to tell which organizations were effective or even legitimate. The use of the internet made it easier for hosts to advertise their needs, but it also made it easier for matches to be made without a rigorous vetting process, or any other steps necessary to ensure reliable and meaningful placements for volunteers. Previously, a sending organization's staff needed to either travel overseas to meet with a partner, or arrange a series of phone calls to design and manage volunteer placements. Now, all that planning could happen in a matter of hours through email and web chats, or be skipped over entirely, with volunteer sending organizations selling

LEARN

Volunteer sending organization
Also called a Volunteer Placement Organization. In the context of volunteer travel, 'sending organization' describes organizations that arrange volunteer placements overseas. They may be NGOs, for-profit businesses, or government agencies. They vary in how much involvement they have in selecting, training, and supporting volunteers, and in their processes for selecting, supporting, or monitoring hosting organizations. Some provide valuable support and learning opportunities for volunteers. Others may have little direct contact with the hosting organization, acting only as a conduit for information about a placement.

Volunteer hosting organization
An overseas organization where volunteers are placed and through which they conduct their work. Although not all volunteers use a sending organization or travel agency, almost all volunteers will work with some sort of host organization, which might be a large and established NGO, local community group, business, educational institution, government program, or faith-based organization.

Non-government organization (NGO)
Also nonprofit. This term is used to describe groups that are impact-driven and have a social mission other than that of making money. In most countries these organizations require legal registration and have special tax categories. In the United States, 'nonprofit organization' is the common term, though in the majority of other countries the term 'NGO' is ubiquitous. We will use both of these terms to refer to organizations designed for a charitable purpose but will avoid the term 'charities,' because, although the term is commonly used in some countries, we feel it has paternalistic overtones.

trips before they have even identified a hosting organization in which to place the traveler. Furthermore, volunteer travel aggregation websites started taking postings from other web sources to add to their sites, often selling trips without ever even speaking with someone at the potential host organization to verify the information, let alone visiting them. Online placement services offered potential volunteers the promise of changing lives, without any quality control in place.

This proliferation of volunteer travel led to increasingly shorter volunteer options, and a new term has developed around this trend: 'voluntourism,' with placements lasting a few weeks, days, or even hours. A recent study found that nearly half of those from the US who volunteer abroad do so for two weeks or less. Short-term voluntourism trips are attractive for their ease of access— while they may be planned in advance, many are chanced upon and organized in an impromptu fashion during a vacation.

Previously, volunteer placements were managed by nonprofit organizations, governments, local communities or religious groups, but now travel agencies are a major provider of voluntourism offerings, which have little context for development work. The main motivation for adding a visit to a school or orphanage might be to simply make a travel itinerary more appealing. They are often customer-demand-driven, looking to find what makes their trip sell, rather than being driven by the relationships and needs of a community. Daniela remembers watching this volunteer travel demand spread across the Cambodian tourism market. "During my time in Cambodia, a number of mainstream travel companies reached out to me, interested to learn about volunteer vacations. 'We need to start offering these experiences,' one travel company owner told me, 'as our clients are demanding it and all of the other companies have already started offering half and full-day volunteer options at orphanages, schools, and building sites. Where can I find a school to send them to?'"

As volunteer travel has risen in popularity, it has stopped being a niche activity, and has become something more commonplace, or even an expected rite of passage. The 'gap year' between high school and college, popularized in Europe and spreading to the US, is often promoted as a chance to go abroad and volunteer. Researcher Jason Hickel found that "every British student I spoke to indicated that they felt it was expected of them to do volunteering during their gap year—it has become so institutionalized, so ritualized, that it is now written into the established pattern of the modern British life-cycle."

LEARN

> **Gap year**
>
> Most commonly, a gap year is when a student graduates from high school and chooses to delay admission into college for a year to work or travel. The term can also apply to an older person taking a year-long break from study or a career.
>
> **Voluntourism**
>
> This term emerged in the late 1990s to describe a travel experience that includes volunteering along with other more traditional tourist activities. Although people who volunteer internationally for long periods of time still combine tourism opportunities into their experiences abroad, the term is usually only applied to short-term experiences that can fit into a vacation from work or school (maximum about six weeks, most often much less). These short-term programs are sometimes also referred to as 'volunteer vacations.'
>
> **Travel agency**
>
> Traditionally organizes logistics such as flights, accommodation and excursions. Increasingly, travel agencies are getting involved in volunteer travel, acting as sending organizations by connecting volunteers to opportunities overseas, for a fee. A major flaw with this model is that travel agencies have experience in the tourism industry, not in development and so can be unconcerned with, or unaware of, some of the major pitfalls of volunteer travel.

Gap year programs have evolved to become standard fare at the most elite schools, with Harvard encouraging every student admitted to take a gap year before matriculation, and Princeton sponsoring service-based 'bridge-year' programs abroad for its students. Volunteer travel is now seen as a vital element to include in the anxiety-inducing college personal statement. Rebecca Waxman, who went on a learning program for three months to Nepal, said, "Amongst the white, wealthy teenagers in my school, international service was seen as a hook for college admissions."

International service is also becoming part of companies' Corporate Social Responsibility policies. A survey of 240 companies, including 60 of the largest 100 companies in the Fortune 500 list, found that 47 percent have a formal international volunteer program. In this environment, perceptions of volunteer travel have changed from a rare adventure for the few to a routine activity for the majority. These changing norms and expectations have led people who might not be suited to volunteering to participate anyway due to outside pressures.

And here we are at the present day, where there is one final development to explore.

From 'Service' to 'Service Learning' to 'Learning Service'

"The most challenging part was the result of the lack of learning I did before volunteering. I was a volunteer/intern in Uganda in public health with a focus on nutrition, yet I had no extensive background and experience in either subject… I realized how important it is to know a little about the community, culture, and topic before entering a volunteer project."

–Jeomar Montelon, who volunteered for over a month in Uganda

The term 'learning service' has its own history, connected to the history of volunteering we just explored. The word 'service' has been used for centuries, and can be problematic because of its tangled connections with histories of missionaries, governments, and the military. Think about it: people 'serve' in the military, and perform 'community service' as punishment for crimes committed. Nonetheless, in its most common current usage, service has come to mean helping others. In the 1990s, many schools and universities in the United States began to require students to complete a certain number of hours of volunteer work in their own communities. The main goal was to foster empathy and civic engagement. But too often the service performed was superficial, merely a box to check off before graduation was allowed. As service was measured in the number of hours of input alone, activities like erasing the chalkboard for a teacher or babysitting their own siblings could count. In response, educators developed the concept of *service learning*. Service learning was designed to explicitly incorporate learning goals into student

LEARN

service projects. For example, college students might volunteer in a homeless shelter, talk to the residents about their lives, discuss findings with each other, and then write research essays about economic policies that contribute to homelessness. Most service learning models emphasize critical reflection (usually in the form of writing or discussions) as a vital element that is needed to maximize the learning that comes through the service. In the past two decades service learning has increasingly been taking place overseas.

We agree that critical reflection is essential to effectively offer service, but we don't think the model of 'service learning,' with service first in name and action, goes far enough, especially in the international context. In this framing, *learning* appears as a byproduct of *service*—a secondary add-on. With 'learning service,' learning is front and center, which is the emphasis of our approach and a key to mitigating the negative impacts of international service.

A trend we noticed is that through many service learning programs, an increasing number of volunteers are learning the same lessons over and over again. We know many people, ourselves included, who have completed a service project only to learn that the actions had minimal or even harmful impacts on the root cause of the target issue. We don't all need to make the same mistakes to learn lessons taught by ineffective service, no matter how valuable those lessons are. Learning doesn't need to be viewed as the byproduct of our actions. For this reason, we came up with the term learning service, flipping learning and action around so that learning comes *first*.

We hope that in understanding this background and history, it is easier to see why volunteer travel is complex, and why the learning service approach is important for volunteers who want make ethical decisions about volunteering. We want the next stage of volunteer travel history to have a learning-first approach.

Perspective: I Suffer from Development Oscillation Syndrome
By Claire

It's not a medical term, and it is self-diagnosed, but I suffer from a condition I call 'development oscillation syndrome.' It's like a roller-coaster of feeling great about international development work, then coming across something that makes me feel disgusted by it, and then a short time later having my faith restored. I have been thrust along this jagged path since I got engaged in this work, but it has gotten worse over the years. My first experience in development, although I definitely didn't call it that at the time, was when I went to Nepal as a volunteer at age 19. While all I did was teach English to seven-year-olds (probably not very well and certainly without much self-reflection), I became concerned that I might have been propping up an unsustainable system of rotating, untrained teachers. I left the experience wanting to pursue a career where I knew I was actually helping people, and the answer that presented itself was to get involved in development work. That is exactly what I did, first by volunteering again several times, and then by becoming a founder member of PHASE Worldwide, an NGO that supports grassroots empowerment programs in rural Nepal.

However, I often felt uncomfortable. Even though I was doing everything I could to ensure that the organizations I worked with were responsible, sustainable, and locally-driven, I felt uneasy about my involvement. Partly, my unease was due to being associated with an aid sector that included a lot of other work that I didn't agree with—from failed projects run by multilateral banks to the misaligned actions of individual do-gooders. Partly, my unease came from being a foreigner. I worried that the judgments or decisions I made were biased by my culture and upbringing, perhaps making it irresponsible for me to be involved with change in other places. I also wondered whether we were defining progress incorrectly, and if the efforts to develop Nepal were in fact benefiting 'developed' countries more, or whether some aspects of 'underdevelopment' were actually desirable. I wondered if development was actually overly damaging to the planet, cultures, or social bonds. For example, I found people in

LEARN

Nepal to be generally less stressed, less depressed, and have more time for human interaction than people in any of the developed countries I had been to. Was my work playing a part in destroying that?

Even though I felt that 99.9 percent of the impact of the organization I helped to start in Nepal was positive, that 0.1 percent gnawed at me. The more I learned about development and its complexities, the more complicit I felt in the dark sides of aid and the more I began to poke holes in every development project I experienced or heard about.

I actually decided to cease my involvement in development over ten years ago... only to then become overwhelmed with feelings of guilt, knowing there were things I could do to help those that I had left behind. This is at the heart of the (often excruciating!) 'development oscillation'—simultaneously feeling compelled to take action and repelled from doing so. Feeling that I have the responsibility and the power to work for global change, while also understanding the arrogance and ethnocentrism of this stance. By learning about the complexity of global issues and starting to understand the "gray between the black and white," it isn't that I feel neutral or on-the-fence about them, but that I feel increasingly intense emotions on both sides, and debate my role in this work endlessly inside my head.

Although I am still involved in development work, the way I strive to beat the internal debate is to devote most of my time to global education, so that more people can become aware of the complexity of these issues and join the work of solving them. This includes writing this book. I don't think anyone has the answers to the big development issues, but I do think we can start by asking the right questions.

'Development' and the International Volunteer

"When you work in development, you're screwing around with someone else's life. If you make a mistake, you can go home. The people you work with already are home, and they probably can't just leave, so you better know what you are doing. The worst thing to do is just go in and do what you're told without thinking about it."
                    –Steve Arnold, International Development Program,
                    School of International Service, American University

In recent decades, powerful governments have shifted the language describing their interactions with other nations away from outdated notions of colonialism and toward the language of aid and development. Most volunteer programs implicitly or explicitly claim to address the problems of underdevelopment and promote some form of development. At first glance, the meaning of these terms appears straightforward. We can understand *underdevelopment* to mean when the majority of people do not have adequate health care, clean water, food, education, housing, or jobs. It seems obvious that *development* should mean creating societies in which people no longer lack these necessities, and *aid* would be how outside players support this kind of progress.

In reality, however, there is intensive debate about the meaning of development, and even more controversy about the best ways to promote it. In every country, national and international forces influence the direction of what they call development— defining goals, controlling resources, setting the pace, and advocating for specific strategies and outcomes. The process is often contentious, with vast inequalities in power among those involved.

Turning the tables on development
To highlight the challenges that volunteers face in understanding and contributing to another country's development, we offer another scenario in which the tables are turned. Imagine that three groups of altruistic volunteers from other parts of the world come to Dallas to help the city develop. Each of the

LEARN

groups has heard much about the severe problems in the city through media reports about poverty, inequality, drug abuse, homelessness, and violence. Each of the three delegations are asked to assess the city's needs and then come up with a plan for a development project that donors in their home countries will be willing to support.

The first delegation is a group of elders from a rural village in Zambia, a country where most people are church-going Christians. The elders quickly identify the problem in Dallas as a shortage of churches, and a lack of respect for elders. The Zambians plan a project that will involve the construction of 20 new churches throughout the city, and the creation of a council of elders in each neighborhood, consisting of men aged 75 or older. They propose to work with a group of local citizens to promote the churches and councils, seeking to create a society in which all children have to work for the elders for at least three hours a day.

Aid

In its simplest form, aid is synonymous with 'help.' However in this book we are referring to the practice of international aid, which is when one country or group of countries offers money or other support to another country or group of countries. Aid most often flows from more economically-developed, and therefore more powerful, countries, to less economically-developed, less-powerful countries. It is often politically motivated and can be tied to outcomes that also benefit the donor country, such as market adjustments. Aid is a complicated business and although international aid is still associated with 'helping', the results are not always positive.

Beneficiary

A person who is on the receiving end of aid, one who 'benefits' from a project or donation. In the traditional model of volunteer travel, the beneficiaries are the people overseas who are 'helped' by the actions of the volunteer. As we explore, the relationship is rarely this clear-cut and volunteers themselves are often major beneficiaries of their own choice to volunteer.

The second delegation is a group of indigenous women from the Amazon. In their initial study, conducted in the summer, they are horrified to see how much trash is produced in the city, the air pollution, and the lack of green space. Their solution is to tear down tall, ugly apartment buildings and build community gardens with simple but beautiful huts for people to live in.

The third delegation is a Rastafarian youth organization. Their analysis identifies the main problems of Dallas to be too much focus on money and power and too little focus on spiritual and community connections. They decide to help Dallas by promoting a reggae dance every evening and developing an educational program to train community leaders and local politicians to grow and smoke ganja.

Although this sounds farcical and unrealistic, it's not that far off from the disconnect between many volunteer travelers and the needs of the places they visit. In these examples, all of the visitors' assessments of needs may be based on elements of truth, and all of the visitors could probably find people in the community to support their projects. But, as you can imagine, the projects would also create problems. Non-Christians and young people might take offense at the Zambia plan. The people who live in the apartment buildings that the South American women want to tear down would probably be very upset, to say the least, and not many people would like to live through the Washington winter in a hut. The Rastafarians and their local partners would most likely run afoul of local marijuana laws, and risk legal action. In other words, people's ideas about development are connected to who they are and how things work in their own society.

Moving towards a definition

During our travels around the world, we have talked to local community leaders who defined development variously as:

- Living in a society that is free of war and violence
- Gaining recognition for the collective rights of a community, not just individual rights
- Being able to breathe clean air and drink clean water
- Having access to jobs that pay a living wage

- Improving material well-being without being forced to give up cultural practices, spiritual values, or the health of the local ecosystem
- Being able to start and run a small business without having to purchase expensive licenses, bribe public officials, or fear police shutting the business down
- Achieving the right to vote, run for office, form a union, or protest government and corporate policies without fear of persecution, imprisonment, or death
- Being able to have children play outside freely without the danger of landmines
- Gaining the right to study in the local language
- Enjoying the freedom to practice a traditional or minority religion
- Having the power to say no when government or private interests want to appropriate community lands for oil extraction or mining
- Having access to credit and savings programs
- Living a lifestyle that allows people to spend time with their families and friends
- Recognizing the right for girls and boys to go to school without paying school fees
- Having access to health care and affordable medicine
- Building a country that nurtures people's happiness
- Living a life of dignity and respect, free from discrimination.

Some societies, especially indigenous communities, emphasize the idea of sustainable development, often defined as "development by the current generation that does not jeopardize quality of life for future generations." Such development demands careful stewardship of environmental resources, in contrast to mainstream theories of economic development, which often promote rapid exploitation of the environment to support short-term financial gain. A number of groups are trying to move away from economic growth as the main indicator of development. In Bhutan, the government rejected Gross National Product as the unquestioned measurement of living standards and replaced it with their own concept of 'Gross National Happiness,' contending that economics plays only a small part in ensuring citizens have a high quality of life. The Social Progress Index is another effort to better compare how countries provide for both the social and environmental needs of their citizens. Rather than just financial measurements, the tool looks at fifty-four indicators aimed at measuring the fulfillment of basic human needs as well as opportunities for growth and progress, and then compares these indicators across nations.

Some projects that fall under the banner of 'development' can have consequences that are questionable or downright harmful. The clearing of virgin forestland for foreign-owned plantations can be justified as a form of economic development. The displacement of communities that have lived on the land for centuries for a hydroelectric dam can be viewed as necessary for progress. The forcible settling of nomadic tribes, the creation of air-pollution at levels so high it is injurious to health, and the proliferation of sweatshop factories for global industry are all activities that have been termed 'development' by those that stand to benefit from them. Many volunteers we spoke to had some uncomfortable realizations about the complexity of development during their placements. Benjamin Witcombe, who volunteered for nine weeks in Kenya, told us, "My skepticism of the development world increased. I realized that a lot of aid given to poorer countries is tied with conditions that are favorable to the country giving it and that the interest on loans given to poorer nations who struggle to pay back debts is high."

A volunteer's perspective on what constitutes 'good' development may be quite different from the perspective of the people with whom they work, and it may be very different again from the perspective of the organization designing the development initiative or the donor providing the cash. The many layers and perspectives on development, coupled with the hugely unequal power dynamic between countries, often results in outsiders (rather than local communities) setting development agendas. Big problems can occur, in both short-term international volunteering projects and multinational aid programs, when local people are not empowered to take control over deciding what development is needed and appropriate in their community.

LEARN

In our fast-paced and rapidly-changing world, it is impossible to have a static definition of development. For example, has access to internet become an important human right for developing communities? What about cellphone technology? India has experienced rapid economic growth and is emerging as world leader in the IT industry, and yet the World Bank estimates that 58 percent of the population lives on less than $3.10 a day. With inequality on the rise throughout the world and a handful of elites accumulating more and more, an important question might be, "How much development is enough?" or even, "How much development can the world sustain?" Development often manifests as the construction of roads, burning of fossil fuels, and consumerism, and its rise is linked to everything from personal issues such as obesity and depression, to global issues such as climate change.

In acknowledging the many perspectives on the definition of development, we also need to acknowledge the many perspectives on how to achieve it. Economists have argued about whether the best aid to offer should be top-down (large scale programs implemented by governments or international donors) or bottom-up (small grassroots initiatives designed and implemented by the communities who benefit from them), or anything in between. The jury is still out on whether any of these development approaches are successful, and in most cases the answer is nuanced. In short, much development practice is still based on experimentation: even professional development practitioners are still learning.

Development is often defined in over-simplistic terms, such as a rise in average income in a country. This yardstick does not evenly assess how income is distributed – it could be a small minority getting much richer and everyone else getting poorer – and does not measure what local people might value more than higher income. As a volunteer, you should be aware that your assumptions about poverty and development may be quite different from the perspective of the people with whom you work. As Duncan Green, author of From *Poverty to Power* says, "Poverty is about much more than a low income, something that becomes particularly clear when people living in poverty are asked to define it for themselves. It is a sense of powerlessness, frustration, exhaustion, and exclusion from decision-making, not to mention the relative lack of access to public services, the financial system, and just about any other source of official support. Poverty has a deep existential impact—being denied the opportunity to flourish, whether for yourself or your children, cuts very deep indeed."

Grassroots

Also *bottom-up*. A project or movement that is started and led by people affected by an issue, that is, stemming from locally-identified needs, rather than those identified by outsiders. The projects tend to be small, as there is rarely much funding, and to be run by small NGOs or community organizations.

Top-down

This refers to programs that lay out a strategy or plan at the 'top' (at government or aid agency level) that is implemented locally. Top-down interventions are often large-scale and well-funded. They are often criticized for being rigid and unable to adapt to local circumstances, and also for lacking local ownership.

Addressing a root cause, or applying a band-aid

Ideally, organizations aiming to address some of the problems of underdevelopment would work to address the root causes of problems, so those problems don't exist in the future. However, some have such shallow analysis and weak programs that their solutions serve as band-aids that merely cover wounds without removing the obstacle that caused the wound in the first place. Many nonprofits and social businesses have built their whole models around 'band-aid' forms of development assistance—for example, giving away pairs of shoes as opposed to helping people access jobs where they can then choose to spend their money on shoes or any other needs they have. These organizations spend huge resources on problematic downstream solutions (such as an organization that is 'saving' trafficked women by putting them in shelters) instead of upstream solutions (such as an organization working to bring traffickers to justice and to prevent trafficking in the first place). Sam Warren, who volunteered in the Dominican Republic for over four months gave this example: "The

LEARN

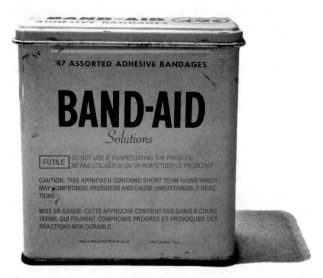

47 ASSORTED ADHESIVE BANDAGES

BAND-AID
Solutions

| FUTILE | DO NOT USE IF PERPETUATING THE PROBLEM
NE PAS UTILISER SI ON VA PERPETUER LE PROBLÈME |

CAUTION: THIS APPROACH CONTAINS SHORT TERM GAINS WHICH
MAY COMPROMISE PROGRESS AND CAUSE UNSUSTAINABLE REAC-
TIONS

MISE EN GARDE: CETTE APPROCHE CONTIENT DES GAINS À COURT
TERME QUI PEUVENT COMPROMIS PROGRES ET PROVOQUER DES
RÉACTIONS NON DURABLE

NEW BRUNSWICK, N.J.   CHICAGO, ILL.

(Do not apply in case of actual development challenge.)

goal of the foundation I was with was to give greater economic employment opportunities to people by teaching them English. I felt like I wasn't that successful... I thought there were other baseline problems with the education system that I couldn't fix." In other words, if the entire organization's premise is only dealing narrowly with a symptom rather than a root cause, it might be considered a band-aid organization.

There are some specific circumstances where band-aid organizations have a role to play—including in a crisis or conflict. Immediate problems often require immediate alleviation to avoid a situation getting worse. After a natural disaster, for example, people may need emergency food or housing. However, it can be quite tricky even to provide emergency relief in an effective way. The relief efforts after the 2004 Asian Tsunami or the 2010 earthquake in Haiti were dogged by a lack of coordination, and waves of unsolicited and poorly-planned donations. Many of the volunteer teams that rushed to help quickly became a burden, using up precious aid resources themselves.

If even band-aid projects seem hard to implement successfully, addressing root causes by shifting the balance of power can be even harder. Shifting the balance of power might mean passing laws that protect human rights so people can advocate for better policies; building strong unions to protect worker salaries and conditions; promoting government investment in education and health; implementing laws protecting the environment; and economic policies that create fertile environments for small-scale entrepreneurs. These tasks are enormous and long-term. Rarely can one individual, or even one organization, claim sole responsibility for an achievement. Success usually requires actors in the public, private, and NGO sectors working together for change.

The Role of International Volunteers: Short-Term Work While Learning About Long-Term Solutions

"Now that I've experienced it, I find I can relate a lot more to news about India and more generally about development, and I can look critically at how the media represents the Global South and aid relief."

-A volunteer who spent six months in India

Combined, local and international efforts can make a real difference, but sustainable development and addressing unequal power dynamics is difficult, sometimes dangerous, and takes time. So what is the role of a volunteer traveler?

Few programs give volunteers the opportunity to work on removing institutional obstacles to development. The vast majority of programs place volunteers in positions where they will provide direct services to a small number of people—building, teaching, playing, training, treating sick patients. Only a few work in human rights, democracy building, or advocacy. The reality is that most volunteers do not have the local knowledge and skills to contribute effectively to these kinds of efforts, and they could endanger themselves and others if they get involved in politically-sensitive struggles in another country.

Other development programs that attempt to be more long term still end up addressing only symptoms. The thousands of programs providing books, wells or goats all have very little impact on the underlying cause of global issues. Even programs set up to improve livelihoods, increase literacy or build entrepreneurial skills may still not change the underlying global systems, such as market protectionism and unfair trade rules, that perpetuate

LEARN

inequality. A stark realization you may come to is that there are entrenched interests eager to maintain the status quo—many of which may be back at home in your own country and not overseas at all.

Allies around the world have an incredible opportunity to shift the balance of power by participating in acts of solidarity—working for a ban on landmines, for example, or advocating against corporate land-grabbing, or changing your own consumer patterns and researching ethical brands. Ron Garcia, of the National Organizers Alliance, said "One of the most important things you can do with your experience is to get involved with solidarity work. Solidarity means people coming together in a process of changing the power structure to benefit the disenfranchised and create a more equitable system. It's a process in which you're learning and growing as much as you are giving back. Solidarity is ultimately an expression of love, a commitment to yourself and to other people that you want a better future." Shifting the balance can also mean working with advocacy networks, that support people around the globe who have come together to create institutional change in their communities—indigenous groups demanding access to education in their own languages, mothers' organizations working against cuts in their country's health budget, or a farmers' union seeking affordable credit.

We believe that in the long term, development can occur only when power is shifted and societies function without corruption, war, human rights violations, or economic exploitation. We also think that it is entirely appropriate that most volunteers in their first experiences overseas focus on mitigating the symptoms of underdevelopment and supporting local community needs, while gaining an understanding of the wider context of international development. It's important to try to find organizations that do this work effectively. Most importantly, in the spirit of learning service, we encourage you to use your time overseas as an opportunity to learn about the root causes of underdevelopment and what local people are doing to address these problems.

When you bring your volunteer experience home, you will be able to use this knowledge to participate effectively in removing obstacles to development and shifting the balance of power.

You may also bring back tools to confront underdevelopment, 'maldevelopment,' and even overdevelopment in your own community or nation. The final section of the book is devoted to the topic of what you can do when you return home, so if you feel overwhelmed by the scale of the problem compared with the time you will have abroad, take a deep breath. You have the rest of your life to make a dent in these issues, and if enough of us make dents, it will lead to long-lasting change.

Solidarity
Solidarity means working 'with' and 'alongside' other people to create a change, as opposed to working 'for' them.

There is Always More Context

As you can see, the context of international volunteering is complex, and can be controversial. What we've provided here is a high-speed tour of a vast and varied subject, but if you want to dig deeper we have added a list of further reading resources at the back of the book that provide a more in-depth exploration of development issues. As these discussions are always evolving, you might also want to engage with the topic through blogs, social media, or by attending events near you.

As there is no 'one size fits all' approach to development and the obstacles and possible solutions may look very different in different places, it's important to take the time to learn about the unique situation and challenges in the place where you are working, to take the lead from local people in what is wanted and needed, and to learn how you can be a long-term ally in challenging the structural causes of underdevelopment.

In the next chapter, we'll discuss some of the issues and pitfalls specifically relating to volunteer travel—so you can learn how to spot them, understand them, and avoid them.

LEARN

4.
THE POTENTIAL PITFALLS OF VOLUNTEER TRAVEL

Perspective: When it All Goes Wrong
By Daniela

It's rare that a volunteer trip gets it all wrong, but one trip that I observed in Cambodia was the perfect storm of worst practices.

An Australian travel company that sends large numbers of volunteer groups abroad had marketed one of its trips as supporting a school in rural Cambodia. The company needed to hire people in-country to run the trip and to identify a project where the young travelers could volunteer. They hired a Cambodian operator to manage all the logistics. They also contracted the founder of the Cambodian Orphan Fund to coordinate the volunteer project. He, in turn, identified a small, international nonprofit organization that had recently funded the construction of a school and offered to have these visiting volunteers help paint the building. At the same time, an Australian foundation had offered to cover all of the costs of the painting and volunteer trip. If you think this sounds complicated, you'd be right, but this convoluted path with many players is not unusual for group volunteer experiences.

Everything was lined up and the volunteers arrived at the school for their two-day volunteer project. Because I knew the foundation, I was invited to come by on the second day to visit the project. Here is what I found when I arrived on the scene:

- The volunteers were wearing bathing suits and bikini tops while they painted, with a crowd of local onlookers. In such a conservative rural area, this attire was likely interpreted by some local community members as offensive.
- The travel company organizers had planned for the volunteers to camp outside the school, but, as they had not done a thorough site visit, they didn't realize the entire school grounds would be flooded during the rainy season. The volunteers had nowhere dry to sleep or keep their stuff, so local community members were called in to help their 'helpers.'
- Because the trip coordinator thought it would be nice to reward the tired, flooded-out volunteers as they struggled to complete the painting, he brought in cases of beer. In rural Cambodia, drinking beer is associated with lazy behavior and even domestic violence. Moreover, the volunteers were on school grounds, a location intended as a safe place for children. The beer was shared with the men of the community who had gathered to watch the half-naked painters and to help fix the painting job that was being carried out haphazardly. The result was a loud group of inebriated painters, both Australian and Cambodian, carousing away while the school's children ran wild beneath their ladders.
- Some of the paint turned out to be indoor paint, even though it was being put on the outside of the building during rainy season, creating a messy scene and a near-worthless paint job that later had to be fixed by the community.

LEARN

I spoke to a few volunteers, and although they complained about their soggy sleeping conditions, they felt it was worthwhile as it was 'all for a good cause.' They were under the impression that the unlivable tent conditions were a measure to save money so that more of their fees could support the school. I checked online to see how the trip had been marketed, and indeed, the website for the trip stated that 'a portion' of trip fees would go to fund the school. This was a lie: I had visited the school with a member of the foundation that had covered the full cost of the volunteer project. None of the travelers' fees actually went to the project or the school; any savings from giving them cheap tent accommodation stayed with the Australian company.

So the group left: tired, wet, a bit tipsy, dripping with paint, and feeling proud of the contribution they thought they had made to that Cambodian community.

Most of these well-intentioned volunteers never found out the truth. They were probably never informed that their choice of attire and public drinking were offensive, that they were using the wrong kind of paint, or that the majority of the money they paid stayed in Australia. They weren't told that community members had to donate their own time to fix the poor paint job after they left. They probably never found out that a project ostensibly set up with the purpose of helping others had been staged in order to offer them the experience they were sold. And although they could have read it in the news, they might never have found out that the founder of the Cambodian Orphan Fund, who had been paid to coordinate their project, was deported back to the UK a few months later on charges of child sex abuse. In fact, the most likely outcome is that they left thinking they had done a great thing, and perhaps they signed up for another volunteer trip, with more money going to an Australian travel company that had little insight into or oversight of the volunteer trips it profits from. Those of us who knew the truth complained to the travel company, but we weren't telling them much they didn't already know. It is unclear if they did anything to change their future trips, apart from quickly removing the previous Cambodia trip details from their website.

Sadly, this trip was not an isolated incident. Although it was one of the worst examples I have experienced, the contributing factors – poor planning, corrupt management, profit motives driving poor execution, lack of community engagement, and lack of cultural sensitivity – are elements repeated again and again in volunteer travel projects around the world. This has to stop.

Being Willing to Learn About the Pitfalls

"This work has a tendency to attract people who want to 'save the world' but have little training in international development and social work, nor knowledge of the specific community that they are working in. Then they only stay three to four months. That leads to a huge amount of time being wasted, with people... working on projects that are unoriginal and doomed to fail, and resisting the suggestions of those who have been here longer simply because people need to see this for themselves before they will believe it is true. This takes a lot of patience."

–Volunteer Hosting Organization

It is a hard truth to swallow: volunteers do not always do good. Positive intentions do not always result in beneficial outcomes. While researching this book, we heard story after story of overseas volunteer projects that were at best ineffective and at worst harmed the very people they were intended to help.

Our claim that volunteers can cause damage may seem shocking. We certainly do not blame individual volunteers for the many structural problems we explore in this chapter. However, when repeated thousands of times, the small mistakes and oversights made by individual volunteers – such as a lack of willingness to do adequate research or prepare properly – create problems of considerable magnitude.

We know that at first it can feel disheartening to realize so many harmful consequences can come from genuine good will. But we invite you to stay with us, and not become dejected by what you learn. This is an important piece of the story, but it is not the entire story. We also honor and believe in the positive potential of volunteer travel, as we explore in the next chapter. Subsequent chapters will help you avoid these pitfalls by carefully researching options before you decide whether and where to

LEARN

volunteer, choosing an effective placement, conscientiously preparing, and volunteering with awareness and humility—all essential to the practice of what we call learning service. In keeping your eyes open to the problems, we hope that you will not only have a better experience as an individual, but also that you will be part of the process of promoting learning service principles and improving volunteer travel.

Negative Effects on Communities Overseas

Poorly-executed international volunteering can create problems for both the host community and the volunteers. We'll start by exploring the negative effects on people, projects, and organizations abroad—that is, the local schools, nonprofits, and enterprises where volunteers work, and the broader communities where they stay.

Wasting organizational resources

> *"Our staff don't have time to hold volunteers' hands, so it is a real burden to us when a volunteer needs a lot of direction... We do our best to offer support when necessary, but our priority is community development, not babysitting."*
> —Volunteer Hosting Organization

For host organizations, volunteers do not come free. Even if they are not paid, the costs of training, supervising, supporting, protecting, entertaining, and following up on a volunteer's visit can often amount to more than what the volunteer has 'donated' in cash or time.

Volunteers often do not realize how much energy it takes for organizations to host them. Let's imagine a volunteer arriving in Guatemala City where she expects to teach English. She is 22 years old, studied Spanish in high school, and recently finished a four-week course to learn some English teaching skills. Her local hosts may well have to arrange her room and board, pick her up at the airport, orient her to the local culture and to the school, train her in specific teaching skills, assist with improving her Spanish, help her get through culture shock, take her to the clinic if she gets sick, and deal with the inevitable snafus: she gets robbed of her passport on her day off, she has a kid in the class who is disruptive and she seeks advice on how to respond, or she has a conflict with her host mother and needs different accommodation. Feel tired reading this list? Imagine how tired the school principal feels adding these responsibilities to her long list of to-dos that already includes everything required to run a school!

Now imagine the extra burden on the principal when the volunteer is not well prepared. Maybe the volunteer made no effort to brush up on her Spanish before leaving home. She didn't make time to practice teaching as a volunteer in her own community. She forgot to go to the travelers' clinic and get the recommended shots. And she did not bother to contact the Guatemalan school's last volunteer to get tips about the students, culture, and teaching. In other words, she expects her hosts to pick up the slack – her slack – thus dumping an extra burden on her supervisor and colleagues.

If our volunteer stays for a long time, then gradually she'll be able to handle more of these challenges independently, and hone her skills through experience. But suppose she stays for just two weeks. Local hosts frequently complain about ill-prepared short-term volunteers, as they can require the same amount of support and training as long-term volunteers, but they don't have as much time to make that investment worthwhile. Even highly-skilled volunteers often require extensive staff time and other resources, such as translators, assistants, or supervisors, for them to be able to use their skills effectively in a new context overseas. One volunteer host said: "The language barrier is often a huge challenge to effectiveness as [volunteers] are often reliant on our staff, taking us away from our work. They also often need a lot of guidance in their work and their free time and even just daily living." Not surprisingly, volunteers who are under-prepared often take more in time and resources than they add in value.

LEARN

Under-qualified and mismatched volunteers

"I was left to manage and organize classes myself with little authority or knowledge of how the system worked... I didn't really manage to teach that much or very well. I wasn't, and still am not, a trained teacher."

-Jessica Pratt, who volunteered in Sudan for seven months

In addition to simply wasting their hosts' time and energy, volunteers can cause even more serious problems when they go abroad to perform a role that they are not qualified to do at home. We have come across countless cases where volunteers with no teaching experience have been asked to train teachers, volunteers with no management experience are asked to manage local staff, and volunteers without a public health background are told to lead workshops on HIV prevention.

We are not saying that only highly-skilled people should volunteer. Even the youngest and most inexperienced volunteer may have something to offer in the right placement, with the right support, and with the right framing of the goals and outcomes. The issue is not the skill level; it's the match between the job and the skill, and the level of authority and autonomy often given to these mismatched volunteers. An inexperienced volunteer from a community college in Los Angeles might be a good match for clearing invasive plants from a path in a Costa Rican ecotourism reserve, or assisting in a wildlife rehabilitation program in Botswana. In contrast, a highly-trained and experienced agriculture expert from Iceland could be a mismatch if asked to help cultivate unfamiliar plants in tropical farming conditions in Indonesia.

A mismatch between skill and responsibility levels can risk causing significant harm—for instance, if an unqualified doctor is expected to provide care beyond her expertise. Medical students are not legally allowed to practice medicine without direct supervision from a qualified doctor, no matter where they are in the world. However, when they are on a clinical placement abroad, the boundaries and extent of their role are not always clearly defined. One report from the *Journal of Medical Ethics* found that "in countries where healthcare provision is hugely under-resourced, students have found themselves under pressure to exceed their role." Unscrupulous mismatched volunteers who are placed in a position of power can take advantage of this lack of monitoring or accountability, sometimes with disastrous effects. Julian Sheather, Ethics Manager for the British Medical Association, describes one such medical student overseas: "He altered a prescription written by a local doctor; he photographed patients undergoing intimate procedures without consent; and he performed an unnecessary lumbar puncture because he fancied 'having a go.'"

In some cases, volunteers specifically choose not to use their main skillset while abroad, either as a break from their normal job or as a way to gain new experiences. Some use their time abroad as a testing ground for a new career. For example, an accountant might want to learn if he can handle the emotions of life in a hospice in India, in preparation for a possible career change. That might be okay, if he is assigned (and willing) to file paperwork, scrub the toilets, or help with fundraising, all while learning more about end-of-life care. It would be a mismatch, however, if he were expected to administer medical treatment or emotional counseling.

Often the volunteer placement organization is responsible for the mismatch. A large number of organizations advertise placements without requiring volunteers to have any qualifications or experience—often for roles such as teaching or project management, which are specialist skills that in the volunteers' home countries require formal training.

The negative effect of under-qualified volunteers can be serious. Zahara met volunteers in Kenya who gave out inaccurate information about AIDS transmission. Volunteers who know nothing about construction can build poor-quality, even dangerous, structures; volunteers who lack business experience can give damaging advice to local entrepreneurs; volunteers without teaching skills can disrupt students' learning. Of course, supporting an organization as an assistant, in a learning and support role, can give both the volunteer and the organization a valuable experience, but unfortunately, many volunteer

LEARN

placements are designed in a way that gives volunteers a level of authority or autonomy beyond their qualification.

Bad role models

> "Please advise female volunteers not to wear sleeveless shirts and to keep their legs covered. Males should wear long pants; in our society, only young boys wear shorts. When volunteers dress here the way they do at home, they set a bad example for our youth."
>
> —Frank Matoro Nyatiwa, volunteer host in
> Dar es Salaam, Tanzania

Volunteers don't often realize it, but behaviors that seem totally normal at home can be perceived negatively in another country: wearing shorts, visiting a local bar, or eating by yourself without offering food to others. We've heard over and over again from volunteer hosts that some volunteers provide bad examples of how to behave. These hosts worry about the effects, particularly on children, who often look up to volunteers because of their status as exotic and empowered outsiders. What's more, if parents take issue with the behavior of volunteers, the host organization's reputation and standing in the community may be harmed.

Gender issues come into play here, too. In many parts of the world, women who drink (even a little) or smoke cigarettes are seen as morally depraved—not the kind of person local parents would want to have as a teacher or youth leader for their children. A volunteer might see having a local girlfriend as an act of cultural integration, but in some societies, dating is not a normal practice, and the girlfriend left behind may be forever tainted by her brief relationship with a foreigner.

Finally, some volunteers engage in behaviors that would be unacceptable even at home, and are even more problematic in the context of international service. A volunteer who spent more than a month in Haiti told us, "Local community relations in Leogane were strained. Heavy alcohol consumption immediately in front of an internally-displaced persons camp struck me as rude and insensitive. Drunk foreigners would make noise on the roof all through the night while Haitians living in tents were trying to sleep... Some individuals came to a disaster area to party and they did party. A number of long-term volunteers close to the organization got drunk and high, stole a local fisherman's boat, and sank it without repercussions." Such volunteers can wreak havoc—generating bad will, tainting the reputation of a host family or organization, and harming local individuals.

Although volunteers don't explicitly ask to be role models, as visiting foreigners they are often on display, and what might seem like just a small bad choice for one volunteer could have ripple effects when judged or emulated by the local community.

Disruptions to local power dynamics

"I was working in Nepal on an education project. I thought that empowering a parents' group was the best way to ensure my project's success, but it had widespread unintended consequences. The employees of the central office in Kathmandu were unhappy that the power and money was being taken away from them. The parents were unhappy with the central office and were worried that money was being misused there... A journalist asked me a few questions on the issue, but in the article he totally misrepresented my answers, suggesting that I criticized the central office and some of its top members. The central office was so angry I had to go to Kathmandu to meet them and was almost kicked out of the country. Volunteers need to be really careful in what they get involved in and should really understand the local power dynamics."

–Bridget Sachse, who volunteered in
Nepal for over a year

LEARN

Most volunteers begin their placement without understanding the power structures of the community in which they volunteer—or the shifts they can cause as outsiders. Volunteers who jump into action before they learn about these complex relationships risk upsetting local power dynamics in ways that can be problematic. Volunteers leave after a few weeks, months, or years. Locals may have to live in the community forever.

A volunteer who dives in to help a local church club with a gardening project may be unaware that there is tension between the pastor and the youth club director. If the volunteer's work reinforces the youth director's power, she might inadvertently undermine the pastor's leadership and threaten the future of the club.

Volunteers may rightfully see injustice in local power dynamics. Girls may be pressured to drop out of school, people of a minority ethnic group may be denied access to the political process, or landless farmers may have to work hard on other people's farms for a small percentage of what they produce. While we certainly do not condone power dynamics that oppress, we have seen situations where, because volunteers want to act quickly and independently, before they have understood complex local realities, their best efforts end up making things worse. For example, one volunteer travel company we came across that runs trips to Asia had a program that gave out goats to local families. The company director ran several trips and only later found out that the local coordinator paid to implement the plan was actually charging people for the goats, and only selecting the families he knew. The coordinator sold his friends discounted goats and lined his own pockets along the way. Because the company director didn't understand the local power dynamics, he chose the wrong person to implement the plan, turning what he meant as a generous and helpful gesture into an additional imbalance of power. Even something as simple as setting up a scholarship fund for girls who have dropped out of school can have serious, negative consequences if done without an understanding of the varied local needs and power structures (not to mention a realistic long-term plan for how the program would continue to operate equitably into the future). Imagine local families pulling their daughters out of school to try to access the scholarship—which is exactly what happened in one program Daniela encountered.

The possible negative repercussions of stirring things up are exacerbated if the learning stages of learning service are skipped over and the action is ill-informed. Effective volunteer engagement in social justice work, in particular, takes a lot of patience and learning. There may well be local individuals and groups already working to challenge injustices; jumping in too soon could disrupt their sensitive work. Volunteers can learn over time whether and how to support them in their mission, considering that real change may be gradual and require ongoing solidarity long after volunteers have returned home.

Reinforcing cultural stereotypes

> *"I was cognizant of the negative impacts I felt I made that were prolonging the 'Western-dominant' ideals that seem to accompany volunteering. In South Africa, I was seen as 'smarter' than my black peers (who actually had more experience than me) simply because of my race. I felt uncomfortable with the subconsciously oppressive role."*
> -Katie Larson, who volunteered in Costa Rica, Peru, Cambodia, and South Africa

Offering help automatically creates a relationship: giver and receiver. This unequal relationship can be imbued with the sense that the 'helpers' – the volunteers – have superiority over the people being 'volunteered for.' Problems arise when volunteers fail to recognize this power dynamic, especially when local individuals, groups or entire communities become stuck in one role: 'receiver.' The net results can include disempowering local leadership, as well as reinforcing negative stereotypes and historical patterns of racism.

Volunteers often arrive on site with their own set of unconscious (or explicit) assumptions about Western cultural, linguistic, and technological superiority. Volunteer placement organizations frequently reinforce these assumptions through images on their websites. A typical photo often features a Western volunteer at the chalkboard teaching English to smiling local children—implying *how lucky these children are to learn English and ideas about the outside world*. The reality is more complex: the unintended results of such a language program might include students prioritizing English over their own language, using English-language textbooks that have no relevance to local experiences, and believing that foreign cultures are superior to

LEARN

their own. Sadly, the myth of the 'white savior' continues today in too many media images of volunteering.

Volunteers can walk into situations where, due to the long legacy of colonialism some people in the local community buy into the attitude that 'West is Best.' Claire encountered this problem in an island on the Mekong River, where the presence of foreign volunteers gave one school such high status in a community that it became overcrowded, while the other school on the island had empty seats, even though the volunteers were not necessarily better teachers. On another trip, Claire met people along trekking routes in the Himalayas who referred to tourists as 'doctor' and requested medicines from their first-aid kits instead of going to the local health post, in the belief that Western medicines are always superior.

Sometimes volunteers themselves make dangerous assumptions about the superiority of their own culture, labeling local ways of getting things done as illogical or deficient, and in need of change. Because of a lack of awareness or learning, volunteers may not even realize that the differences are cultural. These volunteers can get frustrated if the changes they suggest are not implemented, or if they are and they fail. Volunteer hosts can also get frustrated with volunteers who have strong ideas of the 'right' way to do something. One volunteer host said, "Volunteers… want to change the systems to Western ways of doing things, which do not always work. This makes local staff feel uncomfortable and can sometimes create an adversarial working environment. Volunteers do need to understand cultural differences and how things operate within local context."

Fostering inefficiency and dependency

"On one hand it was great to remove rubble for people so that they could potentially start rebuilding soon. On the other hand, couldn't the organization have just paid those local people to remove rubble instead of having a bunch of (let's be honest) ignorant foreigners doing this work?"
-Volunteer who spent more than a month in Haiti

Organizations sometimes rely on a steady stream of short-term foreign volunteers to fill important roles. We have seen schools where the only English teachers are volunteers, and nonprofits where all donor relations are done by volunteers. In many instances, when there are no volunteers, no one fills that role. This can foster an unsustainable dependency on external support. A void is created when the volunteers leave, which can put the organization and intended beneficiaries in a precarious position or make long-term planning impossible.

We have also seen examples where volunteers prop up organizations that are completely ineffective. Often, these are groups founded by outsiders who are quite ignorant of local culture, inexperienced in nonprofit management, and unable to plan strategic and thoughtful programs—in other words, well intentioned, but incompetent. Because of connections back home, they might be adept at recruiting volunteers, whose presence can prolong the life of an ineffective and perhaps harmful organization. Daniela learned this first hand through her experience coordinating PEPY's educational programs with a whole bunch of foreign volunteers who made decisions with limited input from local educators. One visitor commented that the work was "exuberance in place of thoughtful planning." Daniela now agrees with that insight: the volunteers and their fundraising kept PEPY going, even when the organization wasn't doing fantastic work. It took the PEPY crew some time before they learned the lessons shared in this book, transitioned to local leadership, and embedded their work in the local culture, rather than relying on exuberance in offering 'help.'

In many instances, local people could probably do the job more effectively than volunteers, but the abundance and perceived status of foreign volunteers leads to a reluctance to hire local people. However, the argument that volunteers *always* take away local jobs doesn't hold; in some cases volunteer programs create jobs, and in others the job the volunteer is doing was designed precisely for volunteers. Nonetheless, skilled labor (such as teaching or house-building) can be devalued if there is a supply of outsiders willing to do it for free.

LEARN

'Band-aid' approaches instead of addressing root causes

> *"I went to a remote village in Nepal to run a training course, and was surprised to see two foreigners at the back of the class, taking photographs. Afterwards I tracked down the guy who was responsible for them and asked what the photos were for. He said that the photographers were volunteers, and every day he has to make up something for them to do and tell them it is useful."*
>
> –Bikash Koirala, Teacher Trainer in Nepal

In the previous chapter, we discussed the difference between 'band-aid' approaches and solutions designed to address the root causes of problems. One of the common pitfalls of volunteer travel is that volunteers engage in tokenistic 'band-aid' tasks or, worse, work for organizations promoting 'band-aid' approaches that perhaps patch up an immediate need, but make the root cause of the problem worse.

An organization may take on volunteers to do superfluous tasks chosen simply because they appeal to volunteers, are easily achieved, or have a 'feel-good factor.' As Joe knows from his experience in Nicaragua, increasing literacy rates is a goal that involves changes in human behavior and education systems, which usually requires long-term efforts and resources. An organization working on root causes of illiteracy through advocacy for free primary education might feel pressure to add a project that volunteers can easily work on, such as building a library. That 'solution' may look impressive, but is not necessarily a contribution to the long-term goals. Where do the books come from? Who are the teachers and librarians? Who will use the library? Who will maintain it? Will staff resources be taken away from advocacy efforts? If the answers are unclear, then the volunteers may be engaged in 'band-aid' tasks.

A frequent observation of returning volunteers is that they feel their time abroad wasn't as valuable to their hosts as it was to themselves. Two-thirds of the volunteers we surveyed in researching this book felt this way. There is nothing inherently wrong with this outcome. In fact, if you follow the learning service model, the learning you receive may be so transformative that it will supersede any short-term contribution you make, and it is honest and healthy to acknowledge the limits to how much you have helped. However, many volunteers reported that the work they were asked to do seemed designed to fit the restrictions of a short-term visit rather than to provide lasting benefit. As well as wasting time, this can actually steer local organizations' staff and other resources away from addressing root causes.

Sometimes the volunteer coordinators know that the volunteer project is superfluous, but need to find something to fill the time of visiting volunteers. Daniela admits to having done that when running PEPY Tours as a volunteer travel company. She recalls a time she asked their school partner to put their fence-building project on hold until the volunteers arrived. After that, she and her team moved away from service trips and starting offering development education tours, in part because they realized that they were wasting people's time.

Perspective: The Rise of Scam Orphanages
By Elizabeth Becker, author of bestseller Overbooked: The Exploding Business of Travel and Tourism

For more than three decades I had covered Cambodia's wars and revolution as a journalist and author. When peace finally returned after 1991, I went back for repeated visits to the soaring temples of Angkor Wat. On my last visit in 2010, something didn't make sense: despite the relative peace and security, and signs of nascent prosperity, the number of orphanages I saw had increased dramatically. Where were these orphans coming from?

The answer came from a marching band of orphans walking through the streets of Siem Reap, the nearest town next to the Angkor temples. They danced to a drummer and passed a hat among entranced tourists who gave generously. They also invited the tourists to the orphanage for a full dance program.

I traced the orphans to a modern villa on the outskirts of town. This villa was nothing like the real orphanages that I had previously volunteered at in Phnom Penh. The children were unsupervised and even though it was a school day, no one was studying. I went upstairs and looked at their rooms—all a

LEARN

mess. The bathroom was locked. The toilets were broken and the children had to bathe outside under a pump.

All of the children I spoke to told me they had at least one parent, but their families were impoverished and had been persuaded to send their children to this sham orphanage by promises of a good education. Instead of studying, these 'orphans' found out that their job was to 'play with foreigners,' as Sophan, an 18-year-old boy, told me.

One year after my visit, UNICEF released a report, *With the Best Intentions*, which confirmed my fears and revealed that what I had discovered was not an isolated case. The report described how tourists were being fooled by these scam orphanages all over the country, donating money in the belief that they were helping to fulfill the dreams of vulnerable children. But the sad truth was that their donations were condemning the children to separation from their families and no access to schooling.

Four Ways Volunteer Travel Can Harm Children

The damaging effect that poorly-planned volunteering can have on children is one of our biggest concerns about volunteer travel and is probably the ugliest and most saddening distortion of good intentions that we have seen.

Some of the most popular forms of volunteer travel involve working with children, usually in an informal caregiving position or in a teaching role. This kind of work can seem more exciting than other volunteer roles such as office work, which may not provide direct interactions with 'beneficiaries.' As the vast majority of placements with children do not require qualifications or prior experience, for many volunteers, a placement overseas is an opportunity to work directly with kids in a way that they might not be able to at home. Isobel, who volunteered for five months in India, told us, "I saw a lot of interest in working with children... as if that was the only 'legitimate' way to feel like you'd done something worthwhile."

The high demand for child-based volunteering has led to a number of serious problems, all with the same genesis: volunteer-sending organizations are reluctant to highlight risks because people are willing to pay, directors of institutions cave in to pressure to host volunteers due to the money and connections it brings, and businesses flagrantly act against the best interests of children for profit. Here are four of the most harmful outcomes to children caused by international volunteering.

Increasing institutionalization of children

"Children in Nepal are being deliberately trafficked and displaced from their families to meet the requirements of well-intentioned orphanage volunteers. We believe it is no coincidence that orphanages are being deliberately set up where paying tourists can most easily be lured in."
-Martin Punaks, former Country Director,
Next Generation Nepal

A large body of research shows that institutional care for children, anywhere in the world, should be the last resort. The reasons to avoid supporting orphanages are detailed in numerous studies including Save the Children's seminal 2009 report *Keeping Children Out of Harmful Institutions: Why We Should Be Investing In Family-Based Care*. Institutions are by nature fertile grounds for emotional neglect and abuse of children. In some cases, adults have good intentions but not enough training, insufficient funding, or too many children to care for. Even in the most well-run orphanages that cater to all the material needs of the children, the ratio of caregivers to children is almost always much higher than in a family setting, and consequently many children in orphanages suffer developmental delays and problems of social integration later in life. In other, more troubling, cases, adults responsible for orphanages knowingly neglect or deliberately abuse children in their care. These problems don't just exist in low-income countries; extensive evidence from Europe and North America reinforces the conclusion that institutional care is dangerous for children anywhere. This evidence includes recent exposures of sadistic behavior by 'caretakers' in institutions in Ireland and use of institutional care to promote cultural genocide in Canada. In recognition of the dangers of institutions, the UN Convention on the Rights of the Child enshrines the right of children to be raised in a family setting.

LEARN

'Orphanages' and 'institutional care'

Institutional care for children goes by different names, including 'children's homes,' 'care homes,' 'residential homes,' and, of course, 'orphanages.' Although data indicates that the majority of children in these institutions in many low-income countries – from Indonesia and Sri Lanka to Ghana and Liberia – have at least one living parent, we'll mostly use the term 'orphanages' to refer to these facilities, as it is the term most commonly used in international volunteering. Institutional care is contrasted with family-based care, including the options of kinship family care (placement with relatives), foster care (placement in a non-related family), or programs that support financially-struggling families so they can care for their own children.

In many tourist areas around the world, 'orphanages' are no longer places for parentless children with no other place to go; they are marketed to parents as a place where their children will be well cared-for, get a good education, and have exposure to learning from foreigners. In some cases, orphanage owners put considerable pressure on disadvantaged parents to give up their children, with families split apart through deception, coercion, or deliberate trafficking. Children can be permanently separated from their families through this process.

Despite all the evidence of harm, many wealthy organizations, from faith-based groups to family foundations, still invest in orphanages above other options. In their own countries, laws and regulations may prevent people from investing in orphanages, due precisely to the reasons we have explored. Overseas, there may be no such restrictions. Also, donors may not be aware of community-based alternatives for care, or may not be willing to invest in more complex, longer-term solutions that can be harder to measure. Marketing and fundraising materials perpetuate the problem by making orphanages seem like a positive choice for donors, volunteers, and struggling families.

The growing trend of orphan tourism is pouring money into the institutionalization of children. Well-meaning tourists pay for the chance to attend an orphanage dance show, tour buses stop off at a children's home for a photo opportunity, and huge welcome signs call in visitors from the street. Volunteers are recruited through online advertisements, placement organizations, or heartstring-tugging fliers slipped under the doors of youth hostels and hotels.

Volunteers who want to help vulnerable children can end up incentivizing harmful institutional care as the first option instead of the last resort. In several countries, research suggests that 'orphans' have literally been *created* because of the actions of foreign tourists. In Nepal, reports estimate that around 85 percent of children living in orphanages had at least one parent, and 80 percent of orphanages are based in the five main tourist hot-spots of the country. Between the years 2005 and 2010, as the number of foreign visitors increased dramatically, Cambodia saw a 75 percent increase in the number of residential care institutions. This increase occurred despite the number of actual orphans declining over that same period. Rebecca Smith, an advisor with Save the Children, wrote, "We're worried about unskilled and untrained volunteers having access to extremely vulnerable children—and that the demand for this kind of volunteering is contributing to the harmful practice of building and funding orphanages." Extensive research from around the world documents that foreign money, material donations, and volunteers are fueling the drive to separate children and families. Thus orphanages attract volunteers, and foreign volunteers attract more orphans, in a sickening loop that turns good intentions into a travesty.

The advocacy group Better Volunteering Better Care, led by international child protection organizations Save the Children and the Better Care Network, campaigns solely on this issue, working to end the revolving door of volunteers visiting children's homes. There are also many organizations around the world working towards more sustainable solutions to keep vulnerable families together, such as keeping children in schools, helping parents gain skills and access to increased income to be able to afford better care for their children, lobbying to increase factory wages, and assisting communities to provide family-based care. However, these organizations can seem less appealing to donors and do not easily lend themselves to volunteer travel offerings.

LEARN

Supporting corrupt organizations that profit from keeping children in poverty

> "I had a feeling that the orphanage was run more like a business rather than a real home for the children. The primary focus was getting funds rather than the wellbeing of the children."
>
> –Natalia Gligor, who volunteered in Nepal for more than a month

Because so many volunteers and other travelers are attracted to offer money and time to projects with children, there is a cash incentive for corrupt and exploitative organizations to engage in nefarious practices. Some orphanages offer a dance show where the children perform for tourists *every evening* in order to convince them to donate money. Some even send the children out into clubs and bars in the tourist centers, late at night, to beg or to convince drunken tourists to volunteer at and donate to their orphanage. It is difficult to imagine how the children could be placed at more risk.

In this context, unscrupulous individuals and institutions actually have an incentive to keep children in poverty, in order to attract more donations from foreign volunteers, tourists, and other donors. In an article discussing the phenomenon of for-profit orphanages in Haiti fueling the separation of children from their families, Jennifer Morgan of the International Rescue Committee said, "A colleague from another international child protection organization recently told me about a troubling visit he made to a residential center for children in the south of Haiti. The children, my colleague said, were all painfully thin. He asked the head of the center if they had the means to feed the children adequately, and the director replied: 'We have lots of money. But if we keep the children thin, when we send pictures to church groups in the United States, they send more money. If we send pictures of children who look healthy, they don't send as much money.'"

Even when money does not change hands, foreign volunteers can fuel corruption in less direct ways. Philip Holmes, the former CEO of Freedom Matters and producer of the television documentary *Nepal's Orphan Trade,* aptly points out that "a volunteer can bring a stamp of respectability, apparent transparency, or language skills that can be used for orphanage marketing."

Exacerbating attachment problems for vulnerable children

"At the end of my stay, I remember talking to two long-term German volunteers. We each had a child in our arms. (Often the children would fight one another to be carried.) We were discussing our impact on the children. The question that had started the conversation was: Who had benefited more from our volunteer work? Us or them? We had to ask ourselves whether exposing these children to a series of parental figures who appear for a few months and then disappear, never to be seen again, was not, in some profound way, complicating their emotional and mental development."

-Jeremy Frey-Wedeen, who volunteered for one month in Tanzania

Children, especially those who are already vulnerable, can suffer long-term damage from bonding with a series of short-term and unqualified caregivers. This negative impact was recognized in a seminal study by James Bowlby, a researcher for the World Health Organization—in 1951! More recent research has consistently confirmed his findings.

Allowing a group of people into residential care facilities to play with children for a short visit might seem like a way to bring joy and have a fun international exchange, but, in reality, especially when repeated over and over, it fuels attachment disorders and other insecurity issues. Children who grow up without stable primary caregivers are more likely to have trouble forming relationships in later life. Many of the volunteers we spoke to saw evidence of this problem, and felt conflicted or uneasy about their time volunteering in an orphanage. One volunteer in Nicaragua said to us, "I believe I had a positive experience, but leaving was hard. The children got very attached to the volunteers and you could tell they didn't understand why we had

LEARN

to leave. It was heartbreaking and eye-opening." Another, who volunteered in Kenya, said, "The children I worked with became attached to me very quickly... I think that if they will remember me at all it will just be as another white person who was in their lives and then left."

A common theme in our interviews was how volunteers found it difficult to leave children they had become attached to. Can you imagine multiplying that feeling of attachment and separation, several times a month, throughout your childhood? Karjit, a youth from Nepal who grew up in a series of children's homes despite not being an orphan, talked poignantly about his experience in a publication from Next Generation Nepal. "There were so many volunteers: short-time, long-time, middle-time... Sometimes they organize programs and I don't want to go. Children sometimes feel angry because they want to do what they want. There is a nice movie and children they want to watch, but volunteers organize a football program and house managers say you have to go. And all children were angry... Why foreigners come to Nepal? Why do they go in orphanage? That time they come for short time and they give love to us, but then they leave, and when I write they don't reply. I say to a volunteer, 'Sister, I am very lonely,' and they say, 'No problem I am here,' but then they go their country and I write but they don't reply. When I was little everyone can love me, now I am big and I need love."

Creating conditions for abuse through poor vetting and regulation of volunteers

"I did see a few volunteers, including two older guys who made me very uncomfortable regarding the safety of the kids. I know that there is a paper on the wall regarding police checks, but I can't see how it can help..."

–Christine Fletch, who volunteered in
an orphanage in Nepal for five months

Institutions with inadequate child-protection procedures in place (including all those that allow tourists and short-term volunteers to visit and play with the children) risk exposing children to dangerous individuals. In the US and other Western countries, there are strictly enforced rules regarding who can even enter places like schools, let alone institutions that house vulnerable children. In low-income countries, few organizations have the capacity to conduct background checks, or enforce rules regarding photography. There are cases of children being abused by volunteers, as documented, for example, in a 2008 UNICEF-backed study about the rights of children in Nepal. Although most foreign volunteers have no intention of harming children, when they participate in programs without proper screening, they reinforce a system that is wide open to abuse and encourages children to easily trust outsiders. Remember this if you speak with a volunteer travel provider and they don't ask you for any documentation or background checks, but offer you a chance to work with children.

In volunteer travel, there is no issue we feel is as black and white as that of volunteering with vulnerable children. Prospective volunteers often ask us, "How do I find a legitimate orphanage where I can volunteer?" The stark answer is, "If the orphanage is legitimate, they will not let you just walk in and volunteer." There are a small number of instances where experienced childcare and health-related professionals can have a positive impact working directly with vulnerable children, especially in a training role or a more formal capacity than the 'playing' and 'caring' that makes up the majority of child-focused volunteering. As we've mentioned, the growing number of opportunities to volunteer with children is a response to the increased demand from travelers who are willing to pay for a feel-good experience. We need to stop this trend.

Volunteering with children might seem like it's not a big deal if you, as one sole person, visit an orphanage to help for a few days, but it's the collective impact of that happening over and over again that is causing harm, and the only way to stop the trend is to stop individual actions. If you are going to give your time to any organization that serves children – even for tasks such as building a website or fundraising – make sure it's a group that honors the UN Convention on the Rights of the Child and works to keep children in families. In the chapters on researching and selecting an international experience, we'll provide tools to

LEARN

help you avoid volunteer placements that may create harm to children, or cause other damage to communities overseas.

Perspective: Impact is Short Term, Disappointment is Long Term

By Julie Rausenberger, author of Please Mind the Gap! (In-)Consistency in Gap Year Volunteer Tourism

My first experience with 'voluntourism' was when I interned as a volunteer group leader in Ecuador as part of my bachelor's degree in Tourism and Leisure Management. I loved my experience and thought the work we were doing was amazing. In June that year, I was transferred to Asia to continue working as a group leader for the summer program of the same company. There, my eyes opened to the complexities of volunteer travel.

After finishing one of our water projects in a community near Siem Reap, I had an evaluation meeting with my supervisor. I told him that we finished digging two wells for some local families, and we added the name tag of our company on the wells. I showed him the pictures of the volunteers and their accomplishments.

"Excellent work," we all thought, "and a job well done." However, when I asked my supervisor some follow-up questions about the longer-term prospects of the program, my enthusiasm began to wane. "Are you delivering water filters to families who had wells dug for them before?" I asked. "What happens when something goes wrong?" We had seen a few broken wells on the road. "Is there any follow up?" The answers were simple, but alarming: "We do not have a budget for water filters, we do not have staff to keep up with the list of wells we have built, and we do not have the time to follow up." The conclusions I drew were disheartening and put the real impact of our efforts in perspective—there were no long-term plans, and any impact from the volunteer projects was going to be short lived at best.

Now I see that building wells in a country with a weak democratic system can be like a cheap playground for volunteer placement companies. The companies make the travelers believe that they are doing humanitarian work—the companies earn a lot of money, but the effect of the work is purely superficial.

Failing the Volunteers

The failures we explored above relate to negative effects on the communities that volunteers aim to serve. But poorly-planned volunteer experiences can also have damaging effects on the volunteers themselves and their potential to be drivers of positive change in the future. We have seen too many examples where volunteering fails the individuals professionally, emotionally, or morally. A common theme is that volunteers are failed when they do not have meaningful opportunities to learn. We believe this leads to what we call 'the three overloads.'

Poverty overload

> *"It was the most challenging experience of my life seeing the poverty in Kolkata, India. At times it was deeply frustrating seeing people struggle so much."*
> -A volunteer who spent more than three months in India

Volunteers may be woefully ill-equipped for the extreme poverty they encounter overseas. Some feel paralyzing guilt for the way they live at home compared with the lifestyles they witness while volunteering. Others are so deeply affected by their direct encounters with people suffering the effects of poverty – malnourished infants, street children, adults dying of curable diseases – that they become overwhelmed. We call this 'Poverty Overload.'

Without learning about these issues (and themselves) prior to departure, and without proper reflection and debriefing to help them make sense of their experience, exposure to extreme poverty can leave volunteers vowing to have nothing to do with this type of work again. Flimsy pre-departure preparation can also leave volunteers blind to the many strengths of communities that face a lack of material resources; this blindness can further demoralize and disempower volunteers. Some are so overwhelmed that they shut down and miss out on opportunities to engage with further learning during their placement. We met volunteers who dealt with Poverty Overload with escapism (hiding out in Western enclaves, drinking, or using drugs), some

LEARN

who left their placements early, and many who just disconnected intellectually and emotionally. Thus, they were unable to explore the wider global context of the issues they faced—how and why this scale of global inequality exists, and how it relates to themselves, their lives back home, and their future actions.

Failure overload

> "I would think that our presence ultimately made very little impact on anyone. We were just another group doing a one-off project that was of minor benefit, but didn't really change anyone's economic prospects, health, welfare, or education."
>
> -Volunteer who spent more than three months in Guyana

Volunteer companies often sell an inflated promise of how volunteers can help—a simplistic vision of volunteers' power to solve other people's problems. Problems that are far away often seem easier to solve than problems close to home, where the complexity of the issues and the barriers to change are easier to see. While researching this book, we came across many volunteers who were disillusioned when they discovered the depth of the problems that they had traveled across the world to solve. Marketing materials that deliberately shield volunteers from this complexity contribute to the disappointment: volunteers are set up to fail if they are told they are going to help solve a community's deep problems and then are channeled to superficial tasks such as painting walls and playing with children.

Unrealistic expectations inevitably result in failure. Coming to the realization that their volunteer project may not be needed or sustainable, that it does not address the root causes of a problem, or, in the worst cases, is harmful or corrupt, can be upsetting enough to deter volunteers from wanting to try to help again. It can be especially upsetting when the volunteers have traveled with the support and blessings of their wider community – maybe their school held a fundraiser or a local newspaper trumpeted their altruism – which can make the disappointment feel particularly humiliating. Zahara experienced this problem after she asked friends and family to donate to help her travel to Zambia to plant fruit trees and contribute to the nutritional needs of low-income rural children there. But the project was ill-conceived: among other problems, the fruit trees were not suited to the local environment and very few were hardy enough to survive the Zambian dry season. Zahara felt dismal when she had to explain the situation to her donors, and even worse when she reflected on the vast distance between the lofty goals of her project and the reality of the results.

Savior overload

"The trip was marketed to us as an opportunity to help Sri Lanka after the Indian Ocean tsunami. That is exactly what I thought we were doing—for the duration of our fundraising, and for the two weeks we spent at a school, mainly painting and helping to refurbish a library. I was convinced that we were going to help that I didn't ask a lot of important questions: for example, how much more effectively the work could have been done by members of the local community, how much profit the company that sent us made—or how much outsiders could possibly help Sri Lanka recover from the tsunami in two weeks."

-Alice Robinson, who volunteered for two weeks in Sri Lanka

Some volunteers buy into the simplistic vision of quick-fix solutions found in volunteer marketing materials, and never realize their efforts were – at best – superfluous. They fall into another missed opportunity for learning that we call 'Savior Overload.' In this case, volunteers leave their placement feeling good about themselves, but without understanding the ongoing work it takes to sustain real solutions. Believing that they have already 'done their bit,' they then lack the impetus and drive to carry change forward into the rest of their lives.

Privileging volunteers' contributions over everything else can give volunteers inflated ideas about the value of their labor. Development work becomes a non-professional pursuit, with roles that anyone can fill as long as they have a big heart and a

LEARN

bit of time. Going abroad to 'help' local people, without stressing the need to learn from those same people, or follow up on that impact, fosters feelings of superiority ('they' always need 'our' help), which can remain with the volunteer when they return home. This can perpetuate unhelpful stereotypes that hold back development and are a major barrier to cultivating a learning mindset—a key to working across boundaries to find sustainable solutions to global challenges.

Beating the overloads

All three 'overloads' can be avoided by re-balancing the goals of volunteering to focus on learning. Volunteers can see their own responses to poverty as learning experiences that spur them to action, not excuses for paralysis. In addition, if volunteer programs provided different metrics of success, volunteers might frame and reflect on their experiences more constructively. Instead of the main criterion being to 'help,' what if volunteer experiences were framed in reverse, so travelers understood that *they* might be the ones who need help at first—help to learn about the country they're visiting, the problems confronting people there, and how they might contribute to solutions in the long term? In that case, challenging and discouraging experiences could be seen as part of the learning process, not as a sign of failure. Finally, volunteer programs that are honest in their marketing and provide education through their websites – such as stating that learning is a central goal of volunteering, and that volunteers will probably learn more than they contribute – can avoid perpetuating volunteers' paternalistic beliefs and 'savior' mentality.

Ultimately, the three overloads harm not only the volunteers, but our collective society as well, if volunteers do not get the tools they need to learn about and participate in the long-term struggle for a more just world. Volunteers who focus on learning as a way to contribute to long-term change not only feel more effective, but they are also more likely to stay engaged for the long haul by developing a more realistic idea of how to contribute to the multifaceted and ongoing process of change.

If it's This Complicated, Should I Do Nothing?

"My philosophy is that everything is more complicated than you thought."

-Kwame Anthony Appiah, *Experiments in Ethics*

After reading about the complexities and pitfalls of volunteering, you may feel dazed, even paralyzed. Maybe this thought has already crossed your mind: if making positive change in the world is really that difficult, then might it be better just to do nothing? If you are feeling like this, then we urge you to stay with us and read the rest of this book.

There *are* things you can do to improve the world. There are many ways you can make a positive difference in other people's lives, some of them without even leaving home, and there are indeed many talented, thoughtful, humble, and self-reflective volunteers around the world right this very moment having a positive impact through their work.

If you do decide to engage in volunteer travel, the remainder of this book is dedicated to exploring how you can do so in a way that is effective and empowering for all involved, guided by the principles and practices of learning service. We needed to unpack some of the pitfalls of volunteer travel to establish a shared understanding of why this new framework for volunteer travel is needed. We'll focus next on the positive potential of volunteering, and how the learning service approach can help you best use your experience for a positive impact, plan for safe and meaningful travel, and set out to create positive change in the world through how you live, travel, and give.

LEARN

5.
THE POTENTIAL PITFALLS OF LEARNING SERVICE

Perspective: Why I Am Glad I Did Not Give Up on International Volunteering

By Claire

I have spent over half my life somehow involved with international volunteering. During that time, I have experienced just about all the ways in which it can cause harm. After several years (on and off) volunteering in Nepal as a young adult, I had seen both myself and other volunteers fall into every pitfall in the book. It was disillusioning and demotivating, and I started to feel as if everything I tried, even with the best of intentions, could end up causing harm. I got to the point when I was ready to give up on international volunteering altogether.

I am so glad I didn't.

I was 22, back in England and completely broke. I needed a job and wasn't sure whether any of my volunteer experience overseas amounted to much in the UK job market. And then I stumbled across Development in Action (DiA), a grassroots, youth-led volunteer initiative. On the surface, DiA wasn't doing anything much differently than all the other volunteer-sending organizations. It sent young volunteers, usually students, to work in development organizations in India for two or five month placements. Instead of emphasizing 'giving' and 'helping,' however, DiA focused on the exposure to development issues that volunteers received. The goals of the volunteers' short time abroad were clear—they were there to learn from the experts, to bring back knowledge with which to educate others, and to help out when they could. In short, the primary goal was *learning*, not *helping*. All participants committed to designing and running development education projects in their hometowns after they returned. Volunteers ran photography exhibitions, led classroom workshops, and hosted speaking debates. For example, Stephen Jones, an engineering student at Cambridge University, spent his summer with a project in Indore that supported rural women. When he came back, he developed a presentation about rainwater harvesting that was used in schools. He went on to become involved in running Engineers Without Borders UK, organizing learning opportunities for young engineers in organizations around the world. I was inspired!

I worked with DiA as an employee, then committee member, then a board member. I trained and supervised scores of volunteers. In India, volunteers did work that our partners found useful: they made or updated websites, compiled research reports, and assisted teachers in classrooms. These volunteers came back with remarkable stories to tell and lots of learning to share. What's more, inspired by what they experienced and empowered by what they learned from the experts abroad, many of these individuals went on to do extraordinary things with their lives. Like Stephen, many are now leaders in local or international nonprofits. Some have organized or led protests, campaigned on important global issues, or became involved in direct action. Tom Grundy embarked on a lifetime of activism before he started the *Hong Kong Free Press*—a news outlet that aims to provide an alternative to government-owned media in Hong Kong, where he now lives. They are teachers, lawyers, politicians, horticulture experts, and almost every one of them talks readily about how time volunteering overseas changed their perspectives and shaped their lives.

LEARN

Volunteering overseas and getting it right is not easy. But as well as experiencing the challenges and difficulties, I also have seen how powerful volunteer travel can be in inspiring positive change. I was slightly older and slightly wiser when I decided to volunteer again myself, this time with VSO in Cambodia—with a more humble attitude and adjusted expectations of what I was there to do. Even though VSO recruits professionals and emphasizes skills transfer, one of the main qualities they look for is a 'willingness to learn.' In my time in Cambodia, I learned the skills of indirect communication from my Cambodian colleagues, I learned about the realities of subsistence farming from people in the rural communities we worked in, and I gained an insight into Cambodian culture by being part of a small community.

I like to think that because of this learning I was able to make a positive contribution to the Cambodian Rural Development Team, the nonprofit where I volunteered. I started to see that learning was the key to getting it right.

While I have never come across a situation in which an international volunteer has 'saved' a place or group of people, I have seen positive impacts of volunteering on communities overseas. I have known professionals who skillfully built capacity, enthusiastic young people who offered much-needed support with basic but essential tasks, and dedicated individuals who provided creative, problem-solving ideas in difficult times. I think of Gerda, a doctor from Austria who has volunteered for most of the last decade building healthcare systems in the remote Himalayas, and the groups of young Australian students from the Oaktree Foundation who came to Cambodia to learn about issues that they could raise awareness of and money for back home. I have also seen real and lasting relationships formed, where volunteers return year after year.

In chatting with my local friends and colleagues in Nepal, I have learned that a benefit of hosting international volunteers, mentioned time and time again, is the friendship and connection across cultural boundaries. After all, the reality is that most of the people international volunteers interact with will never have the opportunity to travel or volunteer abroad themselves. And yet, they have had the chance to learn from, share stories with, and share their wisdom with people from diverse backgrounds across the world. That's pretty amazing. In fact, that is the very definition of global citizenship: the ability to glimpse our interconnected world, where many people from many walks of life believe in, and are contributing to, a better future for all.

The Value of Volunteering

"I have had the opportunity to work with a number of fantastic international volunteers. Our organization was formed based on the spirit of volunteerism, and that has been what has brought us to where it has come today."
-David Pwalua, Director of Programs for
Afrikids in Ghana

In exploring the pitfalls of volunteer travel, our intention is not to undermine or dismiss it as a worthless activity. We are highlighting the problems in order to improve and transform the way global volunteering is practiced, as we believe it has the potential to become a major force for positive change in the world.

The learning service model accepts that we don't yet have all the answers, and that we need to take a longer term view of impact. Learning service looks to minimize negative consequences while keeping a humble view on what positive changes are possible during a volunteer experience. Moreover, it expands the assessment of impact to include a volunteer's learning and increased capacity to positively contribute to the world in the future. Francesca Morgante, who volunteered in India for five months, said, "It's important to appreciate the positive impact on the traveler and their view on the world, which will undoubtedly be changed, even just by being exposed firsthand to a completely different way of life."

During our research, we met volunteers who offered valuable support, solidarity, and fresh perspectives to communities and organizations abroad. We were inspired by the impact responsible volunteers in well-matched placements could have, and we pulled out the following themes that highlight their range of positive experiences.

LEARN

Two-way skill-sharing

"Initially upon arriving I felt that my impact was negative. I really questioned, why am I here? Why am I taking a Bangladeshi job away? Am I just reinforcing the idea that nursing is so bad here that foreigners have to look after the problem? Am I doing more harm than good? I still struggle with a lot of those questions, which makes me quite skeptical about most volunteer organizations. But then I realized… the whole point of the project is to train the potential nurses that can change the image and role of nurses in Bangladesh. I felt I made an impact by just being there, being me, being professional and responsible as a registered nurse… my behavior reinforced the view that nurses are intelligent, professional, and reliable, and are to be respected and valued."

–Ricki Hagen, volunteered in Bangladesh
for five months

When a volunteer is qualified and experienced in a certain field and commits enough time to transfer knowledge effectively, they can use their time abroad to build the capacity of others. In fact, Erin Barnhardt's survey of 248 volunteer hosting organizations found that 91 percent either agreed or strongly agreed that international volunteers contribute needed skills. It is a reality for many countries that there are not enough trained healthcare professionals, skilled teacher trainers, or other specialists. When the needs of a host organization are well matched with the skills of a volunteer, volunteers can strengthen systems by mentoring local staff. Heather Perry, a health educator in New Zealand who volunteered in Cambodia for more than a month, said, "I felt like I was passing on my skills to women who could continue to grow with them, and use them in their work, and pass them onto even more women."

Volunteers can also offer fresh ideas and inspiration. Erin's research found that 89 percent of hosting organizations surveyed either agreed or strongly agreed that international volunteers provide a new viewpoint or perspective. Wen-Xin, who volunteered for over six months in Ecuador, gave us this example.

"My host family and school learned about recycling and started recycling papers. They bought paper cups and plates instead of polystyrene cups and plates for parties and gatherings."

The skill sharing goes both ways. Many of the most effective volunteers learn skills and gain important perspectives from their hosts, and they often reflect that what they learned far outweighed what they were able to share. A volunteer who spent over a year in Uganda said, "I was able to gain field work experience and learn on the job... Every person I got to know had a different background and different skills, which I could access through working with them." The beauty of viewing your learning experience as lasting well beyond your time abroad is that you can apply those experiences and skills once you return home.

Cultural exchange

"There was a cultural exchange from both sides. A lot of the Tibetans I was working with were not legally allowed to leave India, so [through our exchanges] they were able to learn about America and other countries and I was able to learn about their lives."

-Matthew Graylin, volunteered in India for two weeks

The best volunteering placements create a platform for exchange and look very different from unequal donor-recipient relationships. In Erin's research, 88 percent of hosting organizations either agreed or strongly agreed that international volunteers provide an opportunity for local people to learn more about other nations and cultures. A volunteer who spent over a year in Panama told us, "I know that my community changed their perceptions of Americans, they now have a better understanding of the US and the culture."

Through their experiences abroad, volunteers often recognize the limitations in their current knowledge and perspective, and by embracing a new culture, view their own culture in a new light. They might have the same impact on their hosts, both expanding their perspectives on what is 'right' or 'wrong' and forming new opinions about the other's culture, replacing stereotypes and generalizations that might have shaped their

LEARN

prior views. Amy McLoughlin, who volunteered in India for over a month, said, "Working in India made me more patient and gave me a better understanding of cultural differences," and Morgan Canup, who volunteered in Namibia for over three months, said, "I was able to leave with my eyes and heart open and more accepting to different cultures and ways of life." The positive potential of volunteer travel includes the expansion of cross-cultural acceptance and learning.

Solidarity

> "My NGO is based in a poor postwar area... People here do not travel much, the children have limited resources and opportunities. Volunteering brings in individuals from other cultures and opens up this closed area... Volunteers help us kick-start the community, individuals from the local community get involved and we learn from one another... The communities we work in feel highly isolated from the outside world due to ongoing occupation and conflict, they often feel they are forgotten and no one cares about them, which adds to the psychological impact they already experience. The presence of international volunteers helps break down that barrier and makes the students we work with (and their families) feel part of a global community and realize that some people really do care."
>
> -Volunteer Hosting Organization

Host communities benefit not only from the work that volunteers do but also from the sense of solidarity it can bring. In our research, host organizations repeatedly mentioned the creation of strong bonds between people from diverse backgrounds as one of the most highly valued aspects of hosting foreign volunteers. The fact that volunteers care enough to show up and offer support to their cause is recognized as a benefit by activists and communities overseas—people who are often overstretched, tired, and in need of a motivation boost. Grace, a volunteer host in Lebanon, said, "One thing I hope foreign volunteers take away from their service is how to learn how to listen to others and how to be empathetic. The problems of the people are not ours but being there to listen and support is very important."

Moreover, international support can bring with it money, influence, and political leverage. Of the host organizations surveyed by Erin Barnhardt, 79 percent either agreed or strongly agreed that volunteers from overseas bring international attention to their work. One representative of a host organization commented, "I love the enthusiasm new volunteers bring to our organization. It helps keep me motivated more long term." As such, an opportunity to maximize the potential of your time abroad is by balancing the *doing* of the volunteer work with your *being* with the community and finding ways to have a positive impact through both.

Contributing vital resources

"I was able to kick-start some projects that the villagers had wanted for years (but lacked the resources to start) and that they are committed to maintaining."
-A volunteer who spent over a year in Senegal

Volunteers often bring with them access to money and resources. This may be through a fee paid directly to the organization to offset the costs of hosting them. Even when no money changes hands, organizations get financial benefits from volunteers who fundraise, talk to donors and connect them to opportunities. This is another reason why it's important to find out how much of the money you are paying goes directly to the local organization who is hosting you or who you are working with. Erin Barnhardt's research showed that 52 percent of hosting organizations either agreed or strongly agreed that international volunteers generate revenue for their organization. Therese Arkenberg, who went to Ghana for two weeks, said, "My student fundraising team was able to collect an amount that covered a full round of microloans to 50 women in the community, so I know our hard work made an impact by enabling their project to go forward."

Furthermore, 54 percent of the hosting organizations that Erin surveyed either agreed or strongly agreed that international volunteers help their economy by spending money locally, which

LEARN

suggests that organizations think about the impact of volunteering in a broader sense than the volunteers themselves.

Creating long-term activists and educated advocates

"The experience furthered my passion in the field of development and poverty reduction. I have since become an activist, and the path that I want to take in my life has changed dramatically. Nothing has ever impacted me so much in my life."

–Stephanie Kenealy, who spent three weeks on a learning trip in Cambodia

Learning through working abroad can lead to insights and inspiration that no amount of reading could teach you. You create life experiences rather than read textbook definitions of concepts like 'poverty,' helping you move from a vague term in the media to the nuanced realities of daily living in your host community. Likewise, no amount of academic discourse on grassroots empowerment can teach you as much as meeting strong community leaders and experiencing the impacts of their work. Through an experience volunteering overseas, you can connect to and learn deeply about global issues in a way that could affect the rest of your life. A volunteer who went to Nicaragua for over a month told us, "Working with the 'absolute poor' of the world (the UN's definition being living on less than a dollar a day) completely changed my perspective on what was important to me and those around me. I became more solidified in my political beliefs and less afraid to 'make waves' by standing up for what was important to me. My long-term goals changed, and I have dedicated my life to educating and inspiring young college students to take on these opportunities and how to go about doing so."

The vast majority of the returned volunteers we talked to felt that their time overseas had an impact on their life, and many could point to specific changes they have made as a result. Furthermore, many of the activists, development workers, educators, and social entrepreneurs that we know have been deeply influenced by experiences overseas. Many felt that once their eyes were opened to an issue facing the world, there was no going back and that their ongoing passions and drive for social and environmental justice continue to be driven by the grounding of these experiences. Host organizations also recognize this as an important impact or benefit of volunteering. In Erin's survey, 76 percent of hosting organizations either agreed or strongly agreed that international volunteers become advocates upon return home.

Another important role that returned volunteers play is to connect others to these global issues. Returned volunteers can bring seemingly remote issues to life for their friends and families back home and those who have not been able to travel abroad or experience those issues themselves. By sharing their learning, they can inspire others to take positive actions for change. Ricki Hagen, who volunteered in Bangladesh for five months, told us, "I have also been able to educate friends, family, and colleagues about current issues in Bangladesh and surrounding areas— broadening everyone's knowledge about the world."

Reshaping perspectives on how volunteers want to live their lives

"This year might be advertised as a 'service-based' program, the most important thing you will do in these nine months is to learn. Don't get frustrated if you don't feel that your presence is making a difference, and don't be pessimistic about your overall impact, especially if you read some of the development books on the bookshelf, which you really should... These months will be transformative, and be woven into the fabric of who you are."
-Adrian Tasistro-Hart, who spent nine months on a
learning program in Senegal with
Where There Be Dragons

Describing volunteer travel as a 'life-changing experience' might seem like a tired cliché, but it is also true. People often return home wanting to form closer relationships with the people they love, eat more healthy or environmentally-responsible food, have less screen time, or take time to get to know someone who has recently emigrated to their country. These changes in

LEARN

how people choose to live after their time abroad are hard to measure, but can be profound. Often the changes relate more strongly to personal development than global. Hanna Jacobsen, who volunteered for over a year in Brazil, said, "My volunteer experience reinforced my values, taught me to be more patient with myself, and with others, and with my goals." Sarah Gibbons, who volunteered in South Africa for over a month said, "It has made me more humble and appreciative of what I have… and it has made me confident in meeting new people and working within a professional environment."

Even if the changes are small, and seem only to relate to you, they can be significant. Many returned volunteers found that the small changes they made upon returning home paved the way for a more meaningful and connected life. And the collective impact of all those small changes repeated thousands of times should not be underestimated. What if we all consumed more consciously, ate more healthily, or ensured we welcomed our new neighbors? A volunteer who went to Ukraine for two years said, "I have more patience, confidence, and my scope of reality has been broadened, and my time-horizon for decision making both lengthened and shortened: lengthened in that I am more comfortable allowing life and events to develop with a more hands-off approach—shortened in that I am much more able to focus on the here and now, enjoying daily moments, victories, and surprises."

If you find at the end of your volunteer placement, or even at the end of your life, that all you have done is learned and used that learning to positively inform your actions, without being able to pinpoint any broader impact on the world, then that in itself is enough. Humble action, which is informed by genuine learning, is valuable and can make our world a better place.

Positive Trends in International Volunteer Travel

Thankfully, it is not only us in the *Learning Service* team who are calling for change in the way volunteer travel is viewed, marketed, and practiced. There are a great number of thoughtful and reflective returned volunteers using social media to express critiques and suggestions. There are investigative journalists exposing the pitfalls and giving a platform to those offering solutions. And there are a growing number of ethical volunteer organizations striving to offer volunteer opportunities that minimize the negative impacts and increase the positives.

Some volunteer-sending organizations have come together to share best practices and establish guidelines of conduct for the field. While there is no certifying agency for volunteer programs, some of the most reputable organizations are helping each other to implement ethical advertising strategies, better screen volunteers, and improve training. Steve Rosenthal, Chairman Emeritus of one such network, the Building Bridges Coalition, told us that "the Building Bridges Coalition has brought together hundreds of organizations to work together to improve the quality of our programs, to share our stories... and maximize the positive impacts of service abroad and at home... Thanks to people in our field caring deeply about our work and having a collaborative spirit, we have seen unprecedented cooperation of people and organizations working together to develop standards for our field."

Other positive trends that are emerging include how volunteer travel is being made more accessible to those who have traditionally been excluded. We are seeing an increase in diaspora volunteering (for example, when the daughter or son of Ethiopian immigrants in the US goes to volunteer in Ethiopia) and South-South volunteering (a sharing of skills between two countries that are usually the 'beneficiaries' of volunteer efforts— for example, someone from the Philippines volunteering in Zambia). A member of the Indian diaspora who volunteered in India for over three months said, "I was able to get in touch with my Indian roots in a way that I had never done before." Shruti Manian, another diaspora volunteer who was in India for one month said, "I really understand the socio-economic diversity in India now and am very aware of my privileges."

Diaspora volunteering takes advantage of the linguistic and cultural knowledge that children of immigrants usually have, which can make them more effective volunteers in their parents' country of origin. South-South volunteers may be especially effective for similar reasons—cultural barriers and differences in backgrounds may not be as high, and ideas and skills may

LEARN

be more relevant. South-to-North volunteering still hasn't taken off, but there are interesting examples of the potential of skilled volunteers from low-income countries volunteering in wealthier countries, such as Atlas Corps, which emphasizes a two-way exchange of skills.

A Manifestation of Hope, Peace, and Global Connections

"While the quantifiable impact may seem small, the non-quantifiable impact – such as spreading hope, optimism, changing perspective – seems very evident at times."
                    –A volunteer who spent over a year in Ukraine

The passion and idealism that fuel volunteering are tremendous forces for good. A world without people who believe in change – and are prepared to personally do something about it – is a world without hope. It is heartening that the numbers of people willing to take action on issues they care about are increasing. We believe in the power of this growing movement to do good in the world; if practiced with humility and a learning mindset, it could be just what our divided world needs to usher a new era of empathy, justice, and cooperation.

As we have seen, the positive benefits of volunteering are not automatic. Good intentions are not sufficient on their own, but they are not to be disregarded. Imagine what a powerful force for positive change this movement could be if these good intentions for service were harnessed with a learning mindset! In this section and throughout the book, we have included voices of volunteers and hosts who believe in the power of volunteering. These voices inspired us to write this book. By opening discussions about volunteering, offering suggestions, and encouraging you to add your voice, we believe we can create enough impetus for the widespread change of practice—and, in doing so, channel the good intentions of volunteers to create lasting positive changes. Learning service is a way that we believe can get us there, and the rest of this book is devoted to introducing and exploring this model.

PART THREE:

LEARNING ABOUT YOUR OPTIONS

"Having seen both the positive and negative impacts of volunteering firsthand, I am passionate about ensuring that people are selective and careful about the volunteering experiences that they participate in. I encourage people to do as much research as possible."

-Rachael Wölffel, who volunteered for
a year in Cambodia

Sifting through volunteer travel options can be daunting. There are so many starting points, so much information and so many varied opportunities that it can quickly get overwhelming. Many people end up choosing the first or the easiest option over the best one because they don't know where else to look. The volunteers we interviewed tended to agree on the strategy for finding the best placement: know your options and research them well. This section will help you heed their advice and make an informed decision about which opportunity or program is right for you, giving you the tools to research and ask critical questions before deciding if and how you want to make a commitment.

Potential volunteers often ask us, "Where is the biggest need for volunteers?" The learning service model flips that back around and asks, "What is the impact that you are qualified to make—or are going to *learn* to make?" Taking that as your starting point, the next step is to identify an opportunity where you can both contribute and learn in an effective and sustainable way.

If you were hoping that this section of the book would include a pre-vetted list of the best volunteer travel options out there, we have some bad news: it isn't that simple. Not only do the thousands of opportunities change on a daily basis, also everyone is different and looking for different things. Only you will know what might be the right fit for your experience and needs—or how that might match with responsible volunteer and learning opportunities. What we can do, however, is guide you through a clear process that includes what to consider and the questions to ask, until you arrive at a decision you are happy with. Though it's more work, we promise it will result in a more rewarding placement.

To make the process as easy as possible, we have created the Learning Service Decision-Making Flowchart!

| Compare volunteering with other options | Understand the role that volunteers play | Learn about different types of volunteer travel offerings | Compare and evaluate opportunities | Sign up! |

As you can see, the process starts with helping you decide whether volunteer travel is the right option for you, and if so, to learn what volunteer opportunities are out there. Then it offers guidance on how to narrow your choices, and how to make the final decision of choosing a placement abroad. We will walk you through the questions to ask, suggest some things to consider, and offer some tips for how to make your decisions. If at any point you feel like you have made a wrong decision and are on the wrong path, you can go back to a previous step, re-examine your thoughts, and continue learning about what might be right for you. Remember, changing your mind isn't a bad thing: it's a key part of this learning and evaluation process. Think back to the balance of learning and action represented in the vajra.

6.
DECIDING ON THE RIGHT PATH FOR YOU

Perspective: The Young Person at the Back of the Room
By Joe

As I traveled around the country talking about my book *World Hunger*, I knew always to expect someone in the audience, usually a young person at the back of the room, to ask a version of this question: "I understand the problem. Now, I want to know what I can do about it. How can I make a difference in the world?"

With only a couple of minutes to answer, I would direct them to a short book we had created at the Food First institute, *Beyond the Peace Corps*. But I knew this book was inadequate—sure, it listed volunteer programs we had heard good things about, but we had not had the resources to do field research to assess which ones were truly effective and which would be a good fit for a particular person. In fact, the book didn't even help someone decide if volunteering was the right choice for them. The research Zahara, Stefano and I did for our book How to *Live Your Dream of Volunteering Overseas*, confirmed that for many people, volunteering overseas is actually not the best option.

Even now, many years later, I still get the same questions: "How can I help solve global problems? Should I go overseas to work on these problems? Is volunteering abroad the most effective way to solve these problems? How can I find the opportunity that is right for me? What is the best way to make a difference?" This chapter is for that person at the back of the room.

Step 1: Compare Volunteering with Other Options

| Compare volunteering with other options | Understand the role that volunteers play | Learn about different types of volunteer travel offerings | Compare and evaluate opportunities | Sign up! |

Volunteer travel, when done well and with a learning mindset, can be a powerful and authentic way to see and contribute to the world, but it's not the only way to achieve these goals. There is no need to limit yourself to only considering volunteer travel as a next step. The learning service philosophy can be applied to a much wider range of activities and can guide other decisions you make in your life. A narrow view of what 'helping' looks like restricts the learning and actions that will be needed to tackle future global challenges. There are many paths to impact, and different paths fit different people at different times. There is no one-size-fits-all solution or paths that are 'better' or 'worse.'

As you reflect honestly on your capacity, ability, goals, and priorities for engaging in working for social change, you may realize that it will not be in your best interest, or the best interest of your intended host community, for you to commit to a volunteer placement overseas. For example, international volunteering may not be the right choice for you if:

- You realize that you're not emotionally ready to deal with the stress, challenges, and changes of volunteering overseas, or that the expected living conditions will be too difficult for you to endure.

LEARN

- You have health, psychological, emotional, social, financial, addiction or other issues that might make you a burden on your host community and organization.
- Your situation at home will not be conducive to you spending time overseas. For example, you have a very young child or a sick parent who needs support.

It is important to come to this conclusion in the early planning stages, so we encourage you to take seriously the task of bringing a critical eye to your current situation and readiness. Happily, volunteering abroad is not the only way, or even the best way, to engage in learning and service for causes that are important to you.

We encourage you to consider a range of alternatives. Maggie Mahoney explained her choice to not volunteer this way: "I was concerned that volunteering abroad in the first semester of freshman year would isolate me from my campus community. The transition to college was hard enough without going to a completely different country." Find a path that fits your needs, priorities, and skills, that does no harm and ideally brings benefit to communities overseas. Here are a few suggestions to consider:

Travel

If adventure, seeing new places, and learning about culture are what most attract you to volunteering overseas, you may want to consider simply traveling. Traveling can be a powerful way to learn, clarify life goals and open up options for engaging in social change. This is especially true with travel that engages you with local communities and is 'close to the ground' such as a backpacking trip across a country, staying in basic accommodation and using public transport, or getting to know a city intimately by hanging out with local people. Raj Gyawali, who runs ethical travel company socialtours in Nepal, said, "If you don't feel that you have the right skills or have done the right research to volunteer right now, you should definitely still consider traveling in a country, doing experiential learning that will deepen your local understanding and appreciation—similar to the outcomes you get from volunteering too."

Specifically, we encourage you to travel mindfully, considering your impact on the local culture and environment, and being thoughtful about where you spend your money. Also consider what you are choosing to learn about by being selective in where you hang out and whom you interact with. (Hint: Hanging out at local places and learning from local people may require more bravery at first, or a commitment to learning a new language, but overall may be more enriching than always going to places full of other tourists!)

Travel now includes a wide range of possibilities: ecotourism (visiting a low-impact lodge in the Costa Rican rainforest), cultural tourism (living with a family in a traditional village in South Africa), and adventure travel (a camel trip through the desert of Rajasthan), or even a *staycation* where you take a week to travel to all the historical sites in your own town. Many people find that spending time traveling helps to clarify life goals and open up future options. Francesca Morgante, who volunteered in India for five months, said, "Many people find that the conscious traveling option is the closest to 'helping' or 'giving back' that they feel comfortable with at a certain point in their life. Starting off the journey with an open heart and an open mind will undoubtedly bring an expansion and a transformation in oneself through connecting with different people and places."

If you really just want a holiday or to experience another culture, or do not have time to carefully research service options, there is no reason to have to squeeze volunteering into your vacation agenda. A responsible travel option would probably be a better decision.

Educational travel

If you know your primary goal is to immerse yourself in another culture, and you would benefit from structured learning opportunities, you might look into taking a trip specifically designed around learning outcomes. Learning trips can have a theme, such as learning about a region's environment, art, cuisine, or history. Some focus entirely on international development issues. The learning components may be offered through lectures, lessons, and discussions, or more experientially

LEARN

through homestays, visits to local organizations, and meeting local activists.

Most learning trips are organized for groups—either through an educational institution or as a sign-up tour. While study trips for students are common all around the world, many academic institutions also offer learning trips for adults. Alternatively, if you are self-motivated and have specific interests you may want to look into arranging a learning trip by yourself: as you travel, you could assign yourself relevant readings, visit projects and organizations, and set up interviews with local changemakers. If you do this, remember that you may be using people's resources to fill your learning goals, so consider how you will honor or compensate those who give you their time on your travels, such as making a contribution to an organization. Emily Dunning, who designed her own six-month learning trip overland from the UK to Hong Kong, then on to Japan and New Zealand, said. "I didn't want to just do a volunteer trip—it didn't allow me the flexibility or the opportunities that a 'DIY' travel experience did. Having gained an understanding of the seriousness of climate change and the disproportionate effect of flying on an individual's carbon footprint, I went overland from Europe by train. I saw this as a way to expand my horizons, experience new places and cultures, as well as meet and learn from people working on environmental challenges along the way. It took a lot of time and research to bring it together, but it was so worth it—not only did I get the incredible push-you-out-of-your-comfort-zone experiences that travel brings, but I also got the insights from locals passionate about the same things as me."

A learning trip to a specific place may act as an important first step before committing to a longer period of volunteering, and it can be a way to begin unraveling complex development issues. You can start to explore a country before you commit to living there, and understand the context in which organizations that host volunteers are working, in a much more authentic way than doing internet research. You can also assess your own readiness to volunteer.

Stephanie Kenealy, who went on a learning trip to Cambodia for three weeks, had this to share about her experience: "I returned home with more for myself than I could ever imagined. I gained an enriched sense of myself and my values, and am still gaining from my experience—two years later! The trip also impacted my personal views. It made me challenge things and not just accept what I am told. My entire family and friends noticed a difference in the way I approach things and how I evaluate different situations."

Study abroad

If you are a current or potential student, a university-affiliated study abroad program might be an option to consider. While some study abroad programs incorporate service learning in their curriculum, most have a wider focus encompassing both experiential and academic learning. You might decide that this type of program is right for you at this stage in your life, balancing a travel experience with formal classes through which you can build your knowledge about a new place, language, and culture. Study abroad can also be a good option if you need to earn academic credit.

Study abroad opportunities can be sourced through your own university, or you can apply directly to programs that place you in universities around the world. There are programs that combine any number of learning goals you might have in addition to your normal studies: studying in Costa Rica where you can help grow an agricultural business, a semester in China where you can further your Mandarin skills while also working as an intern for a local organization, or placements in top African universities where you can learn with the future leaders of the continent.

There are also dedicated language schools around the world providing structured opportunities to start or enhance your mastery of another language. They usually require less of a time commitment than traditional study abroad, and often come combined with immersion opportunities like homestays and one-on-one teaching.

With so many options for studying abroad, consider what aspects of the experience are most important to you. Are you only considering programs with academic credentials that are transferable to your home university? Do you want to study within a university setting abroad, or are you seeking out a more travel-related experience, moving between locations, or even

LEARN

circumnavigating the world on a boat as part of your studies? Do you want to study in a place with many other foreigners, or somewhere that will be more conducive to learning a new language?

Find an internship

If you are looking for a medium-term, structured placement that prioritizes learning, you may want to look at internship opportunities. Interning is similar to volunteering, but it is usually differentiated by a more formal work setting, more structured learning outcomes and often a longer minimum time commitment. The work of an intern is more likely to be office-based rather than a hands-on building, painting, or teaching role. Although it may seem less exciting, you will be well-placed to learn about the wider structural issues tackled by an organization, and depending on your skills and commitment, you may be more likely to effect change.

Responding to a structured internship advertisement is different to offering help as a volunteer, for a number of reasons. Internship placements are often conducted much like job interviews, carefully selecting someone for a role based on the match between their skills and the specific need. There is usually only one position available, or at most a handful, so application procedures can be lengthy and competitive, like a job.

Additionally, well-structured internships fit well with the learning service model because they are often designed with learning as a primary goal. Although the intern might be given a number of useful tasks, there is an understanding by both the hosts and the interns that they are there to learn. Many people who are considering a career in international development pursue internships abroad as a way to learn more about possible future career paths. Lily Lapenna-Huda, founder of MyBNK, said, "I did an unpaid internship in Bangladesh with BRAC, the largest NGO in the world and one that is very well respected. I learned so much about monitoring and evaluation, and when I later started a finance education program for youth back at home in London, I was more successful because of that experience. Now, when students interested in social impact work ask me for career advice, I often suggest that if they can afford to intern, at home or abroad, with a well-respected organization, they will almost never regret it, as the skills and experience they gain will be incredibly valuable and will give them the tools they need to tackle other challenges in the future."

Interns may be paid or unpaid, which blurs the line between interning and volunteering. So one final word of advice: just because a role is advertised as an internship, there is no guarantee that it is structured any differently from other volunteer roles. The learning service processes of researching and continual learning is just as applicable to internship opportunities—so if you decide to go for this option, continue reading the rest of this book!

Work abroad

If you have specialist skills that are globally sought after, working abroad may be an option for you. Applying for an advertised and compensated position is one way to be more certain that your skills are matched to a need. One popular option is to gain a certification (and preferably experience) in teaching English or other languages abroad.

Take into consideration that many countries across the world have high unemployment rates, so jobs may be scarce, with preference given to local people. Salaries may be much lower than in your own country. More highly paid jobs, in businesses, large NGOs, or donor organizations, usually require years of experience in the sector. Before making a long-term commitment to working abroad, you might want to spend some time living in the country to make sure your expectations and skills align with the realities and needs. In fact, a common path to working abroad is to start out with a stint of volunteering to gain the cultural competencies you need for employment.

Volunteer at home

If you are looking for a flexible opportunity that can work around other life commitments, you might consider volunteering in your own country. Staying at home may not sound as glamorous as a trip halfway across the world, but there are several reasons why it might be what you are looking for. It can be easier to evaluate and compare offerings closer to home and ensure your skills and experience are a match for the need. Communication is usually easier within familiar languages and cultures, as is the possibility for you to follow up and really see the impact of your work. Finally, volunteering locally does not require as big a life change as settling into a new culture (although the culture shock of working in a different part of your own city or country can sometimes be as big as going abroad). You can even choose a part-time or even online commitment.

Volunteering at home can also be a great first step to volunteering abroad, helping you gain experience and insight that is useful for volunteering anywhere. Many organizations also have excellent training programs for volunteers.

If the appeal of volunteer travel is partly the feeling that you can contribute in a small way to solving a global problem, the assumption that you need to travel in order to address these issues is not upheld in our interconnected world. The truly global nature of most problems means that the root causes may stem from actions taken elsewhere. Supporting efforts on the other side of the globe might require working for changes in politics, law, or trade policies back at home. Raising awareness about how your own country may be contributing to problems overseas, or lobbying for a change in policy that impacts issues abroad, may be a better use of your time and power as a citizen.

Go back to school

If researching volunteering has piqued your interest in international development or related topics such as politics or the environment, you may want to sign up for courses to study these things academically rather than immediately going abroad to volunteer. Taking a course that explores the interrelated topics of aid, development, history, social entrepreneurship, international law, foreign policy, or any number of topics that shape our world can help you get to grips with their overlapping complexity. By taking formal courses, e-learning modules, open masters programs, or self-led learning opportunities, you can work out where you stand on controversial issues at the same time as gaining knowledge for future roles. Alternately, you may decide to learn a technical skill or gain a professional qualification so you have a tangible skill to offer in a future job or volunteer position.

Choosing to volunteer abroad

If, after looking at all your options, learning about the potential challenges, and taking the time for some self-reflection, you feel that volunteer travel is the best next step for you, then we are with you all the way. Using the learning service model, you can have a positive experience contributing and learning abroad, which you can use throughout the rest of your life. The next step is wading through the many international volunteering options. The flow diagram continues by helping you narrow down options based on your personal and global development goals.

LEARN

7.
VOLUNTEER ROLES & PROJECTS

Perspective: I Did What Was Useful

By Rachel Springer, who volunteered in Lebanon for a year

My official title was Emergency Response Assistant, and when I told this to one of my professors who had experience in the field of humanitarian aid and development she said, "Oh, so you'll be doing all the paperwork." It was true. When I arrived in Beirut and began my orientation into my new city and office space I was quickly told that most of my days would be spent behind my computer screen editing proposals, progress reports, and stories for our local partners. I spent hours sitting at my computer receiving proposal drafts from partners, adding my comments to the margins, sending it back, receiving an updated copy, and finally working with them to clean it up into a final copy. I worked to help build their capacity so their organization would be able to independently apply for larger grants through NGOs and governments. When I did venture out of the office, it was to visit a partner's office or one of the projects they were running nearby.

I would return from those visits with a better understanding of the project I had only read about in reports.

My work behind the scenes allowed our local partner organizations to focus on the people. These local partner organizations are comprised of individuals from the communities they are assisting, individuals who know the needs of that community better than anyone else. If they are able to focus more on their new trauma class for women and less on whether their stories and photos are reaching the right people, the community will be more resilient. If they are focusing more on recruiting children for the new kindergarten class and less on putting the finishing touches on a proposal, the community will be stronger. That's where I came in. I prepared with them, met with them, and heard their hopes for a project. We would outline the proposal together, creating achievable and trackable outcomes and outputs. When we finished a draft, I would work to edit it for submission or clean up the language to read better to an English-speaking audience while they focused on getting on with their many other projects.

Step 2: Understand the Roles Volunteers Play

| Compare volunteering with other options | Understand the role that volunteers play | Learn about different types of volunteer travel offerings | Compare and evaluate opportunities | Sign up! |

What do volunteers actually do? The range of roles is broader than you might expect—from weeding out invasive plants to training surgeons in a large hospital, from creating a social media campaign to counting butterflies in the rainforest. A qualified teacher volunteering overseas could choose to work directly in the classroom, train local teachers, support curriculum development—or take on a role entirely unrelated to teaching.

Choosing the right role is one of the most important factors in the success of your volunteer placement.

Hands-on vs. supporting roles

One overarching question about your volunteer role is whether to contribute to an organization indirectly, by doing behind-the-scenes work, such as helping out in an office, or doing more direct hands-on work, such as picking fruit on an organic farm. Most people see hands-on work as more exciting and glamorous than office work, but in many cases foreign volunteers are not best placed to do this kind of work. Local people usually have the better language ability, technical skills, and capacity to build long-term relationships than a volunteer traveler, and a better understanding of the local dynamics and culture. Katie Boswell, who volunteered in India for five months, said, "I quickly realized that I was not the best person for the job of program delivery (i.e. teaching or managing education projects!) and that my direct impact was going to be limited. So I switched to a research/ evaluation role, where my position as an outsider was useful in some ways—people saw me as being more neutral and so opened up to me."

Office work isn't for everyone. But if you have some talent in fundraising, administration, management, or technology, we encourage you to consider the value you might have for an organization in one of these fields. In most cases the office work will be more valuable to the organization than another set of hands digging a well, for example. Shelia Hu, who spent three months in China volunteering for a conservation organization, reflected, "Although many of the projects involve fieldwork, I did all of my work at a shared desk in an office working in communications. Knowing I was doing my part in contributing my skills to the necessary areas was enough for me." As an office worker, you might have the chance to help an organization build sustainable systems for longevity and capacity. And, just as Rachel illustrated with her story at the beginning of the chapter, it can be just as rewarding to know that you are helping to make an impact, even if it is behind the scenes.

> **Hands-on**
> We use this term to describe volunteer work that is delivering a direct service to beneficiaries overseas (such as building, harvesting, or teaching) instead of working indirectly for a cause (such as working in an office).

Gaining experience vs. offering skills

A volunteer role may seem exciting because it offers the opportunity to do something different from life at home. If you never studied sciences you might be intrigued to be part of a marine biology project. If you spend all your days on computers you might be itching for the chance to get your hands in the mud. If you are not an engineer, a carpenter, or a painter, but you want the experience of building a house, you will find many sending organizations willing to accept your money and provide you with that experience.

From a learning service perspective, there is nothing wrong with being open with yourself and others about volunteering in order to learn new skills. The key is making sure the opportunity you select is actually designed with a focus on teaching you the skills—rather than one that really would be a better match for someone who already has a high level of experience in the area. A good rule of thumb is the following: if you are not qualified to perform that volunteer role in your own country, ask why you would be qualified to do it in someone else's. For example, in Kenya, we met a group of young volunteers who had been assigned to train students on HIV/AIDS prevention in local schools. But the volunteers knew very little about how to train others, let alone how to talk about sexual issues in the local culture, and they didn't even have a high level of knowledge about the HIV virus and its transmission. They would never have been invited into a school in their home country to teach students about HIV. On the other hand, we met another group of volunteers in Tanzania who supported local volunteers to run an after-school club. Their program had an in-depth cultural orientation and daily group reflection that focused on helping them develop the skills they needed to be effective in their role.

At the opposite end of the spectrum, your motivation to volunteer may be less about you wanting to gain experience

LEARN

and more about you wanting to offer your skills. If you have skills and experience that you want to share—with a bit of research, you should be able to find a volunteer opportunity where you can contribute effectively to a good cause. For example, if you are a nurse, you might seek a placement in an under-served rural hospital in South Africa. An accountant might make a real contribution at a small business development center in Jamaica.

In reality, most volunteer roles are a combination of both offering and learning skills. Even the most skilled nurse will have plenty to learn when immersed in the medical system of another country. And the least skilled student, with a willingness to work hard, might provide much needed help with decorating a classroom, weeding a demonstration garden, or preparing sandwiches for a homeless shelter. Crucially, you should look for a 'skills match'—you should feel confident that you have the skills required for a role, however menial, and the willingness to offer and adapt them.

What Kind of Work Do Volunteers Do?

If you have already started looking at possible opportunities, you will have noticed the dizzying array of sectors in which you might volunteer. Below we explore some broad areas of work that international volunteers commonly get involved in, and help you assess if they could be a good fit for you.

Education
Volunteer roles in education are widely advertised, with English language instruction a popular option. We talked to teachers, like Eric Lee, who taught English to highly-educated Vietnamese government employees in Hanoi, and Sahar Khoury, who taught low-income children of various ages in a one-room schoolhouse in rural Ecuador. Education is also a tool that is used in other types of community work, for example health education or environmental education. Volunteers are also used to teach various vocational or artistic skills, in areas ranging from food processing to fashion design.

If you are considering a teaching role, something to keep in mind is that having a skill and teaching a skill are two different things. This disconnect is prevalent when it comes to teaching English—many people think that if they can speak English, they can teach it. Unfortunately, it's not that easy. Remember the mantra: "Am I qualified to do this at home?" If not, do more preparation or change your role. The best preparation is a teaching certificate plus significant classroom experience. You could start by investing in an in-person or even online English-teaching course.

If you do not have teaching experience but want to learn classroom skills, then you might consider volunteering as a teaching assistant, or working as a classroom language partner. Nicko Gladstone, who volunteered in Argentina for six weeks, told us, "I was only a teacher's assistant, a small cog placed into a larger, more permanent framework of teachers who had been at the school for years, which meant that I could be gradually eased into a larger role so the kids wouldn't suffer from my initial inexperience." As a teaching assistant, you get classroom experience, the chance to learn from a professional, and an opportunity to share new ideas. On top of this, you may be providing much-needed support to an overstretched individual or system, and perhaps bolster the position of teachers in their community rather than replacing or undermining them.

In considering the growth of English teaching programs, it is important to question who is driving the demand for English education. On the one hand, millions of people overseas see English as an essential skill in today's economy, and it can open up opportunities including connecting to the vast stores of knowledge on the internet. Teaching English can be part of a sustainable development plan, like a project we explored in the Yucatan region of Mexico, where volunteers were teaching local fishermen English so that they could supplement their dwindling earnings from fishing by guiding tourists through a rare flamingo habitat.

Conversely, some development professionals suggest that the push to teach English is contributing to the devaluation and demise of indigenous languages. When Daniela first started working in Cambodia, their nonprofit partner hired an English

LEARN

teacher to teach in the first school they helped to fund. She recalls that, after a few months, she saw students speaking English, learning to read and write, and advancing their skills at an unbelievable rate only then to realize that many of these same students couldn't even read and write their own name in Khmer. She and her team decided that they were doing a disservice by incentivizing English studies rather than helping students learn their own language first, so they shifted their model. Think through your perspective on this issue if you plan to teach English.

Childcare
We have already discussed the harm that can be caused by volunteering directly as a caregiver for children. Opportunities to play with children in orphanages, to arrange after-school activities in slums, or to provide daycare for children in refugee camps are all options that come up high in internet searches. As we have explored, however, this is the area of volunteer travel that comes with the biggest hazard warning.

It is easy to understand the appeal of volunteer work with children. Working with children is seen as less constrained by cultural boundaries. The work seems fun and easy, especially for people without training or qualifications. It is emotional, as children are easy to love. And children are vulnerable: research shows that children suffer disproportionately from the brutal effects of extreme poverty.

All of these reasons, however, should be red flags to the informed volunteer. Yes, children are vulnerable, and that is exactly why care from non-professional volunteers can be dangerous. Think about the training that counselors and social workers in your own country have. Yes, it is emotional—for the children as well, whose attachment to short-term caregivers can cause long-term psychological damage. Organizations offering these opportunities often do so irresponsibly, sometimes knowingly using the children in their care as profit-making commodities that will attract volunteers and inspire hefty donations.

In general, we do not recommend volunteering directly with children in a caregiving role. This should be left to long-term workers with professional training with whom the children can safely form bonds. Qualified professionals with experience working with vulnerable children may be an exception to this—although even then your skills may be better put to use training staff than working directly with children.

Health

"By working with and alongside isolated and often disillusioned health workers, and sharing professional values and standards, volunteers can demonstrate that it is possible to achieve something locally. But I also saw many well-intentioned health professionals go to remote Nepal and struggle with the unfamiliar lifestyle, health system and social context. They often faced clinical scenarios beyond their experience. I was worried that these programs only created dependency, destabilized existing provision and demoralized rather than motivated local staff. Ultimately, it is only the people in low-income countries themselves that can achieve development goals, but volunteers can support them and accompany them on the journey."
-Dr. Gerda Pohl, Trustee of PHASE Worldwide,
and long-term volunteer in Nepal

Volunteers in the health sector are often trained professionals, such as doctors, physical therapists, and nurses. Those without a health background do non-specialist work such as assisting outreach experts who are teaching people to search for and eliminate mosquito breeding groups in their neighborhoods.

Experienced healthcare workers have a unique opportunity to make use of their transferable skills. Many countries suffer from urban bias and brain drain; local professionals such as doctors and nurses often prefer to live in large cities, and many leave their country of origin to work for higher salaries in wealthier nations. This means that international healthcare volunteers can sometimes fill a void, especially in under-served rural areas.

Effective health volunteering is not a simple matter of applying health skills you learned in a rich country to low-income setting. The effective medical volunteers we met recognized that the conditions overseas can differ dramatically from those typically found in medical practice at home, and they embraced the

LEARN

opportunity to learn from and about these differences. In many communities around the world, health may be viewed more holistically than Western allopathic medicine, incorporating herbal traditions, alternative therapies, and spiritual treatment. Medical volunteers can learn from these practices and explore how modern medicine can work within or alongside these systems.

In some countries, clinics and hospitals may lack basic equipment and medicine that is standard in facilities at home. Volunteers are likely to encounter diseases that are rarely seen in their own country such as intestinal worms, malaria, and tuberculosis. Other conditions, such as malnutrition and chronic diarrhea, are linked closely to poverty and thus cannot be cured with medicine alone. Medical student Eric Stein said that as a volunteer in Kenya, he learned that "food is medicine."

Well-meaning health volunteers can do all kinds of damage when directly practicing medicine overseas, including inadvertently harming patients by not accessing medical records, not being able to provide a high-level of bedside care due to language barriers, and accidentally subverting local practices by feeding the idea that international doctors are better than local doctors. Practitioners who are not trained in local realities can risk subverting or undermining local health systems. Directly treating patients outside of local institutions like government-funded hospitals can set up parallel systems of care that compete with the permanent system.

Be particularly wary of the very short-term health-camp model, where foreign doctors are parachuted in and out of a remote area to deliver a service for a matter of days. These kinds of camps do very little to contribute to the sustainable provision of healthcare, and can wreak havoc on local health systems. According to United for Sight, "When a visiting medical team arrives, overburdened local staff may see an opportunity for a break, or they may reallocate their efforts, leaving patients without a trained clinician familiar with the local spectrum of disease and in local diagnostic and management algorithms."

We've seen some best practices in the health sector, such as organizations working closely with local health workers, using volunteers to build up local health capacity. A Ugandan doctor who worked with Health Volunteers Overseas commented, "Treatment is just short-term. Training people who live and work here is more long-term. When HVO started here, we had only two orthopedic surgeons. Now we have ten." In her experience in Nepal with PHASE, Claire supported a program where medical professionals with relevant backgrounds came to train, mentor, and give moral support to local health workers in government health posts in remote areas, all in a way consistent with the culture, values, and long-term goals of the organization.

We also recommend the wonderful book, *Where There Is No Doctor*, for all those who will work in the health care field, even doctors!

Agriculture

"We drove past an old farmer in his field. The extension agent commented 'That old man won't listen to me about using fertilizer—he says he has been planting corn with beans since before I was born.' Not too long after that, the Zimbabwean economy fell apart and fertilizer was no longer available to most farmers. The old man with his intercropping would have been able to carry on, while the farmers who listened to the extension agent would have found it hard to get a decent yield. That experience gave me the deepest respect for the old farmers of the world, and made me think carefully about the role of any outsider in telling a farmer how to farm."

-Zahara, reflecting on her volunteering experience in Zimbabwe

LEARN

Volunteers who work in agriculture may provide anything from specialist input on beekeeping, to simple manual labor like helping out with the rice harvest. In the past, many volunteer programs would impose Western farming practices on local subsistence farmers, causing various forms of harm, such as dependency on hybrid seeds, pesticides, and fertilizers. Now, it seems, volunteers are more likely to promote farmers' markets, school gardens, and sustainable agriculture.

Volunteering on a farm is an increasingly-popular choice for people who have little connection to the land in their day-to-day lives, and this type of manual labor is less likely to upset power balances. WWOOF (World Wide Opportunities on Organic Farms) is becoming a popular way to work on farms around the world. For example, Leanne Huneault worked as a volunteer on an organic farm in Brazil, harvesting berries and tomatoes, transplanting basil, and learning about the farm's connections with local restaurants and the community.

As most volunteers know less about farming than their expert hosts, an agricultural placement can be a great opportunity to practice humility and learn life skills through menial but useful work. Even if you have technical agricultural expertise, you will still need to learn a huge amount about the local context (such as soil type, climate, food preferences, and access to markets) in order to apply your knowledge effectively.

Human rights

Working internationally on human rights issues can be a courageous form of learning service, but as with other forms of political activity, it must be done sensitively to avoid putting both yourself and local activists at risk. Don't act alone without a credible organization behind you. First-time travelers or inexperienced volunteers should think carefully about engaging with issues of human rights.

In the best cases, we have seen human rights volunteers do very powerful and meaningful work. Volunteers with 'human rights accompaniment' organizations act as international witnesses who accompany individuals who face threats of imminent harm. The presence of these volunteers, by drawing international attention to the situation, can help reduce the level of the threat. Volunteers in Guatemala, for example, transport indigenous rights activists to meetings, providing a level of safety by letting the government know that the eyes of the international community are watching.

Other volunteers are involved in documenting and publicizing human rights violations. Some human rights volunteers focus on working with the media or international campaigns. All over the world, elections are observed by international volunteers as a way of trying to ensure they are free and fair.

Volunteers in this sector need an extra heavy dose of self-awareness. Carefully consider the assumptions and attitudes you have about how rights are expressed and denied in different cultures, and how to go about working towards more equal rights. For example, as a volunteer, you may see the burqa as a symbol of gender oppression, but as a skilled volunteer you should listen to what local women have to say, and certainly not encourage actions that might put them at risk. Similarly, advice we have had from people working on disability rights is to check your assumptions about the needs and capacities of people with disabilities. As with other groups facing institutional challenges, you may have more to learn from them about how to promote their rights than you initially think.

Enterprise support

Volunteers with a business background can work in a range of settings, from advising start-ups to launching an online marketing campaign. Many volunteers work with 'microenterprises'— for example, farmers selling cash crops or women making traditional crafts. Some volunteers work directly with individual businesses, for example, helping a small company improve its accounting systems or develop an employee training program. Other volunteers work in centers that serve multiple businesses— providing *pro bono* consulting services on tax forms, food safety, or business expansion. Others support research into product development or increasing market access for small producers.

Volunteers sometimes support microfinance programs that offer small business development loans to those who are unable to access bank credit. If you are considering microfinance work, know that while many of these projects have been successful, they have not been the magic bullet to end poverty that some had hoped. In some cases, microfinance has actually created unsustainable indebtedness in vulnerable communities—in the worst instances, it has enslaved rather than benefited disadvantaged people. If you volunteer in the business sector, be sure to look at who is benefiting most from the income generated.

LEARN

Environmental and conservation issues

"Saving sea turtles in Mexico often attracts the kind of volunteers that imagine a nice beach holiday meeting cool new friends in the sun. The work, however, is far from glamorous. While many parts are very rewarding and beautiful, it can be physically hard and you need to get your hands dirty. Whether a volunteer is a good match for us rarely has to do with their skills or abilities, but has everything to do with their attitude."

–Peppi Stünkel, volunteer host at
Yepez Foundation, Mexico

A large number of volunteers work on environmental issues. They may be involved in maintaining public reserves and parks, habitat restoration, or assisting environmental scientists in collecting data in animal reserves. In many cases, the program fee paid can make more of a difference for the research than the actual volunteer service. This isn't always a bad thing, especially if there is transparency around it. You still get a unique opportunity to learn about conservation as part of a project team. Tsina Endor, a volunteer host with SEED in Madagascar, said "Working in conservation is physical work and so you need to really want to do it. It is inspiring and amazing, but also be prepared for the fact that it can be hours of sitting around and waiting for the wildlife, and research takes patience."

As there is a high demand for volunteering with animals, significant money can be involved. Questionable organizations, prioritizing profit over the wellbeing of the animals, have sprung up in response to the demand. There are deeply troubling instances of unwitting volunteers helping to hand rear wild animals so they are docile enough to be shot by vacationers looking for a trophy—all the while believing they were contributing to conservation. Popular tourist and volunteering destinations have been linked to the illegal trading of endangered animals. Learning about conservation and animal welfare more broadly may help you to identify what good practice looks like, and whether appropriate standards are being maintained.

Disaster relief

A large disaster, such as an earthquake, typhoon, or flood, is often accompanied by an influx of volunteers. Some volunteer teams are specifically trained in disaster response and can bring in much-needed skills to an emergency situation. In the vast majority of cases, however, the volunteers who arrive in a disaster zone are wholly unprepared for the situation on the ground. Although disaster volunteering can be motivated by admirable compassion and a desire to help those in urgent need, translating that desire into action is several times more challenging than volunteering under more stable conditions. Post-disaster areas are often stressful, as victims struggle to make sense of what has happened and what has been lost, chaotic, as aid agencies and governments struggle to coordinate a response, and under-resourced, as transport and communication channels have often been disrupted.

The earthquake in Haiti in 2010 was followed by an influx of unsolicited and ill-equipped volunteers. Not only did they lack cohesion, but they often also lacked basic resources—there were reports of teams of doctors that were unable to feed themselves. Thus, the 'helpers' had to rely on the aid that was intended for the victims, compounding their problems, and causing some humanitarian groups to dub them 'the second disaster.' Claire's experience after the 2015 Nepal earthquake was similar—international volunteers that arrived in the immediate aftermath were little more than disaster tourists. Some flew in to see how they could help, realized they had no idea what to do, spent a few days in the displaced people's camps for access to food, and then took advantage of free flights out provided by embassies. In a country with one international airport, clogging up and misusing the main channel for urgent supplies verges on criminal.

In our experience, the main need after a disaster is rarely unskilled labor. There is usually plenty of that in-country. In Haiti, aid money paid local people to clear rubble. It was cheap, it was effective and it supported the local economy. Unfortunately, there were also far too many voluntourists who paid the cost of their plane ticket to do the same job less effectively and more expensively.

LEARN

Our advice to those of you who want to help after a disaster is to wait. Join a coordinated response if and when a need has been clearly defined. Helen Josephine volunteered in Nepal over a year after the earthquake. "A contact who worked at a relief NGO needed some specific support in the communications section of the organization. I wrote reports and press releases on the organization's work. I did not go into the field. I spoke to the project heads who educated me on what they were doing. They allowed me to ask questions about projects and operations; that helped me to write comprehensive donor reports and most importantly, it allowed me to learn about the NGO, their work and how the people of Nepal are dealing with the aftermath of the earthquake. I came to do a job, and left a lot more sensitive to the needs of people in Nepal."

Although the drama and media attention dissipates within a few weeks, the effects of major disasters can last decades, and there can be important roles for trained volunteers in recovery and rebuilding long after the initial chaos has died down.

In the case of conflict zones, untrained volunteers can be a liability that put themselves and others in danger. Unless you have specific skills and experience, and you are responding to a request to fill a niche role, we do not advise traveling or volunteering in areas affected by war.

The Best Role for You

Although we have explored some of the most common sectors that international volunteers work in, the reality is that there is no limit to the roles that volunteers play around the world. Depending on your background, it is possible to find meaningful and responsible opportunities in almost any sector. For learning service, the most important thing is to choose a role where you don't disrupt progress or cause harm, where your contribution is sustainable, and that positions you well for learning.

As well as choosing a sector and role, there are plenty of other decisions that you need to make that will influence the impact of your volunteering. We'll explore these in the next chapter.

8.
EXPLORING YOUR VOLUNTEER TRAVEL CHOICES

Perspective: The Rise of Third Party Providers
By Dr. Nichole Georgeou, Director, Humanitarian and Development Research Initiative, Western Sydney University

Walking through the corridors of an Australian university I pass noticeboards pinned with posters advertising opportunities to travel and volunteer with local communities in developing countries. Across the university grounds I notice stalls staffed by young people urging students to 'make a difference' and 'be changemakers,' with lists of possible locations in Southeast Asia. When I enter a theater to deliver a lecture, I am awaited by an eager twenty-something asking to speak to my class about opportunities to travel abroad and 'help poor communities' and 'change lives.' Pondering this request I look across the lecture theatre and notice my students reading fliers, the same fliers resting on the unoccupied seats.

Australia has mirrored a global trend that has seen a rapid rise in student travel, especially among undergraduate students. The rise of this phenomenon and the proliferation of private tour operators (referred to by universities as 'Third Party Providers') is due partly to encouragement from the Australian government. Travel is now viewed as an opportunity for students to apply the skills learned in preparation for future employment. But I have always been uneasy about students testing their unqualified skills in developing countries.

There are over 100 third party providers active in Australia, with more arriving on the scene each year. Undergraduates can obtain loans for volunteering or study abroad. International offices are often unaware of the extent of programs being offered and promoted around their institutions.

Apart from the ethical issue of private enterprises advertising their business in public universities, the growth of volunteer tourism companies on Australian university campuses over the last decade raises a raft of issues for me. Firstly: the sector is unregulated, so there are no standards of best practice for either student learning or engagement with host communities. Secondly: local needs should be the most important factor in a development action, not the desire to 'help' or test one's skillset. Thirdly: cross-cultural learning does not automatically occur as a natural by-product of study abroad. After years of working in development, I know social change to be a slow, non-linear process, which must occur on the terms of the people who are directly affected—not those of us who will pack up and leave after a couple of weeks.

Back to the fliers, posters and stalls: I know that my students face a difficult task as they wade through all the options, companies and organizations trying to make money by selling impact overseas. Myself and other scholars are currently working to understand these changing trajectories.

Step 3: Learn About the Different Types of Volunteer Travel Offerings

| Compare volunteering with other options | Understand the role that volunteers play | Learn about different types of volunteer travel offerings | Compare and evaluate opportunities | Sign up! |

Once you have decided on the broad sector you would like to volunteer in, and what kind of role is most suited to your skills, there is still a whole range of choices and considerations to factor into your research. How much time you have, where you want to go, and whether you want to spend a lot of time around other volunteers are all important decisions. Here we list some of the choices you have and offer some reflections on how to make a decision that best suits your goals.

Short-term vs. long-term volunteering

"The longer the time period the better. Although two years is daunting in the beginning, it gives the time for a volunteer to find projects really wanted or needed by the community they are in."

–A volunteer who spent three years in Uganda

In general, short-term volunteering is more prone to the pitfalls we have explored. Short-term projects are more likely to be tokenistic, repetitive or wasteful, or else fuel a dependency on a chain of outside volunteers to keep an unsustainable project alive. Serge Dumortier of Handicap International in Cambodia argued, "The problem with short-term volunteers is that every new person who comes re-invents the wheel and the Khmer staff have to adjust to the foreigner's style and teach them things." In some carefully planned short-term programs, the efforts of a chain of short-term volunteers are designed to build on each

LEARN

other, leading to long-term change through a coherent strategy. However, short-term volunteers tend to leave without enough exposure to critically analyze whether that strategy is in place.

Ultimately, choosing a short-term volunteer experience may be shortchanging yourself: not giving you the opportunity to learn while you serve. If you volunteer for a week, you can get an appetizer to a culture, a kick-start in international development learning, and the spark to want to do something more to address global inequalities, but you will not have a rich, culturally immersive experience. If you know that you want to volunteer and only have a short time available, look for opportunities that are part of an organized educational program that can give you the fuel you need to inspire future action.

Volunteer placements that are much longer, perhaps several months or years, offer both more of a chance to learn and a bigger opportunity to have a positive impact on yourself, others, and a cause. A more lasting mutual exchange of friendship and cross-cultural learning is possible. If you know you are sticking around for a while, you will not be in as much of a rush to make an impact; you will have time to listen and learn from local people and the chance to apply things you learned months earlier through asking questions, listening, and observing. Many host organizations specifically seek out only those volunteers who can commit to longer periods because they believe it takes time for volunteers to learn how to add value. Thida Khus of Silaka, an organization in Cambodia commented, "One year is too short. Only after six months do you even start to understand where you are and what you can do."

Though short- and long-term volunteering programs have different needs and impacts, there is no one-size-fits-all answer to which is better. For example, if you end up volunteering in an ineffective organization for six months rather than one month, the length of your stay is less of a factor on your overall impact than your choice of placement. If you have the distinctive skillset that an organization needs, you might be able to have a more substantial impact during a short volunteer stint where you share your skills, than in many weeks of volunteering on a painting project. For example, after participating in a meaningful community-based tour in Zanzibar, Zahara spent a couple of afternoons volunteering with the ecotourism company that had organized and led the tour. The director had expressed a need for assistance with marketing his new website to help travelers learn about eco- and cultural tourism options in Zanzibar, and Zahara showed him how to use positive feedback from customers like her to increase traffic to the site. With this kind of explicit skills matching, value can be found in short-term volunteering.

No matter how long you volunteer for, taking a learning service approach requires research and planning. If you feel that your main constraint is time, you may conclude that the time you need to invest in the planning process is just not worth it. If you are feeling overwhelmed by the research phase, there is no need to put pressure on yourself to leap into volunteering, and you might want to go back and reconsider the alternatives to volunteer travel that will still give you exposure to global issues.

Using an agency to organize your placement

Organizing your volunteer placement through an agency or sending organization may appeal if you have not traveled internationally before, or if you want support in researching, planning, matching, or organizing your placement. There are a range of types of agencies that send people abroad, including tour companies and volunteer sending organizations.

At one end of the spectrum are the organizations that exist only to recruit volunteers and send them to partners overseas. They may be tiny, with very specific aims that specialize in one issue or country, or they may be large government-funded organizations with the capacity to send volunteers all over the world. Some have strong, long-term relationships with the people and projects on the ground. They may support hosting organizations to supervise and utilize volunteers, and provide in-country support to troubleshoot problems and maximize effectiveness.

At the other end of the spectrum are companies that offer a wide range of travel products, sometimes with volunteering being just one option. The most 'customer focused' providers tend to prioritize the choices of the volunteer over the value of the work. Rather than directly operating volunteer experiences, their service might only be to connect you with an unvetted host

LEARN

organization, without ownership or responsibility for the program once you are overseas.

In addition, there are third-party websites and marketing organizations that promote and sell volunteer programs designed and led by others. In many cases, these are sold by people who have never visited the projects, and who have no idea if the program is effective, well run, or even safe. If you buy a product from one of those sites, you might not even be able to tell which organization ultimately gets your money, or where you will be giving your time. Would you buy a car from someone who knew nothing about the model they were selling you? Volunteer travel has many pitfalls, just as a car has many ways of breaking down, so it's better to work with someone who knows the details of the opportunities they are offering.

The best organizations have a robust procedure for how they vet and match volunteers. For example, when Claire volunteered with VSO, she first underwent an extensive skills assessment to ensure that she had experience that fitted the needs of the program. Then there was a group selection day, followed by a one-on-one interview to assess attitudes and soft skills. Claire said, "I appreciated the rigorous selection process as I knew it meant that I was more likely to be placed in a role where I would be able to contribute." Good agencies also provide extensive learning experiences for those who travel with them, with pre-departure training, on-line modules, or in-country learning opportunities such as group reflections. Before departure, VSO required Claire's cohort to attend two multi-day volunteer preparation courses, one covering the mental and emotional side of volunteering abroad, and another focusing on how to apply your skills in an international development context.

The services offered by some sending organizations can be invaluable, especially if it is your first time in a country or your first time as a volunteer. Megan Ohri, who worked for six months as a volunteer coordinator in India, commented, "In a number of places we visited we came across volunteers who had self-organized their volunteering and were struggling with culture shock and a lack of understanding of the issues they were being faced with (relating to feeling isolated and not understanding the poverty that they were seeing, or the way NGOs work). We usually ended up supporting them informally, including inviting one girl on to our induction training." Remember that all agencies are not created equal, and you need to check whether the organization you are considering provides the services you want and does them well.

Finding a volunteer placement yourself

You may choose not to go through an intermediary organization and instead set up a volunteer placement yourself. Thanks to the internet, it has become much easier both for hosting organizations to advertise for international volunteers and for individuals across the world to connect with them directly. Some volunteers we interviewed found that this approach suited them. "Going on your own really lets you tailor your experience," said one volunteer who went to Ecuador. "It allows you to be passionate about what you are doing and doesn't burden you with the history, bureaucracy, or agenda of a placement organization." Laura Parsons, who volunteered in Nicaragua and India, agreed: "The freedom fit my style. Going without a placement organization meant that my relationship with my supervisors was a direct one and what they said was all I had to concern myself with. The rest was up to me."

Others we encountered issued words of warning. Ranjit Purshotam and Mahendra Thetty, of Legal Resources Center, in South Africa, said, "We prefer volunteer interns to come within a structured program... Those who come as part of a program tend to work harder and have better qualities, and they are accountable to some other structure back in their homes." Bear in mind that if you set up a volunteer experience on your own that there is no wider system to fall back on—you will have to set up accountability structures yourself. Also remember that the opportunities you find are basically unvetted, so the next stage of information-gathering, fact-checking, and evaluation is even more critical.

Group travel vs. going it alone

If the idea of traveling across the world on your own makes you nervous, or if you are looking to meet like-minded individuals, you may be drawn to a group volunteer experience. Some

LEARN

travel companies specialize in group experiences, where people all over the world can sign up for a trip. Your school, club, or religious organization may organize a group volunteer project for its members. Most often, group trips are designed around short-term volunteer interventions, such as a health camp or construction project. As the options for a group working together are limited and the trips need to be planned months or even years in advance, group volunteering options can fall into the trap of being tokenistic. Organizing a large group's arrival can also be a huge logistical burden; consider the planning that goes into catering, housing, and transportation for the group, let alone the procurement challenges and logistical set up for a large project.

As volunteers on group experiences tend to live, eat and work together, you may find your biggest challenge to be getting on with all the other personalities involved. A volunteer who spent over a month in Japan on a group trip shared this experience: "Perhaps due to the average age of the volunteers, most nights were like party nights at a university dorm. I had guessed ahead of time that this would be the case, but if that kind of socializing isn't to a potential volunteer's tastes then it would definitely be something that could cause problems."

If you are considering a group trip, find out how the project was created, why it is needed, who is setting the agenda, and what continuity and follow up there is after you leave. Is there a long-term partnership on the ground that creates some sustainability from group to group? Ensure that you agree with the reasoning for why outside volunteers are being used, and that you are confident that the trip has a wider benefit outside of meeting the demands of your group. Ben Keene, Founder of Tribewanted, an organization that offers group travel experiences, told us, "We wanted to get away from mainstream group volunteer travel, as we had seen that putting volunteers to use on 'development' projects could be tokenistic. We saw that what people were often looking for was a sense of community and an opportunity to be part of a group, with shared values, working towards the same goals. We decided not to make our trips about 'helping' others but instead about learning, working together, and building a sense of community, and some of our biggest impacts are probably related to helping people feel a part of a group that fuels and shares their values."

There is a middle ground between group trips and solo volunteering experiences. Some agencies provide the option to volunteer on your own but to have the support network of a group through accepting volunteers in cohorts and offering a shared orientation. Other organizations place volunteers in clusters so there are several volunteers in the same town or district working on different projects. This hybrid option provides a more personalized volunteering experience with a connection to a wider group so that parts of the experience can still be shared. A volunteer who spent three years in Uganda shared his opinion with us: "I think volunteering alone or in a network of people spread out over a large area is best. When people volunteer in groups, they may have fun and get a small snapshot of life in another world, but it's unlikely that they will have an experience of any depth." If, after examining your motivations and priorities, you find that what you are really looking for is a group travel experience, you might want to reconsider the learning trips we explored earlier.

Housing options

"I volunteered with an educational NGO in Cambodia and initially lived in the housing provided by the organization. I became close friends with one of the Cambodian staff members, and found out her family was renting out a room next to their house. I decided to move there, and before I knew it, I was having breakfast and dinner with them almost every day. I learned so much about their family life; their mentality, openness, and customs. I joined them at the pagoda for birthdays and rituals. I feel like finding a way to connect to a local family is the best way to learn about the culture, share knowledge, and integrate into a community."

-Melissa Chungfat, who volunteered
in Cambodia for seven months

LEARN

For many volunteers, their living situation is a major determinant of the quality of their experience abroad. Some choose to live in high-end housing, as the price is often much more affordable than back home, while others prioritize living in more local conditions in order to connect with and learn from their local colleagues. Few, if any, volunteers truly live on the level of the poorest of the poor, who may suffer disproportionately from preventable diseases, crime, hunger, and malnutrition, often with little or no access to health care, clean water, or other basic needs. Living in those conditions is not sustainable or advisable for anyone, including international volunteers.

Most volunteers live in the space between luxury and squalor. This is usually a simpler standard compared to home, but a higher standard than that of their hosts. For example, in rural Zambia, Zahara walked to the river for water and took a cold bucket shower every night. She enjoyed that experience, but she also appreciated being able to sleep in a cement house in a bed with a mattress, which was an extravagance compared to some of her Zambian co-workers. A volunteer who spent over six months in Haiti told us, "We lived in 'local style' accommodations, enabling us to be viewed in a more positive light by the locals because we did not separate ourselves by our living standards."

Some programs house volunteers together. On the one hand, living with other volunteers can have the advantage of providing you with a supportive and understanding network of people. On the other hand, volunteers who live in a group house with other volunteers who speak the same language often find it more difficult to learn the local language or integrate into the local culture. Norris Friesen, who volunteered in Jamaica, commented on the drawbacks he experienced in such an arrangement, "Some would argue that we were too self-contained; that is, we were housed together and ate our meals together. As a result, we had minimal contact with Jamaicans in the evening." If you are seeking a more authentic experience, to learn a local language, or to really immerse yourself in a culture, you might want to look for an individual placement in an organization, a homestay, or a placement outside of the popular tourist destinations.

Homestays can be one of the best ways to jump straight into local life. Some volunteer programs require it, others may not offer it, but you might be able to organize a homestay for yourself once you are in-country. For many people we have spoken with, living with a local family provided some of the most memorable experiences of their journey, helped with integration, accelerated their learning, and staved off the homesickness. For many, their homestay families are still a big part of their lives once they return home.

Claire has spent a good part of the last decade living with a family in Nepal. She said, "My homestay family in Nepal has basically become like my own family. Despite my behavior being viewed as rather strange (being on my computer working on this book at all hours of the night, remaining unmarried well into my thirties, and my reluctance to wash in freezing water in the early morning are just a few of the million things), their love and support has gotten me through any homesickness I felt. The profound respect I have for this culture stems from the experiences I have had with my family here and seeing the world through their eyes."

While it is important for everyone who goes abroad to make the effort to understand the cultural norms of their host country, if you stay in a homestay there is even more need to commit to learning about and fitting in with the local community. If you are living with a family, you might have to conform to certain family rules around times you enter and exit the home, if or when you bring guests to visit, and the volume of your music—to name but a few! These shifts in behavior are usually amply rewarded with the sense of being welcomed into a family, and are a useful reminder that – whatever your living arrangements – you are a guest in another's culture.

As you begin planning your own volunteer experience, think about how you would like to balance your desires for cultural integration, privacy, and community, as well as the balance between appropriate simplicity, safety, and comfort.

Rural vs. urban

"I volunteered in the remote Northeast of Cambodia. We called it the 'Wild East' as the area was sparsely populated and had few amenities. It gave me a chance to learn more

LEARN

about the culture, gave me access to beautiful outdoor experiences, and meant that I made many Cambodian friends as there was a limited number of foreigners to keep me in my comfort zone, but after such a long time, I missed the social life I had access to at home."
   -Sarah Galvin, volunteered in Cambodia for over a year

With the growing popularity of volunteer travel, many popular tourist destinations are in essence overrun with volunteers. Visitors to tourist hubs like Arusha, Tanzania or Chang Mai, Thailand, might find groups wandering the streets each night wearing matching volunteer T-shirts. Some volunteer providers specifically place volunteers in more remote, less developed areas. These placements can provide you with an opportunity to get more closely involved with rural development work and to immerse yourself more fully in the more traditional aspects of the local culture. That said, rural living can be tough, so you need to ensure you are mentally prepared to be outside of your comfort zone, at least initially. You may find it difficult to adjust to things like sourcing your own water, using an outhouse, living without electricity, and taking long walks or bus rides to visit a friend or see a doctor, so think carefully about what your limits are.

Alternatively, not all urban areas are as popular among volunteers, and even within tourist cities, most foreign visitors live within a small area surrounded by foreign amenities. For example, if you are living in Cape Town, South Africa, you can choose whether you live in a gated community or a less affluent part of town.

Faith-based organizations

Religious congregations and organizations often send groups of volunteers abroad. The host organization may also be religiously affiliated, such as a church group in one country sending volunteers to build a church overseas. Some volunteers we have spoken with who shared a faith with their sending or hosting organizations told us that they found it comforting to have a common spiritual grounding in a different setting. Among non-religious volunteers, or those of other faiths, some found it uncomfortable to volunteer in a faith-based environment, whereas others found that they had no problems, especially when religion was kept out of day-to-day work.

Daniela helped organize a group volunteer trip to Papua New Guinea with a large organization, to construct a group of houses. She found that volunteers were pressured to pray with the local host organization each day. When she later reported that this made some of the volunteers feel uncomfortable she found that a subsequent group of Japanese volunteers were kept in a room until each of them agreed to sign a document saying that they believed in Jesus, and only then were they allowed to join the building work. Needless to say, this is an extreme example, and when these details emerged the global body of the volunteer organization closed down their Papua New Guinea branch for a period to change and retrain staff and remedy the problem. Before signing up to volunteer, find out if the organization has a religious affiliation and what practices that translates into in terms of volunteer expectations.

We differentiate between faith-based organizations (inspired by religious values) and missionary groups (dedicated to proselytizing). It is impossible to fully embrace learning service if your focus is purely evangelism. How can you embrace a *learning* mindset if you are focused on *teaching* people about your religion? Mark Weber, from Poverty Inc., himself a practicing Catholic, says, "We Christians can be particularly susceptible to the savior-hero complex because of our earnest desire to imitate the ultimate savior-hero, Jesus. But the right effort to emulate must be deeply rooted in humility. We're called to be servants, not masters. In our engagement with those in the developing world, we sometimes get this backward."

Several volunteers we spoke with had spiritual motivations but did not feel the need to put a particular religious label on the work they were doing and could find spiritual contentment working with a secular organization. There are volunteer programs that are explicitly based on Jewish values, such as Tikkun Olam (healing the world), but that do not have religious practice as part of volunteering. As you explore your options, consider what role religion plays in your life and what role you think is appropriate for it to play in your volunteer experience.

LEARN

Free vs. paying a fee

"When I was looking to volunteer, I was frustrated that all of the placements seemed to charge such high fees, so we started Omprakash as a free volunteer placement service. But then we saw that there was a need for volunteer education, so that the volunteers would arrive with the knowledge they needed to not repeat the same mistakes of others before them. Providing training for volunteers is costly, so we charge for that service. It also takes time and money to manage the rest of our site, as we need to find ways to vet the programs we are offering, market them, etc. Striking the right balance between charging and not charging volunteers is tricky, but I always encourage volunteers to make an educated choice by asking where their money is going so they can decide if, how, or when they want to pay."

—Willy Oppenheim, Founder of volunteer
organization Omprakash

'To pay or not to pay' is a much-debated topic in volunteer travel. On the surface, paying a fee to volunteer can seem like a contradiction in terms—if you are already offering your time for free and covering your expenses, why should you also have to pay? However, the learning service approach emphasizes that you, as a volunteer, are a major beneficiary of the process. Volunteers are *not* free—it takes a lot of time, capacity, and money to create and support a great volunteer experience. The costs might include marketing and recruitment costs for the organization to attract the right volunteers, staff to vet partners and provide pre- and post-placement support, and all the in-country costs of hosting volunteers. One volunteer hosting organization said, "Initially volunteers didn't have to pay anything, but we realized after a while that this was limiting the organization in terms of how many volunteers we could host as we couldn't meet their costs. Volunteers now have to pay a small contribution for the accommodation that they stay in (this doesn't actually cover the full cost and is far less than rent in their own country), and a one-off contribution that goes towards the costs of recruiting and hosting them."

Our biggest piece of advice in this area is to find out how the volunteer fees are used. Fees may go to the sending organization to cover the costs of placing you in a volunteer role, to the local organization directly to host you, or both. The fee may include a charitable donation for the cause you are volunteering to support. It may also include a large profit margin for a company. A downside to the spread of fee-charging placements is that unscrupulous organizations take on more volunteers simply for financial gain, even when there are no roles for them. So in addition to finding out where your funds are going, ask questions to find out if your role really is needed. When you have the answer and the fee breakdown, you can reflect on the value for money it represents and your opinion on the ethics of the income distribution.

There are ways to volunteer that do not require a placement fee. Some matching portals intentionally do not exchange money with hosting organizations in the belief that this helps ensure that volunteers are valued and needed, and not relied on to generate funds. Some of the larger government-funded or faith-based organizations cover volunteer expenses or even provide a living stipend. If you do not pay a volunteer fee, think about who is subsidizing the costs associated with your placement. It may be you, taking more time to research and set up logistics yourself, or the organization overseas might be taking on extra costs because they need your skills. Being aware of all the resources and time that go into your volunteer placement and how those might be covered will help you make the right decision about whether to pay a placement fee or not.

A final word of warning: it is not the case that the more you pay, the better quality the service. We spoke with many volunteers who paid a lot of money for their placement and ended up dissatisfied, often because they had assumed that their money was going towards things that it was not. Not all fee-charging placements have effective policies for selecting partners or matching needs, and not all of them offer much support for volunteers or for partners. Sometimes none of the money you pay reaches the country where you volunteer—like

LEARN

in the example Daniela shared earlier, about the volunteers who thought their money was going to help a school when, in fact, those funds stayed in Australia. The bottom line is that good organizations, for a fee, can do a lot of the logistical legwork required to provide you with a positive experience, while the worst organizations might take your money in profit and yet still leave you in a disorganized and poorly planned volunteer placement.

Types of Hosting Organizations

Organizations that host volunteers overseas range from large non-governmental organizations to small community groups, and from for-profit and social enterprise companies to governmental bodies. We'll take a look at some of the different types of host organizations and the pros and cons to consider when choosing among them.

Non-governmental organizations (NGOs)
Traditionally, the majority of host organizations are NGOs. The term NGO covers a broad range of entities, from well-funded organizations with programs spanning many issues and countries, to tiny grassroots organizations based in a single community, sometimes referred to as community-based organizations or CBOs. Larger NGOs are likely to have more complex systems of accountability, hierarchal management structures, and more clearly defined roles, but they might also be more bureaucratic and slower to respond to needs in local communities. In smaller NGOs, you might work with extremely driven individuals with strong community ties, but you might also find that they are functioning without professionally-trained staff, a formal management structure, or sustainable funding. Some volunteers appreciate the flexibility of grassroots organizations; others dislike what can be ad hoc management and planning practices. Shelia Hu, who volunteered for three months in China, reflected, "The organization I worked with was a very large NGO, so I anticipated the local offices being just as bustling and overwhelming. However, it was surprising to find that despite

having dozens of employees strewn over two floors, the team I worked with was small and tight-knit."

No matter their size, NGOs across the world vary widely in goals, programs, philosophy, and organizational culture. Remember that all nonprofit organizations are supposed to have a clear mission, and that the organization's activities should align with that mission. This alignment with their intended impact is sometimes called their 'theory of change.' For any size organization, make sure you understand what their mission is and consider how you feel their stated activities align with that mission when deciding if you want to give them your time and money.

Governmental and multilateral organizations

Some of the larger volunteer sending organizations place volunteers directly into government agencies overseas. A volunteer program staff member we interviewed argued that placements with government institutions are "more sustainable, because you know that the institution is unlikely to lose its funding and disappear tomorrow." A number of volunteers working with UN agencies and government ministries spoke to us favorably about their potential for having a large-scale impact by being part of a long-term endeavor. For example, Heather Branson, who was placed with the South African census program through UN Volunteers, shared with us that she "worked with South African colleagues to provide top-quality census data that is desperately needed at the national and provincial government levels."

Working for government agencies can mean there is a risk of bureaucracy and politics interfering with impact. Policies are usually top-down and can lack buy-in at a local level. Things can move slowly, require wading through a lot of red tape, and seem wasteful or inefficient. If you struggle with large systems or hierarchical structures, you may become frustrated if you decide to volunteer overseas with a government institution.

Some volunteers find the politics of government-related volunteer programs stifling. Alexis Eakright was an activist with strong political opinions who volunteered in Costa Rica with the Peace Corps. She found that the biggest local polluter in the area

LEARN

where she was working was a big US-owned banana company that used lots of pesticides. One day, she joined a protest against the company organized by a local environmental organization, "This was a real problem. I am with the US Government, and this is a big US company. I can't be involved in protests... The Peace Corps says you are going to be out there on your own, but in fact you are part of the government. You are a little ambassador... I resented being a tool – a cheap one at that – for public relations for the US Government."

Social enterprises

The boundaries between nonprofit and for-profit organizations have become increasingly blurred in recent years. In particular, the rise of social entrepreneurship has widened the way we look at solutions to global problems, with many mission-driven organizations now incorporating income-generating models and entrepreneurial approaches to their systems-change work. For example, when solar panels first gained popularity in the international development sphere, they were often distributed freely or subsidized by nonprofit organizations, which had to continually ask for donations to increase their reach. Now you will find many for-profit social ventures selling solar power systems with a goal of improving the scale and speed of their distribution to off-grid communities while generating enough income to run their businesses sustainably. Many NGOs are shifting their models to incorporate elements of social business.

Some sending organizations identify as social enterprises, generating profit from volunteer fees and also claiming a social impact, either through the work their volunteers do or through the impact they have on the volunteers themselves. In addition, while in the past it might have been rare to consider a volunteer placement in a business, increasing numbers of volunteers are placed in host organizations that are income-generating social enterprises. This is partly a demand-driven shift: travelers are increasingly interested in social entrepreneurship as an idea, so demand internships and volunteer placements in this area. It is also due to a shift in mindset in the international development community as there is no longer such a strict divide perceived between business and social impact.

Volunteer-led projects

With the growing demand for volunteer projects abroad, impromptu volunteer programs are increasingly springing up. These are offerings organized by an individual or small group, often foreign visitors, aiming to 'help local people.' While sometimes filling a need, it is difficult to evaluate and understand the implications of these projects from afar. Petra, a volunteer host from Syria, told us, "It is very important to know that not having a local partner is very difficult. You will not know the real needs, the backgrounds, the culture, the traditions, how do they act in situation, or why they act like they do." Be very cautious of joining a DIY volunteer project organized by people who may be well-intentioned, but do not have the experience, qualifications, or accountability mechanisms to organize a sustainable project.

We advise the most caution when considering ad-hoc projects designed by individuals specifically for foreign volunteers. For example, Ky Mohamed found his volunteer placement in Nepal through an advertisement online. It sounded idyllic—a community farm and ashram supporting vulnerable people just outside of the lakeside city of Pokhara. However, when he turned up he found the reality to be very different. "There was no project," he told us. "I was shown some unused land by the 'founder', who admitted that what he'd written online was purely aspirational. His plan was to build and run a farm and ashram entirely using international volunteers—which I could see was doomed from the outset." Individually-organized volunteer projects are more likely to fall into the pitfalls described previously, and, in the worst cases, may have you feeding into a corrupt system.

As you can see the range of volunteer travel options is staggering, and there are plenty of considerations to weigh up in making your choice. Next, we'll look at how to thoroughly evaluate programs to make a decision that is right for you.

LEARN

9.
EVALUATING & SELECTING AN OPTION

Perspective: On Choosing Wisely
By Zahara

As a bright-eyed 23-year-old, I was practically bouncing with excitement when I arrived in Massachusetts to volunteer in Tanzania with the Institute for Cooperation and Development (IICD). In selecting a volunteer program, my top priority had been to find an opportunity to go Africa. I wanted to engage in deep learning, and IICD had a two-month period of preparation, even before we got on the plane, when we would learn to plant trees, speak Swahili, and understand the Tanzanian economy, politics and culture. Also, IICD promised an experience that matched my progressive values—working side by side with African farmers on a collective farm, promoting intercropping of healthy vegetables with nutritious fruit trees, and helping improve the economy of Tanzania by strengthening small-scale agriculture.

I was shocked when the reality did not match the promises. The training in Massachusetts focused less on learning about Africa, and more on bizarre fundraising activities for IICD (such

as selling tickets to gamblers at a race track). The only ,
we got in agriculture was transplanting pine trees on a m
in New England, a skill that would prove virtually useless
temperate zone of southern Africa. Then I found out that
had failed to get us visas for Tanzania. At the last minute, t ,
sent us instead to Zambia, a country where 72 languages are
spoken—but not Swahili, the language we had been learning.
Once we got to Zambia, my dream of participating in sustainable
development was smashed when I realized the fruit trees we
were planting had almost no chance of surviving the dry season.
I saw local workers on the project applying pesticides without
training, protective clothing, or proper masks. And when I visited
local farmers, they told me that what they really wanted was
help creating irrigation systems to more effectively grow the
crops they already knew how to grow, and they did not really
need training on how to make an orchard. The project was not
sustainable, not culturally sensitive, and not effective. And it was
not a match with my values.

How did I make such a grave error when selecting a volunteer
program?

My initial mistake was to volunteer with the first organization I
found out about. My friend's brother was one of the founders of
IICD and I was so eager to volunteer in Africa that once he told
me about the program, I immediately signed up without taking
the time to generate a list of options and compare them.

My second mistake was skipping the step of talking to past
volunteers. If I had done so, I would have found out that IICD is
affiliated with a network of Danish organizations (including the
innocuous sounding 'Teacher's Group,' also known as Tvind),
which I later heard described by many people as a 'cult.' This
network has a long history of allegations of economic misdeeds
and cultural insensitivity, not only in Zambia, but also around the
world.

My third mistake was to take IICD's marketing materials at
face value. The photographs of happy volunteers and happy
children were compelling. I wanted to be in that picture. But I
did not know then, as I know now, that it is really easy to set up
a photograph of a westerner standing in the middle of a group
of smiling children in another country. Virtually all volunteer

LEARN

programs feature permutations of this photographic cliché. It is much harder to set up a high quality program where both the volunteers and community have a genuine reason to smile.

By the time I realized I had made a terrible mistake in my choice, I was already in Zambia and had paid thousands of dollars for the experience. I decided to stay and try to do the best I could in a bad situation. Some of my peers did drop out, and in retrospect, maybe I should have as well. That said, there were many positive elements of the experience—living in rural Zambia, learning the ChiBemba language, and forging deep friendships with my fellow volunteers and our Zambian co-workers. But all of these positives could have been gained by volunteering with a reputable organization if only I'd done better research before signing up to volunteer.

Step 4: Compare and Evaluate Opportunities

| Compare volunteering with other options | Understand the role that volunteers play | Learn about different types of volunteer travel offerings | Compare and evaluate opportunities | Sign up! |

"There are lots of organizations out there—and some are very good at marketing when actually there is nothing behind the spin. Make sure that you really research an organization. If their Facebook page looks great but is actually just a rehash of public articles... it's probably not the organization to volunteer your time for. Look for organizations that back up what they say with reports on their websites, feedback from past volunteers and on the ground posts from the work that they do. Don't believe the hype but really step back and assess the worth of the organization that you are going to be involved with."

—Tsina Endor, volunteer host with SEED in Madagascar

Now that you've got the lay of the land, and understand the wide range of choices available, it is time to do some narrowing. To make an informed choice, you need to get critical, start questioning, and begin comparing. In this chapter, we'll empower you to do your own research and choose your best option.

When we advise people on how to select a volunteer program, we often get the obvious question, "What are the best volunteer programs out there?" Some potential volunteer travelers have suggested that we make a list of the most responsible volunteer organizations to make it easier for people to choose. These requests are understandable—we also get overwhelmed by all the glossy pamphlets and cheerful websites showing happy volunteers riding elephants through the forest, writing on the chalkboard in front of a group of smiling girls, or playing soccer with local children using a makeshift ball made of plastic bags.

But we soon realized that recommending specific volunteer programs would be useless, because programs change, and each volunteer is so different. A volunteer option that would be just right for your 55 year-old aunt who is a practicing accountant might be a complete mismatch for your 18 year-old cousin who is still in high school. So, instead of attempting the impossible task of identifying programs that would work for anyone, we'll guide you through the steps to find a program that is a match for you.

Write down your priority criteria
We suggest you start with reviewing your goals, values, and the personal logistics for your volunteer travel. As well as the obvious logistics, such as timeframe, budget and place, think about what you want to learn and contribute, and what your priorities are for choosing an organization. Mark Dosch, who volunteered for a month in Guatemala, said, "After taking the time to clarify what I wanted, the next steps were easier." Here are some questions to consider when writing down your ideas or 'statement of intent' for volunteering:

- What are your learning goals?
- What experience do you have to offer and what skills to you want to develop?
- What causes motivate you?

LEARN

- Is there a type of organization you want to support or a specific field where you would like to add value?
- What support do you need from an organization? What support is desirable but not required?
- Ultimately, what kind of experience are you seeking?

It is equally important is to ask yourself: what types of volunteer programs you want to rule out? For example, maybe you don't want to work in an area that is known for homophobia. If you get seasonal affective disorder, you might want to rule out any opportunities that would require you to live through a cold, dark winter. If humidity drives you crazy, you may not do well volunteering in a rainforest.

Researching and identifying organizations

Although you can start by browsing the internet to give you some ideas, a listing on a website does not guarantee quality or legitimacy. Some sites are based on pay-for-listing systems, with little to no vetting of what is offered. Organizations with large budgets can pay for their ads to come up first in searches. Other review sites are connected to or owned by volunteer companies that have a vested interest in their own opportunities appearing first.

Talk to friends, family and trusted advisers and ask them to make recommendations of placements or programs for you to look into. Share your statement of intent with them so that they know exactly what kind of opportunity you are looking for. Remember that friends' recommendations cannot replace your own research—they can provide a starting point, but you still need to do some work. Consider what relationship the friend has with the organization. Are they connected to the organization through personal relationships and might therefore have a biased view? Were they short- or long-term volunteers there, and how does that affect their ability to evaluate impact? Do they know of someone who went with them and had a great experience (in which case, could you be put directly in contact with that person)? Or have they just heard of the organization and think it has a good reputation?

Some organizations recruit volunteers in the same way that they would recruit for a job opening, often advertising on sites also used by people looking for jobs. In this case, the organization identifies a need, creates a role description and selection criteria, and usually also conducts interviews for the position. This approach puts the hosting organization in the driver's seat and is more likely to be fulfilling for both sides as the need is more clearly defined and the match more closely vetted. These volunteer positions may require you to have particular skills, and this path can also limit your opportunities on place, cause, timeframe, and role.

Just showing up

An alternative way to find a volunteer placement is to plan a trip abroad and wait and see if you stumble across an organization that looks like it could do with a hand, or to look out for a posters advertising a volunteer opportunity that sounds right for you. These options may just fall into your lap as you travel, but remember that even if you are on the go, the stages of researching and critical thinking are crucial to avoiding the pitfalls we explored earlier. Fliers pushed under your hotel room door that advertise volunteering at an animal sanctuary are just like internet searches, and just because they might be the first placement you see doesn't mean they deserve your time or money. Orla Brennan, who volunteered in Nepal for six months, said "During my time in Nepal I met many travelers who decided while here to volunteer. Many of them told me that after their experience they saw the downsides of volunteering in this way, and would not do it again."

Alternatively, 'just turning up' in the place where you know you want to volunteer can be a great way to start serious research for a long-term volunteer role. You can get the lay of the land, build local contacts, start learning a language, and vet organizations face to face before deciding where you want to give your time. Vanaka Chhem-Kieth, the co-founder of a social media platform in Cambodia said, "I was doing extensive research from my home in London about possible work in Cambodia, getting advice and introductions from everyone I knew who had contacts at nonprofit organizations. But it was so hard to do from afar. I wasn't able

LEARN

to really understand the organization's needs nor did I have the critical information and contacts I needed to understand if the organization was as great as it might have appeared online. In the end, I just packed my bag and headed to Cambodia to do my research in person. Being on the ground did not solve all the challenges associated with choosing the right organization, but it certainly made it much easier to evaluate which one would be a better fit than reading through websites."

The Built-in Flaws of Rating Systems

Although the idea seems attractive, there are many problems with relying on volunteer placement rating systems to identify the best options for you. Ratings may seem like a handy shortcut, but may not provide you with the information you need, or necessarily be a fair assessment. Those giving out the ratings may be using criteria very different from your own.

Many organizations have tried to create volunteer program rating systems in the past, and they have all proved inadequate. Here are a few reasons why:

You usually only hear one side of the story
Most systems where volunteer trips are reviewed only ask the point of view of one person—the volunteer. They don't take into account that the relationship involves other people, including managers, colleagues, and arguably most importantly, the communities that the work is meant to benefit. To truly assess a volunteer opportunity you need to understand the wider impact of the host organization, and you are not necessarily going to get that from the opinions of other volunteers. Getting input from local people in a large-scale systematic way for any project is an enormous and expensive task, and trying to do that for volunteer projects around the world would cost more than any group would be willing to pay. An even more difficult hurdle would be encouraging local people to honestly point out the downfalls of a project, as many wouldn't want to scare away the potential for further support or funding.

Getting the negative stories out can be difficult

Most forums where volunteers can give feedback on a volunteer experience are also platforms that financially benefit from the ads or sales commission of selling volunteer trips. There is therefore a big incentive to promote positive ratings. For example, a colleague of Daniela's worked on the orphanages.no website, and came across examples of corrupt orphanage volunteering projects. When he wrote negative reviews about them on a travel rating website, they were flagged by the company and removed, whereas positive reviews, many of which seemed fabricated, were left up. It took many months and many additional emails before the website realized the concerns were legitimate and began allowing the negative reviews to be posted.

The biggest block to publishing negative reviews is fear. Some of the worst and most corrupt organizations have a lot of power, money, and influence. The website owners fear that bad reviews are fake, from competitors or disgruntled employees, and that negative reviews might leave them open to defamation claims. Volunteers themselves also fear repercussions. Many of the people we spoke to who had uncovered issues such as child exploitation or theft at a volunteer placement are often too afraid to put their names on exposés, or have been threatened to the point where they won't speak out at all. Dur Montoya, who volunteered in Morocco on a project that turned out to be a scam, told us, "The project coordinator waited there while we completed the feedback form, so we felt we had to lie and say everything had been OK. We were too scared to tell the truth."

The ratings track the 'wrong' things

You need to be aware of what exactly is being rated and whether you think those things are important. For example, is it important to you that the organization picks you up with a sign at the airport, houses you in a nice clean room, and is conveniently located near the tourist part of town? Or are you more concerned that your placement matches your skills to a need, and that funding is transparently distributed? A volunteer review that says "this placement was great!" may tell you little about the criteria that were used to reach that judgment.

LEARN

Things change

Volunteer programs change all the time. A fantastic – or unscrupulous – director leaves. A natural disaster causes a program to shut down, start up, or change direction. Voluntourism is so popular that new volunteer options bubble up every few weeks. Even if a rating program did an assessment of the tens of thousands of opportunities that exist right now, by next week we might have uncovered hidden corruption in one program and found another that has cleaned up its act. Nothing can replace your own careful research into what a current opportunity is offering.

Ultimately, relying on rating systems means outsourcing a key part of the process that is essential for learning service—doing your own research.

Red Flags in Marketing Materials

"I have developed a critical eye for other volunteer projects that simply 'pick and drop' a volunteer into an environment with the idea they can 'change the world' through short-term projects. The importance of understanding the limits to your work and that you will undoubtedly learn more than you can offer (especially in the first few months of finding your feet) is often ignored by organizations hoping to attract volunteers."

–Frankie Rushton, who volunteered
in India for five months

As we have mentioned, the lines between traditional tourism and impact-driven volunteering are blurred, especially in the way they are marketed. We cite an age-old proverb, "A nice brochure does not a reputable organization make." Many companies choose to market volunteer opportunities in a way that promotes a rather lopsided and simplistic view of complicated issues like development, poverty, and aid. These companies shy away from opening up debates on these complexities, because it is in their interests to convince as many people as possible to sign up, not deter customers by revealing complexity.

One study of volunteer travel marketing explored volunteers' reactions to the language used by volunteer programs, noting that "volunteers felt impressed by the density of buzzwords used in the marketing materials, but there was little evidence of these volunteers searching for evidence of how the volunteer project went about achieving their claims." It is easy for providers to make attractive claims if potential volunteers do not do the research to substantiate them. Volunteers may start to question if the experience they were sold matches the situation on the ground only once they are overseas—and by then it is too late. As a general rule of thumb, organizations that prioritize responsible volunteering are more likely to prioritize responsible marketing, and organizations that include information about learning goals and self-development as well as the long-term impact volunteers can make throughout their lives might align more closely with the learning service philosophy.

In the following examples we have quoted real volunteer websites but have kept them anonymous as we wish to illustrate, not name and shame. Our point is that the kind of marketing we see as problematic is extremely common and the examples we use are by no means outliers. We recommend that potential volunteers seek organizations that have honest, transparent and non-sensationalist materials that avoid any of the following tactics.

LEARN

Overemphasizing the 'need' for volunteers

> "Kibera needs land/tenancy rights, housing, water, electricity, health clinics, education, employment, security plus much more... money cannot help without people to direct it—all the organizations require assistance. They all need intelligent, keen, willing, and compassionate people to help. In the western world it has become common for many students to take a Gap Year out before or after university. More older people are now taking a year out away from their everyday life. Many could work in Kibera where they would achieve a real sense of doing some good. Kibera is crying out for people to help."
>
> -Online volunteer placement marketing

Marketing material that highlight an organization's desperate need for volunteers raises two red flags. One is a sustainability issue: filling vital roles with international volunteers will hinder their ability to provide reliable and high-quality service. In addition, some companies emphasize a critical 'need' for volunteers purely as a marketing tool, when the reality in many placements is that volunteers are at best superfluous additions, and at worst extra visitors to be entertained. If you are considering a volunteering option that is advertising a need, ask who has identified the need, and why and how international volunteers are being used to fill it.

Fueling sympathy instead of empathy

> "Due to lack of support and education around disability awareness in Kenya, many disabled children and adults are hidden from public view by their families... [T]here are increasing numbers of children born with either mental or physical disabilities, such as Cerebral Palsy and Down Syndrome, who do not have access to support and cannot fend for themselves."
>
> -Online volunteer placement marketing

Much of the advertising for volunteer travel is designed to create *sympathy*, presenting people overseas as helpless victims waiting for a savior. We believe this to be a poor substitute for another emotion that is more likely to drive real change: *empathy*. While sympathy builds a desire to help, empathy builds a desire to understand, and only through that understanding are we able to contribute our support most wisely. Natalia Gligor, who volunteered for over a month in an orphanage in Nepal, told us that she now realizes that sympathy can lead to bad decisions: "People feel such pity for children from poor countries, and sometimes feel like doing something about it—having the purest intentions. But it allows individuals... to grow a big business based on children from less-privileged families."

In order to be able to understand what it is like to walk in someone else's shoes, you need to understand what those shoes are like. It is easier to build empathy for people who are similar to yourself and harder when you have few shared experiences. To build empathy for local people, you need to respect and get to know them, not pity them, so look for marketing that seems to offer a chance to share, exchange and learn with local people, rather than save them.

Poverty voyeurism

> *"[The children's home] has approximately 10 children who are currently residing there. It is very poorly equipped and they lack sufficient funds to support all the children's needs."*
> -Online volunteer placement marketing

Poverty voyeurism, sometimes given the more attention-grabbing name of 'poverty porn,' is the practice of using images of poverty unethically. Examples include fundraising or volunteer recruitment materials that have images of run down homes, malnourished and crying babies, or women carrying water on their heads through parched fields, perhaps with an audio voice over giving you shocking statistics and messages about people who 'have no voice.' Such imagery often relies on a simplistic view of poverty, falling back on old stereotypes, and can be extremely damaging.

Learning service means traveling to learn about and understand complex global issues, with a view to taking future action to address them. This is very different from coming to simply observe people facing those issues as part of their daily lives because they seem exotic. Poverty voyeurism is patronizing and exploitative. Seriously question organizations that sell viewing poverty as exciting, or that use disempowering images of local people.

The savior/hero dynamic

> *"The highlight of the trip is certainly the smiles of families when you give them the keys to their brand new home."*
> -Online volunteer placement marketing

LEARN

Another red flag in marketing is when volunteers are presented as the heroes of the story. While of course there are heroic people doing unpaid work all over the world, not all volunteering is necessarily heroic. The media tends to venerate the celebrities who turn up to lend a hand in disaster areas, or the 'everyday heroes' who drop everything to rush overseas to help. The most sensationalist stories focus on aspects such as the distance they had to travel, the barriers they had to overcome, the limited planning they had done, or how young they are. Unlike the qualities that are more likely to make a project successful – careful planning and resourcing – naiveté itself often gets celebrated.

The real harm in the savior myth is the idea that the lack of learning, preparation, and self-reflection is a necessary rite-of-passage for the volunteer hero. In order to be 'heroic,' a volunteer needs to be presented as charting unknown waters when they set out to help overseas. The media celebrates their experiments, thereby encouraging more under-prepared copycats, instead of urging people to learn from the tens of thousands of past volunteers who have gone before them. In short, if society continues to reward *intention* rather than *results*, wasteful actions will continually be incentivized.

If the only stories told on a website are from foreign volunteers, or if the images are all about the visiting traveler saving the day, it is likely a misrepresentation that excludes the main actors— the local people tirelessly working for change within their own communities.

Creating unrealistic expectations

> "Whether you're interested in developing resources in one of the most deprived areas of Thailand or helping to build stronger homes for families having to make do with cardboard and dirt floors in Guatemala—finding your own volunteer building project will be a breeze."
> -Online volunteer placement marketing

Question any marketing that suggests that making an impact will be easy or have immediate effect. Long-term social change, such as improving education systems or increasing incomes, is a slow and multi-layered process, in which outsiders can usually play only a minor role. False marketing of inflated impacts can set you up for failure from the outset. Blogger Rachel, whose post about volunteering in Nepal went viral, wrote, "We were in an area where nobody needed us, and where we could make little to no difference. We couldn't speak the language and had been told beforehand that it wasn't necessary, so we had next to no input. I felt useless."

Look out for organizations that recognize that the problems being tackled are complex, and that whatever skills and experience a volunteer might bring, they are only a small part of a wider solution.

Overuse of the language of tourism

> "As a volunteer in Nepal, you can ride on the backs of elephants through lush jungles, trek through snowy mountains, raft down rivers and participate in an abundance of outdoor and cultural activities."
>
> -Online volunteer placement marketing

LEARN

Although it is fair to recognize that volunteer travelers are *still* travelers, and therefore interested in the sites and attractions of the country they are placed in, it is a red flag when a volunteer placement is primarily advertised using the language and imagery of tourism. If you find yourself drawn to the descriptions of travel adventures, maybe that's what you need and want—an adventure holiday. Or you could choose an organization marketing an interesting, responsible volunteer position and work out other travel plans before or after. Whatever you do, don't conflate the two: your zip-line jungle tour will indeed be a fun and adventurous activity but don't fall for the marketing that makes out that the day you spend teaching in a school is the main point of your trip!

The 'all-inclusive buffet'

"When can I start? Whenever you want to – the choice is yours… [We are] first and foremost flexible. You choose how long your placement lasts, and you also choose your own starting date."

-Online volunteer placement marketing

Beware of companies offering the 'all-inclusive volunteer buffet.' Just like in an all-you-can-eat restaurant, where you can never tell which food items are freshly-cooked, question travel companies that offer do-everything-go-everywhere volunteer options, with placements all over the world that start any time you like. Creating a volunteer placement that is beneficial to both the local community and to travelers is extremely challenging, even in one location. To do that well all around the world is nearly impossible. Broadly, our recommendation is to avoid any organization that sells trips to dozens of locations rather than a selection of strategic partnerships, does not do any volunteer matching, or has commoditized volunteering to the point where they are offering one-click purchasing or 'discount volunteer placements.' Going abroad with one of these high-volume discount providers and getting an unvetted placement may have even greater repercussions than getting a dish of salmonella from the buffet.

Researching Your Shortlist

"Do your research, and get validation: externally, from established organizations or development professionals working in that area; internally, from someone who has worked or volunteered in the organization in the past; and financially, by checking out their financial reports and governance documents. I wish I had given myself that advice before jumping in to support a corrupt organization!"

-Jake Goldberg, who volunteered
in Cambodia for 12 weeks

When you have got a shortlist of opportunities that sound interesting, it is now time to put out some feelers and start investigating! As this is likely to be the most time-consuming stage of your research, try to ensure that your shortlist is not too long—we suggest writing down a maximum of five opportunities to look into further. You can always widen out your search again if your research reveals that they're not what you're looking for.

Compile a list of questions that you would like to know about each opportunity, based on your own values and priorities. Include questions that cover the organization's philosophy and approach to development, community ownership, and strategies for child protection. Also think about questions about the volunteer experience—the selection process, the training and support available, and the opportunities for continued learning and engagement.

As tempting as it can seem, simply emailing your whole list of questions to a volunteer organization won't work. It is exhausting for hosts to respond to potential volunteers asking the same questions over and over again, especially if the answers are easily accessible elsewhere, and few organizations have the capacity for that. You have to put in the legwork and find out most of the answers yourself. Here are some ideas of sources you can use.

The online presence

Although we warned against relying too much on an organization's own marketing material, a transparent organization will be anticipating your questions and put most of the information you need to know on their website. Be sure to read through all the tabs. Check if there is a 'Frequently Asked Questions' page. There may be downloadable project evaluations or financial reports. You may be able to click through to sites that the project is affiliated with, such as parent and sister organizations, and check that their philosophy also matches yours. (If Zahara had done that in the story at the beginning of this chapter, she may not have made the same choice.) Your research may highlight the responsible practices of an organization, or those you don't agree with.

LEARN

Returned volunteers

Talking to past volunteers is a great way to gain a realistic insight into how an organization operates. You might be able to connect to past volunteers directly through social media or blogs, but the easiest way is to ask the volunteer organization if they can put you in touch directly. Sally Grayson, who volunteered in the Gambia for three months, found that her placement organization was a scam. "Why, oh why, did I not ask to talk with previous volunteers?" she lamented. She later went on to found her own responsible volunteer company, People and Places.

Remember, a positive volunteer experience is not the same as an effective one, and one negative volunteer experience does not mean the organization can be written off. Ally Shepherd, who volunteered for a year in El Salvador, said, "Talking to previous volunteers can be helpful, but remember that different people can have very different experiences according to their personalities, so you have to 'connect the dots' between research you do about the organization to be able to decide if the project is for you before going."

Try not to overwhelm past volunteers with a deluge of questions. Two or three pertinent ones are more likely to elicit a response. You could ask questions such as:

- How effective do you think you were in your placement, and why?
- What were the biggest challenges for you in your placement?
- What are the biggest concerns you have about the organization?
- What type of person would be a good fit for this program? Who might not be a good fit?
- What piece of advice would you give to future volunteers doing the same placement as you?

Bear in mind that the organization is likely to only want to offer the details of people who had positive experiences. You can start your conversations with these volunteers, and at the end of the discussion ask if they could put you in touch with a friend from the program who experienced more challenges, so you can get a rounded view. Alternatively you can ask the volunteer organization directly if you can talk to someone who struggled or who finished their placement early. Claire did this before she volunteered in Cambodia, and she found her host organization to be refreshingly honest about the challenges other volunteers had experienced. After speaking to a volunteer who did not enjoy the placement, Claire felt reassured that she and the previous volunteer had very different priorities and expectations, and felt more confident in her choice.

People connected to the organization
Asking a partner organization, donor or expatriate who works in the same vicinity or sector is a great way to get an alternate perspective on an organization. You can track them down through an internet search, personal contacts or past volunteers. Bear in mind that if you ask representatives of organizations that are too similar there may be an element of competition in their response. You could ask questions such as:
- How much do you know about [X organization], and what are your impressions of the work they do?
- What would you say the organization's biggest strengths are, and what are their biggest challenges?
- From your perspective, do you think the organization could support and use a volunteer effectively? In what role?

As with all of these sources, also remember that one person's perspective on an organization is just that, the perspective of one person, so do not take what they say as evidence of an organization's effectiveness or ineptitude without verifying this information elsewhere too.

News articles
If an organization is large enough, there may be news or reviews online. Check news in the country where the organization is based as well, as these stories rarely make international news. Scandals such as organizational corruption are often written as exposés; or alternatively, there may be articles positively endorsing the good work of the organization. When looking for information in this way, bear in mind the date the article or review was written,

LEARN

and remember that organizations can change. You could even bring up any negative stories that you uncover directly with the organization to see if they have another side of the story, or if they have actively worked to address the issue.

Talking directly to organizations

> "Find a project that you believe in and an organization that has a good support structure. Not just logistical support, but social support. Work with an organization that has enduring networks so that you can continue your involvement after you leave the site, and work with a group that you believe in. Demand fiscal responsibility from organizations who you are paying dues to, but do not think that you know all of the answers or the best way to manage the program."
>
> –Whitney Grespin, who volunteered in Tanzania, Ghana, Uganda and Haiti

After you have done your preliminary research, and maybe narrowed your shortlist to just one or two opportunities, you can get down to the nitty-gritty and ask critical questions directly to the sending or hosting organization. Hopefully, from the long list of questions that you started with, only a small number of them remain unanswered.

Remember that asking questions is different from making demands, and that it is reasonable to wait a few days or weeks for a response. You will probably not be anyone's first priority— and if you are, that may not be a good sign! Watch out for organizations that seem willing to accept anyone to get more bums on plane seats and money in their pockets.

Obviously there are incentives for an organization to present itself in the best possible light, so be wary of taking overly positive answers at face value. If an organization avoids answering a question or is not able to provide an answer, this can also be important information, and tread carefully with organizations that don't seem to have the time, willingness or English language capacity to provide the experience you are looking for. Good organizations should be used to answering critical, evaluative questions – and should in fact welcome them – as it will indicate that they are getting volunteers who are switched on, worth their time, and who care about being effective.

Still Undecided?

If you are a perfectionist, striving to find an organization that has never made any mistakes or left any volunteer feeling unsatisfied, you may be looking for a long time—or forever! Instead, in the spirit of learning service we encourage you to identify organizations that express humility in success, honesty in failure, and a willingness to grow through challenge. Also remember that you will never be able to get a definitive picture of an organization, especially from afar, so that your assessment process should continue long after you begin your volunteer experience. Continue to learn and ask critical questions, and don't be afraid to form a new opinion if you uncover fresh information.

If the choice is still not clear:

- Talk with a respected advisor—an international development professional, parent, supervisor, or teacher.
- Pay attention to values—is the tone of the organization in line with the philosophy of learning service? Is it in sync with ideas you value?
- Listen to your gut feelings. Sometimes your body sends you subtle (or obvious) signals that there is something wrong with a certain program. Listen carefully, and respect the wisdom of your unconscious mind.
- Err on the side of caution—choose the organization that seems to have the better support system and orientation for volunteers.

LEARN

Step 5: Sign Up!

Compare volunteering with other options

Understand the role that volunteers play

Learn about different types of volunteer travel offerings

Compare and evaluate opportunities

Sign up!

This is it! You've learned as much as you can (for now, at least) and are ready to sign up with your volunteer program. At the close of this chapter, an important learning step is complete, but this doesn't mean that learning is over. As we move into the next part of the book, guiding you through the service you will do at home and abroad, you will see that the learning mindset is integral to all steps of a volunteer journey. We look at how you can prepare for this in the next chapter.

ON ACTION

"Do the best you can until you know better. Then when you know better, do better."

-Maya Angelou

As you move onto the final part of this book, and the action stage of your journey, we encourage you to remember the message of the vajra: learning and action are intertwined, reinforcing one another in a never-ending loop. Learning through research and reflection can inform your action, just as action can ignite further learning through regular self-evaluation. There are some things that you can only learn by doing, and that includes the learning that happens through making mistakes. Your actions – before, during, and after volunteering – are not separate from your learning, but an integral part of it. Learning service means that all our actions incorporate these three qualities:

- **Being humble:** Not always assuming that your own ideas are correct or appropriate, and seeing that other perspectives may be equally valid.
- **Being mindful:** Being conscious and aware about the impact of your actions on others, being present with the people you meet and being open to learning from them, being intentional about your choices, and being patient with yourself and others along the way.
- **Being self-reflective:** Taking time to reflect on and evaluate your actions so you can adjust future behavior as needed, and always being open to changing your ideas and approaches.

PART FOUR:

ACTION BEFORE YOU LEAVE

Finally signing up for a volunteer opportunity after all your research might feel exciting, empowering, or just a huge relief! Take the time to celebrate your choice. All the research that went into the decision will put you in an excellent position for the next step: humble, mindful, self-reflective action.

When you hear the word 'action' you'll probably think about the time you spend volunteering in another country. In fact, we think that action begins the minute you make your decision about where to volunteer. Between the time you decide and the time you travel, there's plenty to do in order to set yourself up for a successful experience abroad. You probably already have a long to-do list. Your head may be full of questions about how to prepare mentally for time away from home, how to gain experience and useful professional skills, how to gather the funds to pay for your trip, and what to pack. In this part we will explore some of the main tasks to complete before you get on the plane, and how to prepare effectively for a successful volunteer travel experience.

10.
PRACTICING SOFT & HARD SKILLS

Perspective: Be Prepared!
By Isobel Wilson-Cleary, who volunteered for five months in India

It is so important to prepare well for a volunteer placement—if you don't, you will end up wasting a lot of your own time and that of your host organization. I volunteered in India after graduating from university, and a large part of my preparation involved ensuring my skills and experiences were well-matched to the volunteer role, including softer skills of cultivating the useful attitudes and resilience necessary to make the most of time spent overseas.

My degree was in History of Art, but I wanted to get experience overseas before pursuing a Masters that combined heritage with international development. These fields may not seem linked, but I found that my degree came in useful as it helped me to look critically at different elements of society. Art isn't produced in a vacuum and neither are social injustices—there's always a history. It also helped underpin my understanding of communications.

My volunteer position was at an organization called Deep Griha Society (DGS) that, amongst the various projects they run to support local communities, work with vulnerable children and their families. I'd worked with children in an arts setting, as an *au pair* and also as a mentor, so I figured my experience could be of help. I also volunteered at home before throwing myself into an international setting, which helped me have more realistic expectations and a clear understanding of the role of a volunteer.

I knew my communication skills would come in handy overseas. All my previous experience, mostly in the arts, had been very people-orientated where communication was key. I was a careers representative for my department, talking to students of all backgrounds, and had studied a couple of languages at school and during university. This proved to be so useful when navigating the language barrier and engaging with people in India (I can count on both hands, and maybe toes, the number of things I can say in Hindi).

I made an intentional choice to go through Development in Action, a UK-based global citizenship charity, as they take volunteer preparation seriously. I had a good feeling about them from the beginning: the application form was in-depth, and was followed up with an interview, a UK training day and an orientation week. The training was run by previous volunteers who could give me a realistic picture of what life was life in India. The placements fit with a wider mission and they had long-term, close links with their Indian partner organizations, all of which were locally set-up and run. There were opportunities to volunteer with the home side of the organization while I was fundraising and prepping to go.

Though obviously a different environment, and one potentially closer in culture to the UK, where I'm from, I had already spent five months in Italy before my stint in India. This was invaluable in preparing me for the challenges of spending so much time away from home, and also helped me understand what it is like to live as a foreigner.

Overall, the time I spent preparing for my placement was well worth it, as it meant that I got so much out of my time in India—and was also able to contribute my skills effectively to DGS. Good preparation is one of my top bits of advice for any aspiring volunteer!

Cultivating and Practicing Attitudes

"Service is an attitude. The math lessons were concrete examples of service, but they only felt meaningful because of the smile, humility, and open mind that I brought to them. If I had given the same lessons with no emotional investment in the students or willingness to learn from them, it would not have been real service. And the best part of service being an attitude is that you can carry that attitude with you even if you're not 'helping the poor.'"

-Jacob Wachspress, who volunteered for
nine months in Bolivia

You might have already started to think about the skills that you need to brush up on in order to be effective during your placement. You might be planning to take a language class, or develop your knowledge of computer programming. Hard skills like those are important and useful for both yourself and for what you can contribute overseas, and honing your skills in advance is strongly encouraged by many volunteer manuals and sending organizations. We certainly recommend that you identify the hard skills you will need overseas, and learn and practice them. But first, we'll consider the factor most likely to influence the outcomes of your trip—the soft skills that you cultivate and apply. Ally Shepherd, who volunteered in El Salvador for a year, advised that "soft skills such as being open-minded, friendly, flexible, willing to learn and compromise are very useful," and we think they are just as important to develop as hard skills—if not more so.

What does 'practicing attitudes' look like?
When we discuss 'soft skills,' we include attitudes. It might appear strange to talk about attitudes as things that can be practiced,

as it may often seem as if your emotions and attitudes are controlling *you* and not the other way around. It can therefore be extremely empowering to realize that you can control your reactions and nurture qualities and attitudes that you admire.

One thing we can almost guarantee from our own experiences, and from talking to hundreds of returned volunteers, is that there will be times overseas when you will be uncomfortable, frustrated, or bored. It might be hot. It might be dusty. The internet might go out, the showers might be cold, the roads might flood, or the car might break down, and while you can't always prevent those things from happening, it is important to recognize that *you* are responsible and in control of how you react. If you are going to be a grump, all your knowledge of data management or graphic design may be wasted as people will not enjoy working with you. Sidonie Emerande, who works with international volunteers in her native Madagascar, said, "Volunteers who are not open about their personal needs get moody and fussy, which doesn't help anyone."

The ability to re-frame experiences through developing positive attitudes will not only have an impact on you, but it will also have an impact on others around you. Nan Yinn Yinn, who runs a school in Myanmar, said "Volunteers without openness, patience, empathy, and flexibility were the most difficult for me as the school is run according to the needs of the community." Reportedly, Oprah Winfrey had a sign in her studio that read, "You are responsible for the energy you bring into a space." Attitudes and energy are contagious. If one of your motivations for going abroad is to have a positive impact, managing your attitudes is a direct way to impact the people you encounter. When you think about what you want the legacy of your time abroad to be, we are sure that 'spreading bad moods' is not what you want to be remembered for!

Of course, we do not expect you to be happy all the time—this would be impossible. Instead, you can practice being aware of how your interactions affect other people, and be mindful of how you express your emotions. Remain open to the idea that you can create and transform your own experience by choosing to adopt attitudes that will help you. Linda Pinsky, who volunteered in Uganda for three weeks, shared this story with us. "My hosts

ACT

191

would take me to see different research projects. We would go on really long drives on dirt roads that had all these ruts. It would take forever to get there. When we finally got there, the person we came to see wasn't there. The fact that I still felt interested in the research even though we had spent so much time unproductively, made others feel more positive about their own research."

There is a growing recognition that attitudes can be taught and studied. Benjamin Franklin is said to have taken a systematic approach to practicing his attitudes. He created a list of qualities he wanted to embody, and an organized way to track his progress, for example, "Tranquility. Be not disturbed at trifles, or at accidents common or unavoidable." Then each night he would record his successes or failures in living each quality. After some time, he realized that trying to work on all of them at once was not working, and he wasn't successful at efficiently building any of them. (We compare it to trying to learn ten sports at once!) Instead, he decided to focus on one at a time, tracking his progress on all of them, but selecting one to focus on each week in a rotation. In this way, he was better able to achieve growth in that particular area, though he continued to track his success in all qualities each evening.

A more recent example can be seen in the work of Bill Drayton, the founder of Ashoka, an organization credited with fueling the field of social entrepreneurship. One of his passions is promoting empathy education, or education to build skills for empathy in young people. He is working with schools and youth initiatives to teach this quality in the same way as you would a hard skill like math or economics.

You can practice the soft skills you will need overseas by working, volunteering or engaging with diverse communities in your own country in the run up to your time abroad. Joanna Seczkowski, who volunteered in Cambodia for over two years told us, "I had worked already in remote locations in central desert Aboriginal communities in Australia, involving extremely under-privileged families, which prepared me for volunteering overseas. I had already had the chance to practice skills and attitudes I would find extremely useful in Cambodia."

Ultimately, self-reflection is the key to cultivating qualities you want to embody. When you feel yourself getting caught up in a storm of unproductive attitudes or emotions, take a step back. Separate the external reality (what you can't change) from your own internal reactions (what you can). Even if it is difficult to cultivate positive attitudes in the moment when you are angry, anxious, or upset, reflecting on past situations can offer some clarity and help you behave differently when similar situations arise again.

Qualities and Attitudes to Practice

It is important to practice the attitudes and qualities you want to take with you overseas in advance, as it may be much harder to do in a new cultural environment. Here are a few qualities that volunteers have told us were especially helpful for them to work on before their international volunteer experience.

Openness

> *"Go in with an open mind and an open heart, and don't think you know more than anyone else on the ground. Don't think that because a local way is different that it is wrong."*
> -Whitney Grespin, who volunteered in Tanzania, Ghana, Uganda and Haiti

Different cultures can have varied norms for working and communicating. If you are used to one culture's way of doing something, it can be easy to jump to viewing a different way as 'wrong.' An open attitude will allow you to see these differences as learning experiences. For example, in India, you might be annoyed that farmers resist using a new kind of rice seed that has more vitamins, and report back to your organization that the farmers are too old-fashioned to try something new. But if you are open, and focus on listening, you might learn that the last time they tried a new type of seed, the plants needed more water than was easily available, and subsequently yields were lower. You might gain a broader perspective on what sustainable farming means.

ACT

Being open doesn't necessarily mean having to change your views or agree with everything another person believes or says. But it does mean allowing for the *possibility* of this outcome. Meredith Chait, who volunteered in Tanzania, told us, "I wish I had been a little more open-minded on my volunteer trip. I think of myself as a very open-minded and cultured person. However, I was getting frustrated in Tanzania when people or things did not get done at the pace I would have liked."

So how can you practice openness before going overseas? You can practice in your hometown by, for example, visiting a place of worship of a religion you know little about. You can volunteer at a refugee resettlement program. You can even practice openness by watching a news show from a different political perspective than yours and trying to find one thing you agree with—or at least trying to better understand why people have such different beliefs than you. Listening to other perspectives and being aware of how you respond can help you deepen your receptivity and open-mindedness.

Patience

> "I had a chance to live with Americans in Haiti—other volunteers. And I saw how frustrated they would get with things like transportation, tardiness, and overcharging in commercial interactions. I felt pity for them. They'd never had the chance to practice patience with these things."
> -Volunteer who spent over three months in Haiti, who is originally from Thailand

Patience is an essential quality for effectively learning and contributing overseas. Meaningful community development is a long and slow process, and speeding up the pace might actually cause problems. Getting flustered will not make anything happen faster, and if you take a step back you may be surprised at how situations can resolve themselves on their own.

Many volunteers find developing patience hard, especially those who like to see the immediate results of their work, but practicing patience in your normal routine can have wide-ranging benefits. You can start by challenging yourself to slow down in areas of your own life: Leave an hour early and walk to work instead of driving. What adventures do you have along the way? If you find yourself in the slow line at the supermarket, try striking up a conversation with another person in line. Or skip the supermarket, and make a special outing of a trip to the farmer's market where you buy something from every stand, and observe the interactions between the farmers and customers.

Notice when you find your impatience mounting—whether it is trying to put your niece to bed, teaching an older colleague a new computer program, or just sitting in a traffic jam. Be inquisitive and ask yourself: It this *really* such a big deal? What is the root cause of this emotion? Does that issue have more to do with an external situation, or with me? Observe your own responses—physical and emotional. Practice taking ten deep breaths. Say something nice to the person you are frustrated with. And see if sometimes you can actually find a silver lining in the slow downs. A volunteer who went to Albania for two years observed, "Volunteers need to be prepared for slow progress in their missions, but in many cases the patience pays off in personal development for the volunteer."

Humility

> "Too many times we have volunteers who make loud aggressive statements about what they want, who tell us that our work is not effective, who make never-ending demands about how they want things to be different. The most important lesson I could possible teach, and the greatest skill I could ask for from volunteers, is humility."
>
> —Volunteer Manager in Peru

Living abroad almost always requires a healthy dose of humility. At home you may be a straight-A student, an accomplished professional, or a socially-adept community leader, only to feel like an awkward, unskilled novice when you arrive in a new environment. See this as a unique opportunity to put your life experience into perspective.

Humility can help diffuse a situation when things are going wrong. When you are late for a meeting, instead of saying, "The traffic was horrible!" or "I got lost on the way!" why not try, "I should have left earlier." In difficult situations, the best volunteers don't point at external circumstance but look at their own agency. Practice asking, "What could I have done differently?" or "What will I do differently next time?" before you start blaming others.

Showing humility can help you gain respect from your co-workers overseas, and increase the effectiveness of your actions. Aoife Currie, a gynecologist who volunteered for six months in Cambodia, has this powerful example. "The hospital maternity ward was not kept clean, which was a significant health risk for the mothers and babies being treated there. I realized that the problem was that none of the local health staff had the role of cleaning up after the birth of a baby in their job descriptions, and they thought it a menial role for people who were so highly qualified. I decided that if no one else would take the initiative, then I would take on the role of cleaner. I wanted to role-model that no one was too important to take on menial tasks if the outcome would be improved health conditions in the hospital."

To practice humility, try putting yourself in an unfamiliar situation and letting yourself be guided by others who know more than you. Try your hand at a completely unfamiliar skill—for example, ask an elderly neighbor to teach you needlecraft, or ask a young person to teach you a new card trick or video game. Practice being comfortable feeling like a beginner again. Showing humility when you arrive in your new community overseas will help you build relationships and ensure that your colleagues feel appreciated.

Empathy

> *"I am now very cognizant about encouraging empathy, instead of sympathy. But I also know there is a fine line between them, and an art to explaining a foreign culture for those who have not been/cannot go there."*
> —Katie Larson, who volunteered in Costa Rica,
> Peru, South Africa and Cambodia

Volunteering abroad can expose you to the hardships, disappointments, and dreams of others, in a culture and country where you don't (and can't ever) fully understand the whole context. Sibella Graylin, who volunteered for two weeks in India, gave some examples. "You have to be prepared for what you are going to see: poverty, malnourished children, beggars with severe disabilities, dirtiness." Whenever you are faced with the suffering of others, it can be tempting to jump right in with solutions. This is hard even with familiar people and settings, so it can be good to practice this at home before dealing with the cross-cultural complications!

Writer Brené Brown speaks about empathy through her work as a coach. She describes being empathetic as the opposite of trying to fix someone else's problems. Instead of seeing ways to improve something we don't fully understand, empathy is about feeling someone else's emotions. When someone shares their emotions with us, rather than responding with advice, we might start with, "I don't even know what to say right now, but I'm so glad you told me," as Brené suggests. The instinctive efforts to fix other people's problems can lead to difficulties for volunteer travelers. The reality is that most of the symptoms of poverty and daily challenges faced by the people you encounter overseas will not be in your power to solve. Empathy might be the best thing you can offer: a kind moment of deep listening.

Empathy is also a helpful skill for managing potential disagreements. You can practice this before you go overseas in situations that are likely to be the hardest you'll face—disagreements with close friends and family members. In the book *Lean In*, Sheryl Sandberg describes how, as a child, when she and her siblings were fighting, her parents made them repeat back how the other was feeling before they could make their own complaint. This simple act of acknowledging how the other was feeling not only helps you practice listening, but also forces you to articulate the needs or complaints of the other. Sheryl said she didn't enjoy having to do it at the time, but now sees the value in having her own kids do the same. When you encounter something you disagree with, ask yourself questions such as:

- What perspective might they be coming from?
- What arguments could that person make to justify their position?

- What experiences might that person have had that made them think that way?

Writing your thoughts in a journal, and getting down on paper what things might look like from the other person's perspective, can help you cultivate empathy.

Working hard to develop the qualities we have discussed by weaving them into the action you take is essential to the practice of learning service. Attitudes such as humility and openness are at the root of a learning mindset, as they enhance your receptivity to learning and help you to engage meaningfully with new people and places. This, in turn, can make you a more effective volunteer during your trip and once you have returned home.

Preparing for Your Specific Volunteer Role

As well as practicing soft skills and attitudes, another key part of learning service is action to prepare you for the specific needs of your volunteer placement. That starts with proactive background research. By research, we don't just mean reading, we also mean interacting with people in your community who are from or have traveled to the country where you will volunteer, communicating with past and current volunteers at your placement, and using social media to gain a range of perspectives about the culture and context of the place you will be going.

Your research needs will be specific to the place and opportunity you are considering. For example, if you plan to volunteer for a wildlife conservation project in southern Malawi, you may want to learn about conservation work, about the history and politics of Malawi, about the culture of the Chichewa people you will be working with, and about the particular organization with which you will volunteer. Try to find sources that offer a range of perspectives so you don't just get one side of a story. Below are some topics you can look into.

Current affairs
Keeping up to date on news in the country you will travel to will give you further context about your placement and will help

keep you interested, engaged, and excited about your trip. This knowledge will also help keep you safe. A place that seemed stable six months ago when you signed up for your trip might turn out to be a poor choice if there is political unrest, health concerns, or other changes that will impact your experience. Researching news and politics in the country to which you will travel will also help you be more conscious of the constraints within which your host organization is working.

To get up to speed on current affairs, read up on:

- News and politics from the region. Try to look at a range of different sources, including journalists and news outlets based in the country.
- Developments and current trends in the issue you will be working on. You could seek out research reports and briefings from think-tanks, human rights monitors, NGOs, or your host organization.
- Global issues and important global actors. Find out about what happened at recent international summits, or what the current priorities of donor organizations (foundations, governments, banks) are and why.
- Interesting people and ideas having an impact on the world today. Look for blogs or human-interest stories related to development or innovation.
- Travel advice from your embassy and any specific risks or rules that apply.

The historical and cultural context

Understanding how current affairs fit into the historical context will help explain the root causes of some of the current issues in a country. To get up to speed on the history and culture of a place, you could read non-fiction books and biographies, watch documentaries, seek out guide books of the area, and talk to people originally from that place.

Topics to find out about include:

- History: As well as academic books and articles, look for more accessible memoirs or journalistic accounts. Novels or movies based on real historical events can also be an accessible way to delve into a country's past.

- Religion, culture, and lifestyle: Guidebooks can provide an introduction to these topics, or seek out travel writing for a richer flavor. You could even look at magazines local to the area you are traveling to—everything from the interest stories to the ads provide cultural insights!
- The local context of tourism and volunteering: Read blogs, articles, or discussion papers on these topics.
- International development theories, critiques, and case studies: We have a list of further reading about international development at the end of this book.

The organization you will be working with

Look for online reports and publications to learn more about the history, mission, theory of change, and strategy of the organization. Of course start with their website and, for larger organizations, blogs and news articles about their work. Connect with past volunteers to gain insight on what skills would be most useful to develop before you travel, and get briefed on specifics of the project you will work on. Ask your contacts to send you useful project documents or evaluations to help put your assignment in context. As always, if you come across anything in this further research that rings alarm bells, don't be afraid to ask more questions or form a new opinion about whether this placement is right for you. In learning about the organization, you might want to find out more about:

- The issues and goals on which the organization is focused
- Recent evaluations of the organization's work
- The organization's structure, who you report to, what your role is, and who you will work with, be managed by, or mentor.

Developing the hard skills needed for your role

Depending on what your role is and your current proficiency in the skills needed, you may want to put in some extra practice. A volunteer who spent over three months in India said, "Brush up on your skillset before you leave to begin volunteering so you can put your all into the experience." This might mean taking courses, like an English teaching certification, or a class in the local language. If you are unsure what skills would be useful in your role, ask your host organization. Even if you are just in a supporting role, or have signed up for a volunteer program that is more focused on learning than service, you might still want to kick-start your learning by exploring these areas:

- Professional skills and academic qualifications for the job. There may be short certifications in community colleges near you, or distance-learning opportunities. For example, if you will work in a business development center, a class in financial management could be useful.
- Local language skills. We can't emphasize enough the degree to which language skills will help your placement. Consider hiring a tutor, or taking an evening class. At a minimum, strive to learn some basic greetings.
- Familiarity with software or other systems used in the organization. Ask if there is a particular tool for accounting, web development, or database management that you'll need to use.

In our experience, developing your skills and familiarizing yourself with the culture, politics, and history of the region before you leave is well worth the time. It can help you to adopt a learning mindset right from the start, to understand your new home more quickly, and to be a more critically-engaged volunteer.

11.
FUNDING YOUR TIME ABROAD

Perspective: How I Funded my First Trip Overseas
By Claire

My first international volunteer experience was when I was 19, in the summer break after my first year of university. As a typical student, I had absolutely no money, and my parents weren't in a position to support me. In fact, it had been subtly hinted that I should probably get a job over the summer to supplement my fairly meager student loan. Ever the rebel, I managed to fund my flights and a three-month stay in Nepal, and not go completely bankrupt in my next year of study! How did I do that?

The first thing I did was apply for a travel grant from my university—which I received on the condition that I write a report about what I had learned. The second thing I did was to secure a part-time job doing temporary office work. It was low-pay, but over time I could save something. The third, and most important action I took, was to ensure I made extremely thrifty lifestyle choices in the months running up to my departure date. I cooked my own meals, I didn't buy coffee or alcohol, and

I invited friends over instead of going out. I walked everywhere. I shared textbooks. I chose not to go to the end-of-year event at my college due to the pricey tickets. Lots of these decisions were difficult, but I was determined to get to Nepal that summer.

I actually continued the frugal lifestyle when I was in Nepal, and I have to say that it helped me integrate into local society. I lived with a family and ate all my meals with them. I didn't go traveling or trekking during my stay and spent all the time that I could at my placement. I caught the local bus to work each day. Saving for the experience myself and not viewing the trip as a vacation made me value and appreciate the whole experience so much more than if it had been easy to get there.

The Costs of Volunteer Travel

Going overseas for an extended period of time without an income is expensive, and the costs can feel prohibitive. Placement fees, flights, insurance, and living expenses, depending on where you are going and for how long, can add up to several thousand dollars. Due to these high costs, the stereotype of the international volunteer is the über-privileged and sheltered gap-year student. If you are not fortunate enough to be able to easily spare the large amounts of cash required—earning and saving by yourself may seem like an insurmountable task. We believe that volunteer travel should be accessible to anyone interested, not just those who happen to have large amounts of money languishing in their bank accounts. Although volunteers from different backgrounds and income levels may have fewer or more financial barriers, with a bit of creativity, forward-planning and determination, an experience overseas is within your reach.

Many formal volunteer programs recommend that you fundraise to help towards your personal volunteering costs. However, like most of the topics we have explored in this book, fundraising is a field wrought with complexity, posing larger moral questions to the conscious traveler. While we do not rule it out, there are ethical considerations and potential pitfalls. In this chapter we confront the complexity and explore ways of responsibly and transparently funding your placement abroad—whatever your economic circumstances.

What to Do if You Don't Think You Can Afford it

If volunteer travel is a priority for you and you do not already have the funds you need, it takes dedication and an astute financial plan to make it a reality. There is a certain power in working hard for the privilege of this kind of opportunity. The personal investment of time and money will help you value the experience and ensure you don't take it for granted. Furthermore, the planning and build up can be as much of a learning experience as the volunteering itself, and the returns you are likely to get will be immeasurable.

Start by making a budget. List out all of your foreseeable expenses and begin to plan accordingly. Once you have researched the potential costs of your trip, look to see what amount of money you already have in hand to allocate to your trip and how much more you would need before you can comfortably cover the projected costs. Even if you are on a low income, and don't have much cash to contribute from your salary each month, there may be a few lifestyle decisions you can make in order to regularly put something aside for your volunteering trip.

Here are some ideas for what to do if your current bank balance seems like an obstacle to your going abroad:

Work for it

This may seem like a fairly obvious option but it is surprising how often it is overlooked. If you already have a job and your income is being eaten up each month, consider taking on something extra on top of what you are doing. For example, could you work one evening a week or on Saturday mornings, and ensure everything you earn goes towards the trip? You can think about work that is more flexible, such as babysitting or dog-walking if this appeals to you. If you have a skill such as painting or making clothes you could take custom orders for a fee. Even if you have to work a few extra hours waiting tables it will be motivating to know that every penny you earn is bringing you closer to your overseas experience.

Scrimp and save

We have encountered many volunteers who self-funded a period abroad by making some lifestyle changes. Think about ways that you can cut down on your regular expenses. For example, could you bring your own lunch to your campus or office instead of buying it every day? Could you invite friends over to your house for an evening instead of meeting them in a café or bar? By spending money sparingly, you may reach your goal sooner than you think. You might also gain insight into what it is like to live in straitened circumstances, enabling you to better empathize with the communities in which you might be volunteering.

De-clutter

You can get a bit of extra cash by selling items that you own but you may not need while you are away (or ever again!). This may be large items like your car, or smaller things like musical instruments never played, or an old record collection. You could have a local sale where everyone knows that their purchases will fund your trip, or alternatively you can sell your things through online forums.

Look for grants or scholarships

If you're a student, your college may offer travel grants or have other funds available to financially support you. A number of programs and volunteer-matching portals offer a full or partial scholarships for volunteer placements based on need, and some international service organizations are specifically targeted at opening up overseas service opportunities to those who might have financial barriers to joining. There are also funds and foundations set up for this purpose that you could apply to.

Apply for a funded volunteer opportunity

If you have professional skills and experience to contribute, you can apply to a fully-funded skilled volunteering program. The skills you have will need to have been identified as those required by the partner organizations, but this way you will get your travel and in-country expenses covered. As the organization is making this large investment in you, you can also feel more confident of a skill-match.

ACT

Ethical Fundraising for Your Volunteer Placement

Many volunteer programs encourage or require volunteers to fundraise. Sometimes this is for a donation to the overseas organization, as a contribution towards their work and to offset any costs associated with hosting you. Other organizations, especially those that charge a large fee, might suggest fundraising as a way of covering the costs of your flights, accommodation, *and* placement fee. Those companies sometimes provide guidance and materials to support volunteers in doing so. There are some ethical considerations involved in responsibly fundraising for your own expenses . Further, being intentional about the way in which you fundraise could result in your fundraising being educational, shifting attitudes, and challenging predominant stereotypes about the main value of volunteering. Here are some important tips to bear in mind for ethical, transparent, and myth-busting fundraising:

Be honest

One of the main considerations for volunteer fundraising lies in the difference between raising money to cover all the costs of a volunteer placement, and raising money directly for a cause. For example, someone might volunteer for an organization that aims to 'save the rainforest,' or 'stop human trafficking,' but when they raise money for their placement, the funds are actually used to pay a sending agency to offset the costs of marketing and recruiting volunteers, or for the cost of flights. This creates a disparity between where donors think their money is going, and the reality. Realistically, the vast majority of volunteers are not going to save the rainforest, or stop human trafficking. What is more reasonable to expect is that with the right placement and the right attitudes, someone can learn a lot about the issue, raise awareness amongst their family and friends, and be of help to organizations committed to long-term work in this area.

We recommend reconsidering how fundraising is labeled when it comes to raising money towards travel and placement costs, in order to avoid sending messages that might ultimately be damaging to the very cause you want to support. Benjamin Witcombe, who volunteered in Kenya for nine weeks, told us:

"Although we learned a lot from the trip, which we may be able to put to use in future development initiatives, the money was mainly focused on delivering our selfish objectives like a desire to help rather than on actual help itself, which put into question the morality behind fundraising for our trip."

Tell people exactly what their money is going towards. If you wish to combine fundraising for your volunteer costs with fundraising for the cause or organization, it is best to keep these two pools separate so it is transparent to donors where their money is going. Be honest with people about what you see as being the true benefits of your placement. If you are fundraising for your own personal travel costs, make sure that is clear, and make it known that the biggest outcome of that trip will likely be your own learning. If people make a donation and know that they are investing in a future leader and changemaker (you!) – not literally saving a poverty-stricken child in sub-Saharan Africa – it is a more empowering situation for both them and you, and any potential future beneficiaries.

Spread the learning service concepts

If you believe in the core messages of this book, that you have to learn before you can help and that learning is the key to effective service, then do not feel embarrassed if one of your main intentions in going overseas is to learn. Explain that the issues are complex and that you are taking this trip because you care deeply, and want to contribute to long-term solutions instead of doing something surface-level. If you explain that you are not only fundraising for your trip overseas for your personal growth, but for your life-long contribution to a just and sustainable world, you might be surprised by how many donors are excited to support you.

Don't play the sympathy card

Earlier we discussed volunteer placements that aim to evoke sympathy rather than empathy in their marketing. Be careful not to fall into the same trap when you are fundraising! One of the trickiest parts of managing a responsible fundraising campaign is finding a balance between marketing tactics that are effective, and those that are most respectful towards the issues you care about. While images of poor children with distended stomachs might get people to open their wallets, the overall impact of using such images is negative.

You may be traveling to a region that faces a lot of issues and challenges, but defining an area based entirely on its problems or on an outsider's perception of need is not empowering fundraising. In fact, by focusing on the worst-case situations, the aid sector has created a sense of hopelessness and perpetual need, which can actually deter the long-term investments that could contribute to stamping out poverty and disease. This type of imagery can detract attention from the complex, underlying causes of poverty and inequality and foster pity, rather than empathy and action. Furthermore, it fuels the stereotype that people in developing countries are not able to solve their own problems and are waiting around for a savior – maybe even a western volunteer – to pull them out of poverty. Katie Boswell, who volunteered in India for five months, told us, "In my current organization, we run workshops with Americans who are fundraising for overseas community-based organizations and visiting them, sometimes volunteering with them. We do role-plays to get volunteers and fundraisers to realize how it feels to be on the receiving end of service or funds."

One good rule of thumb is never to use a picture of someone in your fundraising unless you would be content with a photo of a family member or close friend (or you!) being used in the same way. If the picture or language is meant to provoke strong emotions of sorrow, then it may be offensive to whoever is being pictured. If you would feel embarrassed to explain to the person in the image how you are describing them (for example, destitute, helpless) then we suggest you reconsider what you say. Anything aimed at provoking sympathy at best misrepresents complex scenarios, and at worst is manipulative. If you received the images from your host organization, try to find out if permission was sought from the subjects to reuse their image in advertising—if you're doubtful that such steps were taken, are you really comfortable using it? Consider offering feedback to the organization about use of images.

Build empathy instead of selling sympathy. Help to educate your audience to understand and respect the people and issues you are working with. Use positive images, illustrating the change and not the problem, and offer context, to ensure the subject and issue are presented in a rounded, multi-dimensional way. Instead of the most important feature of a child being that he grew up in a slum or his mother has HIV, how about mentioning that he is a whiz at math, that he helps grow vegetables in a rooftop garden, or that his mother is an active volunteer in the local health center?

Challenge stereotypes

Ensure the language you use to describe the place you will visit is precise, honest, and non-discriminatory. In this book, we try to avoid using broad terms like 'poor people' when describing others, especially since there are many dimensions to poverty (economic, social, emotional) and a lack of a standard method for comparison (what you might call financially poor, another might consider rich). As a rule, try not to define a person or place purely by what they lack. There are also certain words that tend to only show up when discussing 'others.' Daniela is from the village of Briarcliff Manor, in New York State, yet no one has ever referred to her as a 'villager'—at least not that she knows of! Subtle changes, such as using more positive terms like 'community member' or 'people from x village', are better than unintentionally demeaning terms.

There are also unhelpful stereotypes about volunteers that you can challenge. Even though there is a lot in the public consciousness around volunteers 'fighting poverty' or 'making a difference,' be sure to resist playing into the hero role. Giving the impression that foreign volunteers are instrumental in solving problems in other countries ultimately reinforces an unequal power dynamic, suggesting that local people are somehow incapable of solving the problem themselves and that only foreigners can provide solutions. You may also want to avoid promoting the idea that development is easy and can be done by anyone with a big heart and a bit of time on their hands. If you want your actions as a volunteer to be mindful and humble, this should be reflected in how you fundraise. Ellen Gilbert, who volunteered in Ethiopia for five weeks, reflected, "When I volunteered, I was 19 years old and had never been to another continent outside of North America. As I volunteered I realized I still didn't know what problems I was attempting to solve. I hadn't imagined how my ego may have affected the fundraising for the trip or inhibited me from understanding who I was 'helping' and why."

Be humble and realistic about what you claim your impact will be. During your time overseas you will hopefully be able to offer some level of support to organizations on the ground that are in it for the long haul, plus your passion and commitment to the cause will ensure you continue using what you have learned well into the future. Don't underestimate these contributions!

Report back
If you are asking people to donate for your learning, then the measurement of success for their donations can be found only in understanding what education you have received along the way. Keep people informed about their investment: you! You could keep a blog, send email updates, write a thank you note, or give a call, but whatever you do, those who helped you go abroad will probably be delighted to hear what you have learned.

12.
MENTALLY & PHYSICALLY PACKING YOUR BAGS

Perspective: The Dangers of Gift-Giving
By Claire

One of the things I love about my work in educational travel is that I am able to build relationships with local communities by returning with different groups of students year after year. We stay in homestays, and students learn a tremendous amount through engaging in community activities such as farming, or apprenticing in traditional crafts such as stone, wood or metal carving.

Before heading out for these experiences, students are briefed about the implications of a group of foreigners descending on a community. We talk through ways to minimize any negative impacts our visit might have. I have always struggled to balance offering adequate compensation to the families that host us, and fueling jealousy among those who don't. There is also a tension between wanting to enable learning and sharing between students and community as a fair exchange, and not wanting to draw undue attention to the gaping material inequalities that exist between their different ways of life. An important part of the briefing with students is around gift-giving. I always used to think that bringing gifts from home to say thank you to the families is a kind and harmless gesture, as long as the gifts are small and inexpensive.

In the majority of cases, the students I travel with come from wealthier backgrounds, but once I had the opportunity to work with students from a community art college in Boston, who mostly came from relatively low-income backgrounds. This experience opened my eyes to the problems I had inadvertently created through the exchange programs I had facilitated. I brought the students from Boston to stay with families in an urban area of Kathmandu valley called Patan. I had brought countless groups to this community and up to that point, feedback from both the student groups and families was always positive. The program started off well, but after a few days I heard some complaints from the families, mostly that these students were not as kind as students from previous groups. The students also complained of uncomfortable situations with their homestay families. One girl told me that the children in her homestay had asked for presents, and were not satisfied with the pens and books she had brought. Another student said that her homestay dad had shown her the expensive watch gifted to him by a previous student. It even came out that past students had agreed to pay the school fees for their homestay sibling and was sending money every month. I realized that my concept of 'small and inexpensive' was very different from that of some of my previous students!

Only then I realized that I hadn't been doing a very good job of adequately explaining to students about how gift-giving can raise unfair expectations. As far as the homestay families were concerned, expensive gifts had been part of the deal, and as they viewed everyone from the West as rich, they had no concept of some students not being able to afford it. The gifts, although generously offered, had created barriers and ultimately damaged relationships instead of building them. Although after much explanation, both students and homestay families said they understood why this had happened, I learned a lot from this experience about how to frame exchanges in a way to align expectations.

Gift-giving, just like service, needs to be done mindfully and with an awareness of the implications on both the wider community and future relationships. While ensuring that homestay families are adequately compensated, I also now request students to leave material gifts at home. If students are inspired to give more to the people they have met on a trip, I direct them towards gifts that can't be traced back to an individual, such as a donation to an organization that works towards supporting the whole community.

What to Bring

"No matter what you think it will be, no matter how you prepare, something will be different from what you expected, you'll realize something you brought is 100 percent useless, and you'll wish you had something that you never thought to bring."
    -A volunteer who went to Kazakhstan for over a year

An experience that you have been planning for months often only starts to feel real once you start packing your bags. As you physically gather items that you think you might need for the journey ahead, you might also be sorting through your mind, drawing on previous learning to mentally prepare for the trip. If this is your first trip abroad, or the furthest and longest away from home you have been, you may find the process stressful. It may be impossible for to you adequately prepare when you have nothing to compare the experience to—in which case, 'preparation' may just mean becoming more comfortable with the unknown.

When it comes to packing, the necessities are an open mind, a positive and humble attitude, and some tools for self-reflection… but no doubt you'll also be wanting to know the most useful physical items you can put in your bag. This section has some ideas for things you want to be sure to take with you—or to leave behind.

Packing lightly and appropriately

Some of you may feel most comfortable bringing little with you and purchasing things you need as you go along. For others, you might feel more secure if you can feel as though the items in your bag leave you prepared for any eventuality. Our main suggestions are to *pack lightly* and *pack appropriately*.

WorldWorks in Vancouver has some memorable advice that should serve you well as you go to pack, "When in doubt, leave it out." They go on to suggest that you try to think of the worst case scenario if you left out an item and ask yourself, "Could I buy it locally? Could it be sent to me? Could I do things differently without it?" The answer to these questions will be different in different locations: volunteering in rural Senegal is very different from volunteering in central Bangkok. We spoke to volunteers who bought expensive outdoor clothes to volunteer in rural Indonesia, only to find themselves much more comfortable in the local sarongs. Others said that they spent most of their time in the same two T-shirts. Find out from past volunteers what you can easily find (for example, local clothing and food) and what might be harder to find (your favorite tea, western brands of shampoo) and what might not be possible to get hold of at all (we have found that feminine hygiene products and contact lens solution fall into this category in some regions of the world). In many places you might be volunteering, you can buy almost anything you need when you arrive.

Some other handy tips gained from experience include packing your carry-on bag as a mini-survival kit in case your bigger bag gets lost in transit—a change of clothes, emergency toiletries, toothpaste, and anything else you need to for your first few days in country. One excellent tip from Global Exchange in San Francisco suggests that you pack your bags and "then walk up and down a flight of stairs or around your neighborhood. If you get tired, reconsider what you are bringing and try to pare it down to the bare minimum." As you are navigating your way from the airport in Java, Indonesia, trying to find that elusive bus station in 100 degree heat and 100 percent humidity, you'll definitely be glad you heeded this advice!

Things Volunteers Were Glad They Packed

To offer some concrete examples, we asked returning volunteers to let us know the things they are glad they packed and those they wished they packed when they went abroad to volunteer. Here are a few of the most common items that people mentioned.

A refillable water bottle. In many places across the world, tap water is not safe to drink, so many travelers survive by buying bottled mineral water. Not only is this expensive in the long term, but it also creates a lot of plastic waste that ends up polluting local streets and rivers. With a refillable water bottle, you can get filtered water from restaurants or your workplace, or even buy your own water filter.

Pictures from home. Pictures from home can be useful for ice-breaking and bridge-building in many contexts, especially when you don't have a shared language. Homestay families and colleagues may be intrigued to see photos of your home town and relatives, and sharing part of your life will help you form closer bonds.

A headlamp. The place you are traveling to may not have electricity, and even if it does, there may still be frequent power outages, so a headlamp can be useful to have on hand. You may also find it useful when you are returning home at night down unlit streets.

A journal. Even if you do not keep a journal at home, many people feel inspired to start one when they travel, to record the myriad of experiences and roller-coaster of emotions that they experience. Journal writing can also help you relax and put intense or stressful events into perspective.

A first-aid kit. Although basic medical supplies are easily obtainable in many countries, having a first aid kit with supplies that you know how to use is extremely helpful. It can save you running to the pharmacy and trying to explain in broken Swahili that you have a cut on your finger!

A secure money belt. A pouch that goes under your clothes can be a good way to carry valuables like your money, credit cards, and passport, without having to worry or feel exposed.

Earplugs. These can make a world of difference in getting a good night's sleep in loud and unfamiliar surroundings. They

ACT

won't make that much difference, however, if you find yourself in rural Philippines sleeping on the raised bamboo floor over the family's roosters (only city folks believe that roosters crow only at dawn!)

Spare batteries. Bring good quality spare batteries for your headlamp, camera, laptop, and any other electronic items. One volunteer who went to Haiti echoed the sentiments of many others we spoke to when she said, "I should have brought a battery with me so I could work without electricity." Something else you could consider is getting a solar-powered charger for cheap, green, and accessible energy!

Things to Consider Leaving at Home

"It seemed like a good idea at the time!" is a regular exclamation that we have heard from volunteers when talking about the things they brought with them and found they didn't need. Here are a few suggestions of things that others wished they had left at home.

Expensive electronics or fancy gadgets. Depending on where you are headed, having electronic gadgets or expensive accessories may prove to be a barrier to your integration into your new home. Your digital SLR camera might take better shots, but it will not be as handy as a simple point-and-shoot, and you will be much less upset when it inevitably gets damaged. Insisting on wearing designer gear or flaunting the latest model smartphone may set you apart. Think about how you might be perceived as different to others in the community, or the expectations that may fall on you to provide monetary support, if these signs of wealth and privilege are a very prominent part of your interactions with local people. Susy, who volunteered in Nepal for over three months said, "After the first two weeks the monkeys stole my smartphone out of my rucksack, and after getting over my sadness I learned that you can exist without your phone. Life goes on!"

Your social media passwords. The ease of communication with home, facilitated by the internet, can lead volunteers to try to exist in two worlds at once. You may want to consider simplifying your life by focusing on where you are and limiting your contact with home (of course, still letting them know you are okay once in a while!) Your time overseas will be deeper and richer if you can challenge yourself to be present and not mediate it through screens or the impressions of people back home. Staying present, connecting with a new place and new people, and avoiding excess homesickness are all easier when you are not constantly checking in on what others are doing in their lives. Daniela's experience of working with interns in PEPY was that those who spent too much time on social media had trouble adjusting. Ironically, those same volunteers would be the ones who returned home and wrote on their Facebook that they wished they were back in Cambodia!

There is of course a balance, and whether you are going away for three weeks or three years, you need to make the decision that is right for you. Consider the impact technology has on your own experience, as well as how it enhances or inhibits your interaction with others.

Emotional baggage. It is normal to feel increased levels of stress or anxiety in the time leading up to a big trip, but it is important to try not to allow these feelings to continue and affect your time abroad. Take some time before you depart to do what you need to get into a calm space. It might mean spending some quality time with loved ones to say goodbye, or simply taking some deep breaths and drawing a line under difficult experiences to try and let them go before you get on the plane.

Appropriate Dress

All societies have conventions regarding what is appropriate clothing to wear in different situations (think: would you show up for a job interview in shorts and flip-flops? Perhaps in California...), and what is considered appropriate can vary considerably. Although to you, the way you dress may be an expression of individuality, a response to climatic conditions, or of no consequence at all, the clothes you choose can offer very different messages and it is important to be aware of what they are before you choose what to wear. To avoid offending people, find out about local conventions of dress in the place you are going, and pack accordingly. Bear in mind that what may be acceptable wear on the beach will almost certainly not be acceptable in a classroom or office, and if you are in any doubt, write an email to ask!

It is likely that dress codes will be more conservative than what you are used to, especially for women. Some volunteers we have spoken to complain that restrictive dress codes make them "feel not like themselves", but you might want to ask: is it more important to feel like yourself, or is it more important that local people get to feel comfortable in their own backyards? In your hometown, it might be inappropriate for a woman to walk around topless, in fact, they might even be arrested. Consider how showing your shoulders, knees, or midriff in certain cultures might be equally as scandalous.

Just by being a foreigner and looking different you may already prove to be somewhat of a distraction to the people in the local area. In many communities, if you wear culturally inappropriate outfits, people will form a negative impression of you and maybe your whole country, so you may start off on the wrong foot before you even begin your work! Claire had an experience of having to talk to a volunteer who brought what she thought was standard 'office wear' from the UK to wear to work in Nepal; she was trying to appear smart and professional, and yet her short skirts, tights and high heels were rather shocking for her Nepali colleagues.

Your choice of clothes may be taken as a lack of respect for the local religion or culture. Don't be fooled into thinking that because some tourists wear inappropriate clothing (for example, men wearing shorts or going bare-chested in sacred sites) that it must be okay because 'everybody is doing it.' You may inadvertently feed stereotypes that all westerners are insensitive or sexually available, as that is what your clothing might symbolize.

Find out what clothing you will likely be wearing on a daily basis before you pack, so you can avoid the dead weight of clothes you won't have the opportunity to wear and bring clothes that help you fit in. Even better, why not pack very little and plan to buy local clothing when you arrive! This also can have the effect of making a positive statement about how much you want to integrate into and learn from the culture (as well as generally being comfortable and fit for the climate).

Bringing Gifts for Your Host Community

"It is very important that North American volunteers not bring things to give the local people. One problem with having North Americans as volunteers is that the locals think that the North Americans don't really expect them to pay back the loans. They say, 'But the North American padrinos (godparents) wanted me to have this house, they gave it to me.'"

-Carlos Mejía, Habitat for Humanity, Guatemala

When it comes to giving gifts to the people you meet on your trip, many volunteers want to find a way to celebrate their hosts and to try in some way to repay the generous hospitality offered to them. However, as Claire's story at the beginning of the chapter illustrates, it is important to consider what types of gifts you are bringing with you, who you are giving them to (or not giving them to), and what sorts of precedents your actions might set. Be aware of the power hierarchy created when you either give or receive a gift, especially one with a large monetary value. Gifts given by one set of volunteers can create expectations of gifts from the next set of volunteers. Nicola Andrews, who volunteered for over a month in Nepal, said "I felt that by giving some of the children 'things' they came to expect the 'things' every time I arrived." What you see as a generous offer made to one person or group may create inequality in a community or jealousy on the part of others. If you are working with an organization, the recipients might consider the gift as being from the organization, not from you directly. The result could be that the organization becomes inundated with requests from others who want the same.

In many touristy areas, children have learned to ask outsiders for candies, pens, or money. This can incentivize begging even amongst children that are well-provided-for by their families, as well as reinforce stereotypes of the role of foreigner as donor and provider, not as a learner and friend. Also, be aware of cultures with reciprocal gift exchange systems—the receiver of your gift may feel obligated to give you something back, something denoting your exalted foreigner status, which may be something beyond their means. In short: it's complicated!

Many volunteer placements have clear policies with regards to gifts, so be sure to understand what those are before purchasing items (inquire by email if you haven't seen any guidance). One idea is to bring small gifts that may have some sentimental value, such as a craft or food from your hometown, that you can offer to anyone who you feel made a difference to you. Or you can show your appreciation in non-material ways such as writing letters or postcards. Maybe you can plan to take a picture with your host family while you are there, and get it framed for them. Another idea is to give something that can benefit the broader community as opposed to just one individual or family. Donating to an NGO that you know to be doing good work can be one way of leaving a positive legacy without being responsible for choosing the direct recipients of your support.

How to Prepare for Your Wellbeing When Abroad

One of the most common worries for volunteers before they depart is how likely they are to fall victim to disease and disturbance whilst overseas. This may be due to stereotypes in the media, warnings online, and the concerns of over-protective (but well-meaning) relatives. Anxieties over getting sick, getting stuck in a disaster zone, or being a victim of crime can be on your mind in the time leading up to a trip, and it can be hard to know how to prepare for these possibilities. A part of learning service is thinking through these scenarios in advance so you can prepare both physically and mentally.

Your body will need time to adapt to a new environment. Traveling between time zones, eating different foods, and being exposed to different bacteria all mean that you are more likely to get sick, especially in the first few weeks. Some level of illness, especially minor gastrointestinal problems, are to be expected and although they are uncomfortable, are nothing to be worried about. They usually clear up on their own after a day or two. In fact, once you have had traveler's diarrhea a few times and have realized it is not that bad, you may soon be able to experience a bout and still go about your daily activities!

Some volunteers we spoke to fell victim to more serious conditions, such as severe food poisoning or infectious diseases. In these instances, it is important to have information about the healthcare facilities in the town where you will be staying, and how long it takes to get to what might be considered an international standard of care (which may even be in a neighboring country). Make sure you have the contact details of someone involved in your volunteer placement so you can let them know what has happened.

To proactively prepare for managing health issues when abroad, plan in advance how to ensure food is hygienically prepared (such as cooking for yourself or eating in reputable restaurants) and that you have reliable access to safe drinking water (for example, a water filtration system). If you are going to an area that has malaria, bringing a mosquito net (or finding out where to buy one in-country) is essential, as well as looking into the option of using anti-malarial medicine for the duration of your stay. If you have existing conditions that require regular medication, consider bringing a long-term supply with you, unless you can find out for sure that the same drug is available where you are going.

As well as your physical health, it is important to ensure that you take care of your mental health while abroad. If you have a history of mental health issues such as anxiety or depression, you should prepare in advance for how you will manage these issues if they appear or worsen overseas. Speak to your doctor or sending organization about putting a plan in place for how to stay well, and what to do if you are struggling. This could include knowing how to access support if you need it—for example, who to speak to in your host organization or how to get in touch with your friends, family, doctor, or counselor back home. You could take some resources with you, such as a book on mindfulness or managing depression, or look up some tips online before you leave. And remember to be realistic about what conditions, both physical and mental, can be adequately managed overseas and when you need to spend more time at home dealing with these issues first.

Ready for Anything?

Ultimately, our advice is to take necessary precautions such as those described above, but not to become paranoid or let these worries ruin your upcoming experience. The best kind of preparation is mental preparation. Brace yourself for a bit of sickness as your body adjusts. As the risk of losing or breaking items is higher when you are traveling, be ready to let go of any of the possessions you are taking with you. If you are careful, chances are you will return with anything you still want to hang on to, but it is better if you travel with things you are less attached to. Instead of spending your last few days at home worrying, relax, and spend time with family and friends. If you have been following the learning service model, your trip will be well organized and it will likely be an exceptional learning and growth opportunity for you. So now is the time to get excited! In the next section, we will look at how to maximize the learning opportunities and contribute effectively while you are in your placement abroad.

PART FIVE:

ACTION WHILE ABROAD

It's finally here. Pre-departure researching, learning, planning, and packing are all behind you, and you are now ready for the adventure! As soon as you step off the plane at your destination, the new culture and environment will bombard your senses. Whether you are staying for two weeks or two years, this place will be your new home, and to be of use (and avoid doing damage) you need to do all you can to understand this new place. This section will help you navigate the ups and downs of living in a new culture. We'll look at how to manage this transition and adjust more easily. We'll explore how to get the most out of your time, and how to deal with the myriad of personal and professional issues that may arise. Finally, we'll look at how to maximize your strengths and skills to be an effective volunteer, and how to make your impact sustainable as you wrap up your time abroad.

13.
HUMBLE & EFFECTIVE ACTION

Perspective: A Tale of Two Volunteers
By Daniela

During the years I directed an education organization in Cambodia, I managed dozens of volunteers. The typical scenario was that they would apply for a specific role, usually in our communications and fundraising team, which was where we needed support from native English speakers. They were required to commit to a six-month volunteer period. Over the six years I managed the team, the majority of our volunteers were fantastic: they filled a needed role, contributed to our team culture, and acted in culturally-appropriate ways. Unfortunately, we did have a few examples of team members whose attitudes or skills were not a good match for our needs. Here are two stories based on actual experiences, with names changed and specifics slightly altered for anonymity.

Volunteer 'Anthony': A skill mismatch

Anthony applied to be a communications volunteer for our team in Cambodia. We conducted a brief interview and reviewed his email application prior to his arrival and let him know that the role would be largely managing email inquiries and then organizing and sharing the data and logistical details with the rest of the office. When Anthony arrived, it quickly became apparent that there was a skills mismatch. His writing skills were weak and he was not very good at details or logistics. Managing him began to take a lot of other people's time.

Anthony, however, was humble, honest, self-aware, and positive. He approached his manager and explained the areas where he felt he was weakest. They worked together to create a system that fit his skills, saved the manager's time, and delegated certain aspects of his role to people who were able to complete the tasks more efficiently. Anthony readily accepted and sought out constructive feedback, regularly checking in to make sure what he was doing was in line with the organization's needs. Overall, he was a joy to have on the team. He never complained if someone asked him to help out on an extra project, even if it kept him in the office a bit later. He contributed valuable ideas for improving the office structure, and he took it upon himself to create opportunities for cultural exchange and language sharing. He worked in conjunction with a local team member on these events and safeguarded against them relying on his leadership.

As Anthony had only been out of college for a few years, one of his goals for volunteering abroad was to learn about possible career paths he might consider when he returned. On the weekends, he set up meetings with other organizations working in a range of fields from around the city to learn more about their work. Eventually he became especially interested in health care and was able to secure a weekly volunteer position at a local clinic. Through what he learned, Anthony was inspired to become a nurse, and when he returned home to Australia he was accepted into a program to qualify him to do just that.

Although the original role envisioned for his position wasn't a perfect fit, due to his flexibility and commitment to having a positive impact, he was able to carve out a role where he was indeed able to add value. The role was not glamorous: it involved working on tedious day-to-day tasks needed in the office. But Anthony supported the team with a smile, brought positive energy to the office environment, and was remembered fondly after he left.

Volunteer 'Bradley': An attitude mismatch

Another volunteer, Bradley was accepted for a similar communications role in the organization. He had come from a business background, and through his skills and experience he was quickly able to add value. He noticed that our organizational systems were lacking, that we didn't have a well-thought-out communications plan, and that our contact database was in disarray. He was able to fulfill all the skills we needed and more, and if things had worked out slightly differently with Bradley, we might have benefited more from his knowledge and insight.

Yet, despite the skill fit, Bradley was one of very few volunteers who ended up going home early. Though his expertise was valuable to our team, his attitude was not. He would come to work hungover, having partied most evenings. He would say disparaging things about the culture or local women, and his over-confidence made it very difficult for other team members to challenge any of his opinions. Both local and foreign staff found him rude, and no one wanted to work with him. Soon his negative attitudes started to pervade the office.

We attempted to give him feedback and tried to help him align his actions with our stated values, but changing someone's values is much harder than improving someone's skills or shifting the working structures to fit their needs. We started to feel embarrassed to have him associated with our organization's work. When the first part of his assignment was complete, and his review had not resulted in many visible changes to his attitude, we thanked him for his efforts and asked him to end his volunteer placement early.

Through our experience with Bradley, we realized that our recruitment, vetting, and review process needed not just to screen for our skill needs, but also take into account our attitude and value needs. As a manager, I realized that I'd much rather have a volunteer with the right attitudes and values and less-than-ideal skills, than someone with exceptional skills and less-than-ideal attitudes. A humble, open, positive, and committed team member who is placed into a role that doesn't fit their skills will be proactive about creating a better fit where they can add value. A self-absorbed, arrogant, judgmental, or ethnocentric volunteer, or someone who considers themselves a martyr, is less likely to take feedback well and can poison a whole team's culture.

Transitioning In

Settling into a new culture, community, and workplace all at the same time can be a difficult transition. Although not everything will resonate with every volunteer, you will almost certainly experience emotional peaks and troughs throughout your time abroad. If you expect these emotions, prepare for them, and treat them appropriately, you will pass through the crises. This can ultimately become part of a powerful learning experience.

The honeymoon period

For most international volunteers, especially those with little or no previous international experience, arriving in a foreign country is a dramatic jolt to the system. The smells, the climate, the markets, the traffic, the language, all may be radically different from those at home. These differences can be both exciting and overwhelming. When you first arrive in a new country, a single day can seem like a week, and activities as simple as following directions to an office or having breakfast can be intense adventures.

Generally, people experience a high after their arrival in a new country. The rush of new stimuli tends to push aside any disappointments or frustrations a volunteer might have, at least temporarily. Most newly-arrived volunteers are upbeat and optimistic, which is why this is often referred to as the 'honeymoon' period.

The feelings of adventure and excitement and the drive to have all these new and different experiences is exhilarating, yet the combination of jet-lag and lack of routine can also be exhausting. The honeymoon phase, just like a real honeymoon, is wonderful while it lasts, but usually short-lived. Enjoy your first few days, but don't try to do everything at once. Remember to pace yourself, and eat and sleep in a proper routine to speed up the adjustment process.

The post-honeymoon dip

The 'post-honeymoon dip' may happen anytime from one week to several months after you have arrived in the country. The exhilarating pace of the honeymoon period may catch up with you, leaving you feeling tired and low. Things that were exciting, exotic, or endearing just last week can suddenly seem illogical and frustrating. The temperature, food, cultural norms, and differences in standards of living can start to irritate you and make you crave things that are 'normal.' During this phase, you might feel lonely or homesick. You may experience anxiety as you realize your assumptions and expectations don't always match up to reality. Claire remembers her initial enthrallment with everything on her first trip to Nepal – including the bumpy roads, the garbage on the street, the dust – suddenly being punctured one day when she realized that none of her new friends understood or appreciated her sarcastic comments that she thought were really funny!

There is no quick-fix antidote to these feelings. Given time, you will adjust and may develop a more realistic appreciation for your new community than what you initially saw through those rose-tinted honeymoon glasses. The important thing is to recognize when the post-honeymoon dip is happening and act appropriately: chill out, get your head back in the right place, and move on to the next challenge!

Culture shock

At some point during the first few hours, days, weeks, or months, international volunteers typically experience culture shock. Indeed, you may skip the honeymoon period entirely and jump straight into this phase. *Culture shock* is a term that describes a variety of emotions, such as stress, irritation, anger, isolation, confusion, anxiety, and loneliness. It is a continuation of the post-honeymoon dip, but more pronounced and longer-lasting. Culture shock sometimes stems from feeling ignorant about how to get things done in a new environment, or at least how to get them done 'correctly' according to cultural norms. Behavior that is normal and accepted at home, like wearing shoes inside the office or directly complaining about poor customer service, may be frowned upon in your new surroundings. Vice versa, you may find people spitting in the street or cutting ahead of you in a line unacceptable and rude, whereas your local counterparts may not. Communication can be a challenge, even if there is a common language. It can be exhausting and frustrating. Our goal in discussing culture shock here is not to prevent it – that would be impossible – but rather to help you to be conscious of it and avoid feeling surprised when you experience the first symptoms.

Different people experience culture shock at different times, in different ways, and with varying degrees of severity. Some people find that their pre-arrival research and preparation helped them align their expectations with their in-country experience and find it easier to deal with the frustrations and setbacks they encounter along the way. Some find that maintaining a learning mindset helps them to process their new experiences and to see the positives of being out of their comfort zone. Others are overwhelmed by things they didn't anticipate, such as the climate, their team dynamics, the government bureaucracy, or the way they are looked at on the street. Sidonie Emerande who works with and hosts volunteers in Madagascar, said "Volunteers sometimes cry when they see things that are normal to us, such as poverty or child labor."

You should be aware some people do not experience culture shock until as late as one or two years after arriving in a new culture. Don't be surprised if it sneaks up on you. You may not experience it at the same time or in the same ways as others, even if you all arrived at the same time. In fact, people respond to new cultural environments very differently. Some never adapt, fixating on how much better things seem at home and failing to make any positive connections with the people in the host community. Others enthusiastically embrace the culture of their host country and get very involved, which helps to overcome the initial confusion and isolation of culture shock. Madeline, who studied abroad in Scotland, reflects, "I was sorely mistaken when I thought that I could jump straight into a new life in a new country. I realized that being abroad means that you have to seek out things that make you happy, whether that be a club, sport, class, event, or traveling." Try to throw yourself in, build relationships and keep an open mind. Remember that culture shock is a normal response to the transition from a familiar to an unfamiliar culture, and will usually pass with time.

Navigating Your First Days as a Volunteer

You may feel daunted by the idea of responsible volunteering— avoiding the pitfalls and actually making a contribution can seem like an impossible balancing act. On the one hand, you are trying not to be a burden or drain resources, and on the other, you are trying not to take the lead or impose your own ideas. Jacob Wachspress, who volunteered in Bolivia for nine months, said, "My responsibilities were often unclear and constantly changing. At times near the beginning I felt like a burden because I had to ask so many questions that took people's time." The first few days in a new job can be overwhelming – whether or not you're in a new country – but keep an open mind and trust that with time you'll find your feet. A volunteer for over a year in Kazakhstan had this advice: "Let go of any preconceived ideas about what you're there to do and let your mission come to you. Forcing your ideas and trying to make certain things work can frustrate you and tire you out for really no good reason when there are opportunities in every direction."

Some people arrive at their volunteer placement and have little – or nothing – to do. Maybe the office is empty, or full of people who you haven't been introduced to. Maybe you feel as if your colleagues are ignoring you, seem too busy, or don't want to take on the extra responsibility of coaching you. Maybe they are shy or even a little intimidated by you. How do you break the ice and see if you have anything to contribute?

At the other extreme, your colleagues may have been eagerly awaiting your arrival so that they can pile mountains of work on you that no one else is taking responsibility for. Maybe there is a backlog of reports to be written or an inbox of emails that hasn't been opened in the four months since the last volunteer was in town. Perhaps colleagues bombard you with requests for training in areas that you don't have much experience in, or shove you into a high-level meeting with government officials and hope you can fend for yourself. How do you know when it is appropriate to use your initiative and when to take a step back?

Thankfully, you can take comfort in the fact that if you are aware of these issues and asking these questions, you are already demonstrating some of the qualities you will need in order to be effective in either of these extremes. Our main advice, in either of these situations, is to listen, continue to ask questions, and have the patience to avoid jumping straight into making any judgments or major commitments. This can feel counterintuitive: if you are not being offered work to do, you may want to prove your capabilities by getting something of worth done. Similarly, if it seems like there is a lot of pressure on you to perform, it can feel as though the best reaction is to jump up and meet those high expectations. In fact, the best, though hardest, thing to do might be to take your time to think before digging in too deep. David Pwalua, Director of Programs for Afrikids in Ghana, says, "It is important for volunteers to understand the culture and work ethics of a place before trying to influence things. Understand the pace of work and their systems. Move at their pace, and then you can work with them to quicken or change."

There may always be tension between when to use initiative and when to wait for instruction, which is why ensuring you are working as part of a team is so important. In that way, it isn't up to you alone to make decisions. If you feel like you are waiting for instructions, but want to start moving, use your initiative to learn and develop possible road maps, rather than jumping in and taking action that may or may not be needed. For example, if you feel like you need more information before you can take on a project planning task, why not use your time to research the history of the project and learn about other similar projects so that when you do get a chance to meet with the right person, you have a better basis for understanding and are prepared to ask the right questions. Ramphai Noikaew from Thailand, told us a story of international volunteers who rushed in too early and made a terrible mistake. "They were a couple from Europe who were overconfident in their own skills. Without asking, they went to cut down the fruit trees on the pathway to the farm. Those fruits trees belonged to our neighbors, and the farm ended up having to pay compensation." Keep in mind that some of the most important things you can accomplish are your own learning and growth, and accomplishing that certainly requires you to practice patience. Remember 'getting things done' does not equate with 'being successful' and putting more time into planning and research can help you immensely in the long run!

Attitudes and Actions of an Effective Volunteer

As Daniela's story at the beginning of this chapter illustrated, how you approach tasks and your time abroad is just as important as what you actually end up doing—if not more so. By heeding some of the following advice, you will be a much more effective volunteer, able to give your time and skills appropriately.

Remain humble
A key to successful learning service is remaining humble. Accepting that you don't know all the answers, that your opinion might change as you learn more, and that the lived experience of local people can make *them* the real experts, is all part of maintaining a balanced perspective on your role. A volunteer who spent over a month in Tanzania told us, "The best tip I can give is that volunteers should not enter the community with strong ideas or with pushy attitudes. Some volunteers in my group were too forceful and tried to tell the workers at the orphanage how to do things—which is wrong. Volunteers should help where it is wanted and give suggestions or advice when solicited. They should remember that they are guests in the community, there to observe, enjoy, and help in a kind and generous way." A humble outlook is essential to avoiding the pitfalls of volunteering and becoming a part of a system of change that is much larger than the contribution of one individual.

Listen before you leap
Listening is an important skill to cultivate. It can help you to be aware of how your attitudes and actions impact others and to

better understand the local context. Listening to and learning from colleagues and community members, and developing cultural sensitivity, can help you have an impact down the road. As one volunteer host in Cambodia exclaimed, "Don't come in and tell people what to do! Americans are so bossy."

We have come across many projects that could have been much more successful if volunteers had taken the time to listen to local communities first. Titus Kuria, who grew up and worked in the Mathare slum in Kenya, shared this experience. "I worked on a project that installed eco-friendly solar street lights. It had been very successful in different parts of the developing world, and the founder was in town to receive an award for his work. While he was here, he thought to get some volunteers to install these street lights in my hometown. Everything happened so fast; he called me to have lunch with his volunteers to discuss it, but that afternoon we started the project. Unfortunately, most of the international volunteers were neither experienced nor skilled. The local volunteers were also not aware of what to do. I tried to tell them that most of the materials and tools were not readily available in Mathare, but they wasted a lot of time looking for these materials anyway. The next stage was to try and improvise. That meant using substandard materials and taking a lot of time on one light. At the end of the day, we had only done ten lamps and our target was 50. But the next step was the saddest. After getting the lamps ready and installing them on the streets of the slum, the following night they couldn't be located. Basically, they had been stolen. I later realized that no one had engaged the community to take care of the lights so no one felt responsible for them. It was one of the most frustrating projects I have ever done. Looking back, I realized that going that fast without listening to and involving the community meant that the project was bound to fail from the outset."

Listening isn't just something you want to do in the initial stages of your time abroad but throughout your experience. Listening is integral to learning. It is easy to jump to conclusions about the local culture, community needs, or the way you are perceived, but you won't know if those conclusions are accurate unless you seek out and tune in to a diverse range of perspectives.

Widen your definition of success

Volunteers can fall into the common trap of defining 'success' too narrowly—often something like 'taking full ownership of a concrete project and seeing it through to the end.' This is why so many volunteer projects are discrete activities with a clearly-marked endpoint, like building a school or digging a well, with an outcome that someone can point to and say, "I did that!" Though taking complete ownership of a project can feel satisfying, if that project is not well-integrated into a much larger system that started before you got there and will continue long after you leave, your efforts may have been successful for no one but yourself.

You may have identified expectations and goals for your time abroad only to discover that your plans do not align with what your local host organization managers have in mind. Even if you have been given a detailed job description, you may need to let go of the expectation that you'll be doing exactly what it says. It should be up to the host organization to identify how the skills you bring are put to best use. For example, if you are an engineer volunteering in a renewable energy organization, the first thing you might want to do is see if you can improve the solar technology that is being used. Just because you have the skills to do that, however, doesn't mean it is the contribution the local organization wants from volunteers. In fact, maybe their own engineers understand the resources, constraints, and cultural considerations better than you do and, instead, they need your understanding of the technology and English-language skills to write grant reports or funding proposals. Or perhaps they are hoping you will build staff capacity so that they themselves are able to troubleshoot problems with the technology. Maybe they have seen volunteers in the past who have jumped in too quickly without first getting their bearings on the local context and have made 'improvements' that didn't work in the local context or that prohibitively increased the price of the product.

"Start small and slow," we were advised by one volunteer who spent a year in Uganda. "You won't change anything huge in a week or a month or probably even in two years. This isn't to say you won't make a difference but if you try to do something huge you most likely won't involve the people and you can potentially do more harm than good." Being asked to take a backseat role in the beginning can be healthy, and help ensure you are supporting the organization's overall needs, not just your own desire to feel useful in the areas where you want to help. A wider definition of success might mean carrying out the basic logistics and maintenance tasks around the office that free up the organizational leadership to focus on the core of their work. It might mean learning enough about an issue or an organization to feel comfortable and confident advocating for the organization and supporting it more significantly in the future.

Rather than measuring success based on personal accomplishments, view yourself as part of a larger ecosystem within the organization in which you are working, and also within a wider system of change. The most effective volunteers recognize that their work is part of a long chain of decisions, actions, and impacts, and they are not quick to take personal credit for successes that relied on a system much larger than themselves. A volunteer who spent two years in Panama said, "I think volunteers need to think less individualistically ('I will do X, change Y in my short time') and instead think of themselves as part of the greater picture. You really are a staff member. Individual volunteers may have more or less impact, but the organization as a whole can have a huge impact in a country." Success then stops being about measuring what one person can achieve and becomes more about groups working alongside each other toward common goals.

Consider the power dynamics

> "I disempowered some people and undermined others because I did not understand local dynamics and politics, and the sending organization had no one to advise me."
> —Sallie Grayson, who volunteered in
> the Gambia for three months

The presence of an outsider in a community or work environment will always have an impact, even if it is largely unintentional. In his famous speech in 1968, made to a group of young volunteers, Ivan Illich pointed out that, "By definition, you cannot help ultimately being vacationing salesmen for the middle-class 'American Way of Life,' since that is really the only life you know." People are products of the societies that raise them, and even those who think they have rejected many of the mainstream values of that culture may still be inadvertently promoting them. A traveler bringing a smartphone or expensive camera into a remote community can fuel discontent, incite consumerist values, or provoke desires for emulation. Ways of dressing, speaking, and socializing can also reveal different values, which in other countries may be associated with high status.

Some types of volunteering create less concern in terms of power dynamics than others. Picking trash from a river, assisting a teacher, or helping out with admin tasks in a busy office should not challenge local hierarchies very much, unless the volunteer steps outside the boundaries of their role. You should always be aware, however, that the carefully-balanced power dynamics of an organization or community may shift because of your presence. Doing your best to make yourself aware of the community and organization's power structures will allow you to make informed choices about how you act and what you support. Charbel, a volunteer host in Lebanon, gave this example: "I was working on a project with Syrian refugees that taught computer coding to children and adolescents still learning basic literacy and numeracy. After a while, the municipality started being less and less flexible with us, and we were a bit surprised with their attitude. After all, we were implementing an educational program in the area. Turns out that they were discontent with us teaching coding to Syrian refugee children, while not doing the same with the local (Lebanese) children of the town that was hosting us. The problem ended up getting resolved easily, and we opened three additional classes for Lebanese students."

Another danger is that the presence of a volunteer may shift power away from local structures and transfer authority or decision-making power to the volunteer themselves. Often foreigners are offered respect and authority simply because of their nationality or skin color. Sometimes this is a hangover from colonialism, and other times this is due to the power dynamics that come with dependencies created from foreign donations.

For example, Daniela knew a Peace Corps volunteer placed in a health center in rural Cambodia, who was called 'doctor' by everyone in the area, when, in fact, he had a liberal arts education and had never studied medicine. Fortunately, he acknowledged that he was given an inappropriate amount of status and was respectful enough not to abuse it. If you feel you are being asked to make decisions outside your remit, question this and ask for support from a permanent staff member who can continue being in charge after you leave.

Seek out feedback and give it appropriately

The giving and receiving of feedback are often left until the end of an experience, when it is too late to make adjustments or put any learning into practice. If you are committed to being as effective as you can be in your placement, make sure you give yourself regular opportunities to reflect on and evaluate your action—and change direction if warranted. Actively seek feedback from friends, colleagues, or other volunteers about how you can improve and remain open to feedback that comes through other channels. Sidonie Emerande remembered some volunteers she worked with in Madagascar who asked the street children they were working with for feedback on their work. "Recognizing personal mistakes and apologizing even to the little kids was so constructive for everyone."

In cultures that have a less direct communication style, feedback might come to you via a colleague rather than directly from your boss, or might be expressed through body language or even a polite silence. Ruth Bergan, who has spent many years volunteering in India, remembers an awkward moment early on in her experience. "I joined a local community meeting, and as soon as it was underway I had a feeling that something was up—people seemed uncomfortable and wouldn't meet my gaze. I was racking my brain to remember any cultural *faux pas* I could have made. At the end of the meeting I asked someone that had been sitting near me what the problem was, and she told me that people had been shocked by the way I was sitting. I was on a chair with one leg crossed over the other, and apparently in that community only men sit like that. It made me realize that sometimes an issue that is really important to those around you might not even be on your radar."

There are of course cultural considerations around giving feedback. Your helpful suggestions may just be interpreted as over-harsh criticisms by colleagues. Perhaps the organization has formal writing feedback channels, an appraisal system, or other means of making suggestions. As with many other things, it is better to wait and observe how other people offer feedback before diving in with critiques that could accidentally damage relationships.

Reflect continually

International volunteers can be at risk of sensory and emotional overload as they deal with such a huge range of experiences. Taking some time out to process it all can help you regain balance and perspective. Many volunteers told us that their lives as volunteers were conducive to thinking, reflecting, and journal writing. You might find it interesting not only to write about everything that is going on around you but also your emotional responses, charting the ups and downs of your volunteer experience. Shelia Hu, who volunteered for four months in Vietnam, Morocco, and Bolivia, kept a journal of her experiences. "As someone who can never make it past the second day of journaling back at home, I was especially proud of myself for keeping up with this goal. Sometimes my time abroad was extremely overwhelming, and the activities and days blurred into a mess; so it was important for me to be able to go back to my daily log and make this experience one I would always remember."

You may benefit also from organized group reflections in the form of discussions, retreats, and workshops. If your volunteer sending organization doesn't provide these kinds of opportunities, you might decide to organize something more informally with other volunteers you meet, or create a virtual meet-up online. You can reflect on your new culture, the development situation of the country, or your personal development as a volunteer. Issues of identity such as gender, race, class, and sexual orientation may also come up. Together, you can examine the root causes of the challenges you personally face and the problems your projects address, and increase your sense of commitment and accountability to others.

Here are some questions for journaling or group reflection:

- What are the problems my work here is addressing, and who has defined these as problems?
- What are the immediate causes of the problems my work is addressing? What are the root causes? How have these causes influenced the strategies employed to address the problems?
- What are the barriers to development in this location? How are people working to overcome them?
- What role does the global economy play in the problems and opportunities facing the local community?
- What role do politicians and ordinary people in my home country play in the problems and opportunities here?
- What power, privileges, skills, and resources do I have that local people do not? What do they have that I do not?
- What factors impede or enhance quality of life here? What factors affect quality of life in my home country?
- What do I gain from my work here? What do local people gain?
- What will happen here after I leave? What can I do now in order to ensure I leave a positive and sustainable legacy?
- How can I nurture the positive changes I've made in myself once I return home?
- What can I do when I return home to continue to support the work I am involved in, or to confront the root causes of the challenges being faced here?

Be culturally sensitive

Different cultures define appropriate behavior differently. If you are being welcomed as a guest into a community, you may need to uphold a different code of conduct. This is not to impose external moral judgment on activities you enjoy that may be perfectly acceptable in your own culture, nor does it mean you need to change your own moral code, but it does mean you need to respect the values of others while you are living amongst them.

There are no hard and fast rules for how to be culturally appropriate—not even in a single, relatively homogeneous culture, let alone for all the diverse countries in which you might volunteer. The best advice we can give you is to be aware of how other people are behaving, observe them closely, and when in a setting completely unfamiliar to you, to mirror the actions and behaviors of friends and colleagues. Find out not only what is illegal in your host community, but also what activities are frowned upon, viewed as harmful, or just outright offensive. For example, in some areas, drinking alcohol is associated with domestic violence, wastefulness, or abuse. Before getting caught up in the scene, think very carefully about what message you will be giving to your friends and colleagues.

A consequence of your role as a foreigner is that anything you do is much more likely to be noticed and talked about, and you may even be seen as a representative of your whole culture or country. Being conscious of the local connotations and stereotypes attached to certain types of behavior will help you avoid embarrassing yourself or bringing shame on those associated with you. Although in many communities, there may be circumstances that occasionally make these activities acceptable, unless you are living there for a long time and can work out the nuances, self-imposed abstinence from culturally inappropriate activities is often the easiest path. For example, you may not be able to invite members of the opposite sex to stay with you (even if the relationship is platonic), and maybe you have to limit late-night partying to the times when you are away from the community in which you work. You may have to observe certain eating practices in your community, especially if the institution or community you are in is strongly religious. Your volunteer placement might ban smoking on the premises, require a certain dress code, or enforce other behavioral standards that are likely not meant as restrictions or punishments but rather as guidelines of how to avoid unknowingly offending others.

Stereotypes you Don't Want to Live up to

We thought it would be instructive, and possibly amusing, to get the views of local host organizations and local volunteers about the 'types' of international volunteers they have come across over the years. Though the usual caveats about stereotyping apply, the following may give you some pause for thought (and you may recognize some of the traits in people you know—or even yourself!):

'The prince or princess'
This is the volunteer who expects everyone to cater to his or her needs, without considering that the lack of the things demanded may be the daily reality for others. This is the volunteer who 'can't' eat local food, 'can't' travel on the bus, or 'can't' use the public bathroom. This is the volunteer who diverts precious back-up electricity for their hairdryer, who won't make field visits because of their fear of insects, and who regularly says it's too hot (or cold!) to work.

'The vacationer'
The vacationer may be a fun person to have around, but not a particularly effective volunteer. Always sneaking off early and avoiding being given any useful tasks to do, they love getting pictures with local kids to post on social media. At weekends they are likely found on the beach or at the bar—in fact, this is where they might be found during work time too. The time they dedicate to work is seen by them as more than enough, so they expect everyone to just be grateful for what they do, however little it is. In the words of a host organization in Tanzania, "Some of these volunteers would come and be with us, but just [as] we start to get used to working with them they are already very tired and bored and need a break in Zanzibar. So they tell us they will work for two weeks, but after three days they want to go on safari."

'The expert'
The expert believes that their experience or qualification in a given field makes them an authority on how to do things—maybe

even things well outside of their realm of knowledge. Maybe they studied engineering at Stanford and are now trying to redesign the water system in an urban slum. Or perhaps they worked in public health in Europe and can diagnose exactly what is lacking in Kenya's health system. Or maybe they studied development, and just know it all. The expert's level of confidence can be dangerously convincing to those around them, even if in reality they have little comparable experience, don't know anything about the local culture (and are unwilling to learn), and may know less than many of their quieter but more experienced local colleagues.

'The martyr'

The martyr makes a lot of noise about how much they have given up to be there. It is, in fact, a mystery how they managed to sign up to volunteer at all, considering the number of sacrifices they had to make. Everything they do is for 'the sake of the children' or 'the benefit of the poor,' and they are not allowed to say they have gained anything or enjoyed any of their time abroad, as it would undermine what a struggle it has all been.

'The colonialist'

The colonialist has a jolly good time on their volunteer placement. From their high-up view, peering down at local life, colonialists might think the local people a little dim or a little strange, but otherwise a colorful and happy lot. Of course, they can't quite do things as well as in the colonialist's own country, but it's all okay! With a little bit of coaching, hopefully they'll learn to do it properly.

Final Thoughts

Our most important piece of advice about being a humble and effective volunteer is to continue to cultivate your learning mindset and to view all experiences as opportunities to learn. Many volunteers look into volunteer travel with one set of expectations and motivations, depart for their chosen country with another, and return home with a totally different set of experiences and lessons learned. Focusing on your learning goals can stop things becoming too bleak or stressful and help you retain optimism even when the work is hard. Keeping learning as a central goal of your experience helps you to maintain an open mind and positive attitude.

14.
GETTING THE MOST OUT OF YOUR TIME OVERSEAS

Perspective: Breaking Down the Barriers
By Mark Denega, Filmmaker

I was on the outskirts of Lima, making a film called *H.O.P.E. Was Here: A Volunteer Travel Documentary*. For the first half hour I filmed Johnny, a middle-aged Peruvian man, spending time with his wife, Silvia, and their four-year-old daughter, Minerva. I said almost nothing and just kept rolling. Soon we lost adequate daylight to film, and with sweaty palms I switched the camera off and put it away.

Silvia sewed while Minerva played with the new pet cat, and Johnny disappeared into the back room. I finished packing up my equipment and sat timidly waiting for some interaction to happen. I certainly wasn't going to initiate with my broken Spanish. Johnny emerged and suggested we take a walk outside before the sky darkened completely. He could show me his neighbors' houses. Minerva, curious about this strange interloper, followed.

Their two-room home sat on a hill nestled among the sprawling desert slums that rolled around Lima's wealthy center. The sun fell behind the mountains to the sound of wild dogs barking. It was a familiar setting for Johnny and his family, but far from home for me. We walked up his street not saying much, just appreciating a nice night. Occasionally he'd point toward a home and describe who lived there, and I'd nod along without ever fully understanding. I was afraid to speak, and Johnny could tell. He didn't mind.

Minerva, however, had different expectations of my language skills. Shortly into our walk, she assaulted me in rapid Spanish: "Are you afraid of spiders? Why is your skin so white? How did you become a giant?"

When I didn't understand, she repeated the questions louder. When I shook my head to suggest I still didn't get it, she was confused and frustrated. I felt stupid, powerless, and vulnerable.

Dinner came, and my nervousness at communicating got worse. I tried to keep my mouth full of the takeout fried chicken as long as possible. Minerva was bored with me – her broken toy – and Johnny and Silvia became more self-conscious about speaking Spanish, for fear that I'd feel isolated.

This painfully silent meal came to life when Johnny and Silvia's sixteen-year-old daughter arrived home from work. She put her bags down, and then introduced herself.

"Hi, my name is Grace," she said in English. Johnny, Silvia, and Minerva didn't speak a lick of the language, so this took me by surprise. Grace went on to explain that she loved English and preferred it to Spanish. I immediately felt more comfortable in the room, and Grace was curious to learn some of the idiosyncrasies of my native tongue. I grabbed a pen and paper and wrote out that the present and past tense of 'read' are spelled the same, but the latter is pronounced the same as the color 'red.' Her fascination with this ignited my own curiosity, and I uttered my first coherent Spanish words of the night:

"*¿Hay palabras similares en Español?*" I asked, wanting to know if there were similar quirks in Spanish. There were, and soon the whole family was joining in, taking turns to point at objects around the room and speaking them in both languages.

At the end of the night, Johnny and I rode a rickety car back to my gated volunteer housing center where Johnny worked security. As the car sputtered along, I thanked Johnny for welcoming me into his home. We went on to hold a full conversation, and though I'm sure my Spanish was riddled with errors, I didn't care.

Daily Life Abroad

The last chapter focused on approaching your volunteer work activities with a learning service perspective; in this chapter, we'll broaden the lens to look at the other elements of your overseas experience. Whether you volunteer for two weeks or two years, you'll do more than work; you'll also have a place to live, food to eat, and, most likely, some down time to explore the community you are visiting. This chapter will help you apply the learning service principles to the broader experience of being overseas as a volunteer, even when you are not engaging directly in the work of volunteering.

What you get out of your experiences living abroad depends largely on your attitude. Approach it with a pessimistic mindset and every minor setback seems monumental; approach it positively and with a learning mindset, and you might find enjoyment – or at least meaningful growth opportunities – even when things are testing you. While abroad, you will have the opportunity to do things you would never do at home: eat fertilized duck eggs with fetuses inside, make a fool of yourself dancing in public, attend a traditional healing ceremony. We'll explore some tips for getting the most out of your time abroad, using the tools of humble and thoughtful action, and learning from all your interactions, not just your volunteer work. By the time you return home, you might even be craving duck fetuses!

Tips for Engaging With People and Place

How can you move from being an observer of a culture to an active participant in it? What do learning service principles look like when you are trying to engage and connect with your host community? Volunteer Gabriela Corbera told us, "The most difficult part of volunteering was balancing my job, struggling to speak Khmer language, learning about the history of the country, and making time to just *live* in Cambodia." Indeed, integrating into new social settings, maximizing learning opportunities, *and* giving your all to a volunteer role requires hard work and prioritization. Here are some ideas for making the most of your free time.

Learn the language

Feeling competent in a new language takes a lot of time and effort. No other single factor, however, can affect your international volunteer experience more profoundly than your ease in the local language. As your language proficiency grows, new worlds open up to you. You will be able to interact with people more directly, your conversations unfiltered by translators. Depending on how long you are staying for, taking a few months out for intensive lessons might not be a possibility. But as soon as possible after arriving overseas (or preferably before you leave!), try taking a class, find a tutor, or exchange lessons in a foreign language for lessons in your own native tongue. Even just learning a few phrases can help show that you are making an effort and will create room for your co-workers to teach you more words each day. This strategy is more polite than expecting everyone you meet to speak to you in English; you may be surprised by how much more warmly people respond to you if you at least greet them in their own language. Rachel Springer, who volunteered in Lebanon, said "Taxi drivers were more friendly and accommodating when I would greet them and explain my destination in Arabic rather than English." By learning a new language, you will also be able to learn more about the local culture, as the words people use shed light on cultural as well as linguistic differences.

Be sure that the language you learn is the one that will be most useful to you. A volunteer who spent two months in Morocco reflected, "I thought that I could get by mostly by speaking French as it is the language of business and diplomacy. It turned out that I neglected two things: class dynamics and geography. French, because it's a colonial language, is spoken by the upper class. This meant that if I wanted to grab a cab, the driver usually spoke only broken French (if at all) and I had to get by on the Darija I had picked up. Furthermore, a French friend found his language skills completely useless when staying in the Atlas Mountains as the main language there is Tamazight."

When using a new language, it's good to ask for occasional feedback to make sure you're not saying something that makes no sense, or worse, is offensive. Chris spent three years teaching English at a school for girls in Japan. Every Friday he'd ask the students if they were "excited for the weekend." On the last night of his time teaching, he complained to a local friend about how poorly he was treated at the school and explained that when he asked the girls if they were "excited for the weekend," no one took the time to respond to him. His friend pointed out that he had selected the incorrect version of 'excited' and had actually spent the last three years asking his students if they were 'aroused' for the weekend! He was embarrassed to say the least, and realized that it was his own behavior that had resulted in his lack of integration. If you feel like you might be offending someone and don't know why—ask. The answer might be enlightening!

Don't be afraid to make mistakes

Making mistakes is part of the process of interacting with a culture different from your own. Indeed, it is how you learned your own culture as a child—through a bit of trial and error. Don't let the fear of saying the wrong thing or breaking a cultural norm stop you from trying to connect. We heard countless stories of volunteers who looked back on their actions when they first arrived and noted moments when they felt foolish. Most mistakes were little ones, like eating with your left hand at a formal dinner in Egypt—then having a local friend explain that eating like this is seen as unhygienic. Though you may be horrified at the time, often you can later look back on such an incident with a sense of humor. A volunteer who was in Senegal for more than a year had this advice, "Be prepared to laugh—at yourself, at others, and at the cultural misunderstandings that will inevitably come." Indeed, in some cultures everyone will burst out laughing at your mistake anyway as a way of papering over the *faux pas* – making it seem that, of course, you were making a joke all along – so you might as well join them!

Whenever you do make a social blunder, try to learn from it so you can avoid a repeat performance, but don't let the paranoia about trying to obey every rule of cultural etiquette stop you from going out and making friends. People in most cultures will be forgiving towards foreigners and understand that you are learning. There is often no better way to learn than from your mistakes.

Photo-fasting: Living in the moment

Some travelers rarely step out from behind their cameras. Even though the local kids might love to see their faces on your screen, and pictures can be a discussion topic to help bridge a cultural divide, a camera can also be a barrier to fully experiencing the place you are visiting. By seeing everything through a lens, you remain an observer, and can be viewed as a consumer of a culture rather than a participant in an exchange.

We recommend you consider some situations where you keep your camera (or cell phone) in your bag, or even setting yourself a period of 'photo-fasting.' This can be especially helpful in building bonds with people at the beginning of your stay. Setareh Masoumbeiki, who volunteered in Cambodia, told us, "As a social documentary photographer, it was very hard for me to not want to bring my camera out with me each day. I saw so many images I wanted to capture. But I recognized though that in order to feel comfortable taking pictures of people, and to not feel like I was intruding on their lives, I wanted to know them first. I spent more than six months getting to know this group of families living in a vulnerable urban community; eating with them, sitting with them, watching them. I was invited to their children's weddings. The children asked me to swim with them in the river, to take a walk with them, to nap in their parents' hammock when I was sleepy. I did all that long before I asked them if it would be okay to take photos."

Mindful interaction means becoming aware of how intrusive taking photos can be. Scenes that seem exotic or picturesque to you are everyday life for the people who live in them. Imagine how it would feel if foreigners continually stuck their cameras into your home, taking pictures of you doing household chores, making breakfast, or even having a shower! A good rule when taking photographs is to first ask yourself why you want to capture that scene, and if there is anything exploitative about your intention. Are you photographing poverty for the sake of it? Make sure to ask yourself if you might be documenting something that the subjects might prefer to keep private. If you are happy with your motivations, then introduce yourself and ask permission. Photographs can feel much more significant if there is a relationship behind them, and it can be meaningful to both parties if the subjects choose to participate in the photoshoot.

Eat local

In our own experiences of working in volunteer travel, few things are more frustrating than a volunteer who refuses to try any of the local foods. "Eating insects is wrong" they might say, or "I can't eat a meal that doesn't have any meat," or "Rice, *again*?!" Remind yourself that if you wanted to eat the same foods you eat at home, you could have saved a lot of money and stayed at home! Engaging with a local culture means you need to be willing to try new things, and sampling the local food is one of the best ways to integrate into a culture and make friends. Susy volunteered in Nepal, where meals are flavored with a range of strong spices, and often served without a spoon. She dove in anyway, and told us, "I ate local food and immersed myself in a way of life I enjoyed... When you're out of your comfort zone you gain confidence and feel alive. At 54, I was so lucky to have these experiences."

We're not saying that eating a delicious fried spider or boiled chicken feet is not going to feel weird or downright repulsive the first time. Our Cambodian friends are grossed out by cheese, saying something along the lines of "So, you are saying that you take the liquid that comes out of the breast of a cow, and allow it to grow bacteria, and then you let it go bad until you can even see the mold, and *then* you eat it?" Of course, we do not advise that a vegetarian volunteer should start eating shawarma, or an observant Jew or Muslim volunteer should start eating roasted pork, nor do we think you should eat food you suspect might make you sick, but we encourage you to push your culinary boundaries as far as your morals (and health) allow.

You can further your learning by viewing food choice through the lens of privilege. Local food may be repetitive out of necessity because there simply isn't access to a great diversity of food, or it is prohibitively expensive. In some families, people are genuinely grateful for their *dal bhat* or rice-and-beans twice a day. Rejecting food you are offered can be seen as a larger rejection of friendship or of the culture as a whole, and can cut you off from opportunities for deep learning about the challenges of poverty, or the joys of simplicity, or both.

Live local

Some volunteers find that the more they learn about daily life from local people, and live with and like them when possible, the quicker they are able to build trust, make friends, and become more effective in their work. Titus Kuria fondly remembers working with one international volunteer, JB, in his home town in Nairobi. "JB learned a lot about the people; culture, food, language. There came a point that he was very comfortable walking alone at night. At that time Mathare was not very safe even for some locals, but he embraced the community and the community embraced him right back."

Using local transport is one easy way to enhance your cultural interactions. On well-traveled tourist paths, you might have a choice of local buses or tourist buses. In cities, there might be taxis for the wealthy and shared vans or pickup trucks for everyone else. In many places of the world, the 'local' form of transport is a bicycle or your own two feet. While at home you might have lived a life of rushing – taking the quickest transport possible to get to your next meeting – this is not likely to be the best choice in your volunteer-related travel. Zahara often traveled around Nairobi in *matatus*. Squeezed next to the other passengers, the conversations, sights and sounds provided an education—from the lyrics of the blaring Swahili pop, to the psychedelic and sometimes political paintings on the *matatus*, to the hardworking passion and humor of the *manambas*, who help the conductor attract passengers with wild word play in Sheng, the slang forged in the slums surrounding the city. Taking the slow local bus, walking home by the river, or riding your bike to work and having a group of young monks help you fix your tire along the way—your transport adventures might form some of your fondest memories.

The lifestyle choices you make will also affect your interactions with people in the community. David Chaske, who volunteered in India, recalled that, "Children began to recognize their poverty in the value of my belongings." Lalo (Eduardo) Rodriguez of the Mennonite Central Committee in Mexico reflected, "I recall that, when I was a child, the missionaries from the States always talked about how we were all brothers. Yet when I visited them in their homes, I saw that they lived in another world. In the bathroom, everything – the soap, shampoo, and toothpaste – would be from the US. I asked myself, 'Isn't this a contradiction?'"

How and where you spend your money can have just as big of an impact on the communities you are visiting as your volunteer work. Remember that you vote with your money: whatever you spend money on, you are voting for more of that in the world. Do you want your money to support multinational corporations that import foreign goods? Do you want to 'vote' for more money spent on alcohol in tourist bars? Might your visit to a shady massage parlor put you at risk of supporting illicit sex trafficking? In contrast, are there local markets where you can shop? Can you find a responsible travel operator to book your travel during breaks? Are there social enterprises you can choose to frequent? If you take a holistic view of your daily impact, your positive support to the areas you visit can extend far beyond the time you spend volunteering. Keeping a 'money journal' where you note and reflect on your expenditures for a week can help you be more mindful about how you spend your money... and might even change the way you think about how you spend money at home.

Get out of your comfort zone
You may feel tempted to re-create your life at home. Challenge yourself to get away from that. Do you rush from work each night to watch a TV series from your country? To blast rock music on your headphones? To while away hours browsing YouTube? There is no problem with any of these pastimes—sometimes we *need* to relax and balance a day full of stretching ourselves. But if you find your routine is preventing you from spending time with local friends or trying new things, decide if and how you want to move out of your comfort zone and add more learning into

253

your daily life. Make a list of experiences you want to try: joining in a local religious ceremony, attending a traditional wedding, or learning how to cook a local delicacy. Think about what would expand your experiences so that when you get home you have points of reference to look back on and say, "I learned so much!" even if you also say, "It wasn't easy."

For long-term volunteers, visits home might sound tempting, but some volunteer programs discourage or forbid travel home during your placement. That's because volunteers can experience a second and more severe wave of culture shock upon returning to their placement site after a short trip home. You may also feel unbalanced or experience unhelpful stress if a friend or relative wants to come to visit you in the middle of your placement. You might consider encouraging friends to visit only after you have ended your stint as a volunteer.

Avoid getting sucked Into the 'tourist vortex'

A challenge for many volunteer travelers is to avoid getting sucked into what Josh Morris of the Chiang Mai Rock Climbing Association in Thailand calls the 'tourist vortex' or 'tourvex.' This is the place where foreign tourists tend to congregate, where the coffee shops have a hipster chic, and maybe even where you can find your favorite products from home. As volunteer coordinator Julie Rausenberger observed, "I noticed that the volunteers liked the project work, but once they got back from work, they wanted their comfort—food, shower, beds... and headed to Pub Street or a similar area for a cocktail."

In Bangkok, it's Koh San Road, in Kathmandu, it's Thamel, in Costa Rica it's Tamarindo (so much so that locals have nicknamed it 'Tama-gringo'). In these areas, everything may seem to be tailored to your needs: you can get pizza, salad, and perhaps a decaf soy latte. In fact, it *is* tailored to your needs. International investors and chain stores targeting the lucrative tourist market can drive out local vendors and ultimately have a negative impact on local culture—the culture you traveled across the world to experience!

If you live abroad for a long time you might want to head to the tourvex for a treat meal or to locate your favorite brand of toothpaste. But remember, the more time you spend there the less time you have for integrating into the local community. April Nizlek, who volunteered in Haiti, India, and Indonesia, told us, "Try to have a balance between contact with local people and foreigners. You miss a lot of the experience if you hang out with expats all the time, but at the same time it really helps if you have a few people from your culture that you can talk face-to-face with about your experiences." As you decide how to spend your time abroad consider your choices: another Starbucks, or yak butter tea?

Common Challenges and Concerns in Living Abroad

Even with the great diversity of volunteer experiences, there are some common challenges and concerns about life abroad. Here we discuss some of the difficulties of living in a new culture, and how to navigate them.

Adapting to a different pace of life

Many of the volunteers we interviewed noted that the pace of life in Asia, Africa, and Latin America was slower than in their home countries. Projects in those regions often proceed much more slowly than they would in Europe or North America, and with good reason. A community organization in Haiti, for example, may lack computers, filing cabinets, reliable internet connection, and even electricity. Along the Congo River, some villages may be accessible only by boat, and in the Himalayas, some settlements are a week's trek through severe terrain. Physical barriers and cultural expectations can slow down a project, and a healthy dose of patience is necessary to help you keep going.

In many countries, when someone says they will meet you at a certain time, you can expect them to be late—sometimes by hours! Punctuality might not be as highly valued as it is back home, or people might have other pressing priorities that take precedence. Claire's experience in Nepal is that village meetings don't have start times, they are called either in 'the morning' or in 'the afternoon' and people come after they have finished their household and agricultural chores. It is the act of gathering that is important, not starting on time. Roman Christoforou, who volunteered in Ghana for six weeks, reflected, "There is a concept known as 'Ghana time', which basically means that nothing happens on time and everything is very chilled. You might arrange to meet with someone at noon, and it'd be perfectly normal to still be waiting at one. This can be frustrating at the start, but you grow used to it and eventually welcome being away from the stress of a hectic day in the UK, where this concept known as time takes priority over everything else." When you are in a new culture, try to adapt to the pace of life and see if you can learn to find the value in it instead of pushing against it.

Bargaining

"What price am I supposed to pay?" international travelers frequently ask. We recommend asking local friends to help you understand the average prices and teach you appropriate bargaining tactics. In some countries, bargaining down to half the originally quoted price is entirely normal and accepted, whereas in other places you should expect only a small discount and pushing for more is considered an insult. And in certain scenarios, any bargaining would be inappropriate. Knowing appropriate tactics is essential for any long-term guest in a country.

The feeling of being forced to bargain hard, or worse, being 'cheated,' often leaves volunteers feeling sour or resentful. Remember to put these feelings (and prices!) into perspective—a small price inflation for you may be an important additional income for a local family. Zahara once recalled her guilt from bargaining down the price of a hand carved stool that a farmer sold her in Zambia over 25 years ago. Try to avoid getting upset when you compare the price you paid with what someone else paid for a similar item. Like seats on the same airline flight, it depends on the time and place of purchase, and the customer's willingness to pay. You paid what you felt was right at the time: now go enjoy what you purchased and stop stressing about your five pesos!

Bureaucracy

For some volunteers, a host country's government bureaucracy creates frustrating barriers to effective work. For example, permission to proceed with a project may hinge on the agreement of two government agencies that, apparently, don't communicate with each other. A bureaucrat may expect a bribe for a routine procedure. Negotiations with important officials might require many meetings and rapport-building before the main topic of discussion is even brought to the table.

You need to decide for yourself what your ethical lines are and how to draw them. Some people refuse to feed corruption through bribery. Others discover that what they consider a 'bribe' is considered by their colleagues as a normal cost of business; a 'fee' paid in order to proceed with the transaction. We are not in a position to give rules in this area, because the specifics are unique to each context and often come down to an individual's values and qualms. Remember, as a volunteer you are a role model, by choice or by chance. Your behavior will be scrutinized and perhaps emulated by others, so be cautious about your decisions. If you are solicited for money on behalf of your hosting organization, ask a colleague if there is a policy that can guide you. If you feel you are being asked to act above your level of responsibility, leave it up to those who are more familiar with the local systems.

Heed the rules, even if they seem restrictive. Many volunteers feel frustrated by red tape limiting their actions. Letting rules slide because you think they shouldn't apply to you is a slippery slope. Imagine a youth club letting the children go out and explore the town with foreigners just because they have made a donation. They may not mean any harm, but the message to the children is that it's okay to go off exploring with unknown visitors. In other words, yes, the child protection policies should apply to *you* too, even though you are not intending any nefarious acts.

Sidonie Emerande, from Madagascar, told us about a time a volunteer asked for her help to change his tourist visa within one week so that he could get a residence card in Madagascar. "We were asked to talk with the girlfriend of a politician who asked for a huge amount of money. I decided to quit as his translator because I did not want to be involved in bargaining over the price of the paperwork, especially with the volunteer overreacting and threatening blackmail as he knew about the politician's secret affair." If red tape is getting you down, imagine for a moment what hoops your local colleagues would have to jump through

ACT

in order to get the necessary documents to work in – or even visit – your country.

Security

As you navigate an unfamiliar country, you might worry that you will be a target for crime. Depending on where you are, the reality can vary from you being statistically safer in your host country than you are at home, to having to come to terms with the fact that you may well be a victim of a petty crime, such a pickpocketing, during your time abroad. As in your own country, crime may come down to a matter of luck. Take precautions, such as always being careful with your belongings, using bags that close well, and not flaunting cash or leaving expensive items lying around.

In addition to street crime, as a volunteer you need to be wary of con artists who may scam you into parting with money on false pretenses. Dur Montoya and her husband arranged to volunteer in Morocco and the 'director' of the organization told them their job was to walk the tourist trails and take pictures. "Eventually he extorted $200 from us saying that we need to pay for our tourist experience: he said that if we refused to pay, he would be able to track us down because Marrakesh is a small place. We worked out that this man was not the director of the organization at all, just a good actor who tricked us." Even if nothing has happened to you, it is also a good idea to know what the process is for registering a crime with the police should you need to do so.

Sometimes volunteers ask whether they should plan to get involved in practices that are technically illegal but that others recommend, such as exchanging money on the black market or buying alcohol in a dry region. Although we cannot give you any hard and fast rules, we do recommend extreme caution when engaging in anything you know not to be fully above-board. In addition to possible legal risks, there are ethical and practical considerations. Think about how breaking the rules may be interpreted as disrespect; and if the difference to you is only a few extra dollars or another mint tea instead of a beer, you might decide it isn't worth it.

Perceived vs. actual risk

Risk is difficult to gauge in an unfamiliar context. Dangerous activities, such as sitting on the roof of a bus, may be commonplace. Similarly, there may be things you do on a daily basis at home, such as walking home at night or carrying your wallet in your pocket, that your new friends overseas warn against. It can be hard to make the right decisions to keep yourself safe and not end up paranoid! Traveling with the mindset that people around you are out to rob or cheat you can be tiring, not to mention the stereotypes it reinforces in your mind or the barriers to cultural integration it creates.

In fact, integrating yourself into a community can be one of the best ways of protecting yourself from being a victim of crime, as people start to see you as one of them rather than an anonymous outsider. Claire lived in provincial Cambodia and every morning would go to the market to buy vegetables. She recalls, "One day I noticed a commotion at the other side of the market, but it didn't really interest me as I just needed to buy my cucumbers and get to my volunteer placement on time. As I was getting ready to pay, a man I did not recognize broke from the crowd and walked over to me. In his hand was my wallet. Apparently someone had pick-pocketed me at the previous market stall, and some passersby had noticed, tracked the thief down and reclaimed the stolen item. All the time I had been completely oblivious. I had no relationship with the people who had helped me, but they saw me in the market every morning and knew I lived in the community. I was overwhelmed! I offered my helpers a reward, but they refused, so instead we all had ice-cream together."

Staring competition: Different attitudes towards privacy

Foreigners are often stared at, especially outside of larger cities, in places where outsiders are seldom seen. Chances are you will look a lot different than the average person around town, and that might make you interesting to observe. A volunteer who spent a year living in a farming community in Thailand told us, "I was among only a handful of *farang*, or foreigners, they had ever seen, and because of this I was a local village celebrity." Katrina Donovan, who volunteered in Bolivia, said, "Don't take yourself too seriously. You will be stared at, laughed at, and you most likely will start with the vocabulary of a two-year-old. You should be comfortable being the center of attention... Sometimes I think that maybe my purpose in the village was to entertain people."

Interactions that in western cultures typically make people feel uncomfortable may not be considered awkward elsewhere. Your hosts, for example, may assume that if you are alone you are sad, so see it as their responsibility to accompany you everywhere, not realizing that you might just want some alone time. Alternatively, some cultures are much more comfortable with silence than the culture you may have come from, and a meal without talking may be the norm. As for the kids, whose favorite pastime is looking in your window or even rummaging through your interesting-looking possessions, the concept of 'privacy' may be lost on them.

Grace Cawdry, who went on a learning trip to Cambodia for six weeks, shared this experience: "I stayed with a local family in their home. I thought the family didn't especially want me there. Cultural misunderstanding! They were being extra polite and focusing on making me feel important by letting me eat dinner alone and not speaking to me until I spoke first. As soon as I realized this, I saw their efforts in a different light and the uncomfortable moments moved away, breaking down the barriers."

If you find yourself feeling awkward in a social situation, reflect on whether others also seem uncomfortable or whether your feelings have arisen from different cultural norms. "If you get overwhelmed and want a place to run and hide, arrange to have your own sanctuary – either a place, or within yourself – somewhere that you feel safe," suggests Carol Hansen, who volunteered in India. Escaping for a few hours once in a while may help you maintain your balance and need not undermine your participation in the local community. It can also help you practice the kind of self-reflection that is central to the learning service approach.

Gender

Gender issues can be sensitive for volunteers. Female travelers are frequently warned about the dangers of traveling alone overseas, and in every corner of the world, it is unfortunately true that women are much more likely than men to be the victims of sexual harassment and assault. We have heard from female volunteers about experiences that range from having strangers yell out rude taunts to being groped on a crowded bus. Although these incidents are not your fault, there are some things you can do to lower your risk. For example, one challenge for female volunteers overseas is that they may focus too intensely on trying to integrate and, in the process, inadvertently allow their personal safety to become a secondary issue. One volunteer in Indonesia let her host father put his arm around her when they walked around the village. She let it slide thinking it must be culturally appropriate, whereas he interpreted as a green light to initiate a sexual relationship. In contrast, a volunteer in India who knew it was not acceptable for men and women to touch, learned to not even offer a handshake to members of the opposite sex for fear of it being misinterpreted. Instead, she would press her hands together in a *namaste* as an alternate greeting and thereby avoid any physical contact. As you will already have enough of a reason to attract unwanted attention as an outsider, our advice is to err on the side of caution. Susy, who volunteered in Nepal said, "Traveling as a solo woman I learned that I needed to think things through carefully and trust my gut instinct." Listen to your intuition—it's better to risk offending someone than to put yourself in a precarious situation.

There are various ways to respond to gender-based harassment. Responses can range from saying "no," firmly but nicely, to yelling, fighting, and/or running away. Modify your response according to the situation. We strongly recommend that you ask local women for their advice on safety. In Mexico City, Zahara learned to scream as loud as she could at subway gropers, "Don't touch me," which broke their anonymity and shamed (or scared) them into stopping.

Your nationality, religion, and race might compound the gender stereotypes you face. Katie Boswell said of her time in India: "The most challenging part about volunteering was the assumptions that people had about me because I was a white girl—for example, being automatically seen as 'loose' even though I wore *salwar qamiz* and was careful not to behave in inappropriate ways such as dancing or drinking alcohol." When you confront these attitudes, take a moment to reflect on the stereotypes that foreigners face in your own culture, to put your experience in context, and try to find a supportive friend to help you process the specific challenges you are facing.

Gender roles may be more rigidly defined in other countries. Certain dances, religious practices, and spaces may be designated as the exclusive realm of men or women. Some female volunteers are informally granted 'honorary male' status and the license to participate in some traditionally-male activities such as going out drinking. At other times, women volunteers may be expected to confine themselves strictly to the female realm, for example, in clothing norms. Yet often, female volunteers have easier access to many aspects of local culture, such as cooking, visits to the market, festival preparation, and spending time with children. Male or female, you will probably find advantages and disadvantages to your gender identity.

Some cultural practices may surprise you or offend you. Women, for example, may be expected to wait until the men finish eating before they begin their meal. Sons may receive preferential treatment when it comes to household chores, going out with friends, or university education. In many countries, women get less of a choice in whom they will marry. And in some countries, female genital cutting is practiced. Examine the difference between accepting cultural differences and tolerating injustice, and choose what to accept and what to challenge. If you decide to rock the boat, do so gently, and only after deepening your understanding of the issue and considering how your actions might impact your safety and that of others. One volunteer host told us how international volunteers could be positive female role models. "When we had women volunteers from the US and Europe, they respected local culture but also showed many people in our community that women can be independent, travel alone, be professional and strong, and that these do not necessary entail improper behavior on their part, or a threat to 'family honor.'" Ultimately, you may not be the best person to challenge unfair practices, but you could offer support to local people and organizations that can drive this change in the long term.

Men also have to consider their relationship to gender role politics in their host country. The way you interact with women may come under close scrutiny, so be sure you act with the utmost respect and do not inadvertently reinforce unhelpful gender stereotypes. In some cultures, there may be pressure to go to 'men only' nights out, where business is conducted to the exclusion of female colleagues. Some volunteers we talked to felt pressured by colleagues to engage sex workers. There may be ways you can challenge gender norms without damaging relationships, for example, by cooking for your friends or washing your own clothes—and politely declining to take part in activities that strike you as unequal.

Stereotypes and attitudes about race and appearance

In some cultures, there are fewer taboos around words describing personal appearance. Skin color may be talked about openly, not necessarily in a racist way. Xavier Livermon, an African American volunteer in Lesotho, found that "in some contexts, I was referred to as a Basotho (local African), other times I was considered to be South African or even white." Lucius Walker, the founder of Pastors for Peace, explained how, "in Latin America, people call me 'gringo.' So I had to learn to either own up to or somehow deal in my own psyche with the fact that I was being seen as an American, not as an African American. The distinction between Americans and Black Americans was clearly not being made." A volunteer who is considered 'black' at home might be shocked to be labeled as 'colored' in South Africa, or 'mulatto' in the Dominican Republic.

Unfortunately, racism and racial stereotypes persist. In many countries, white people are informally granted special privileges, while in other cases white people may be openly resented or looked down upon. If you are not white, some people may not believe that you are from a western country. Talk to local people and other volunteers of various ethnic backgrounds so you can become aware of the way others may view your ethnicity. Friends may help you reflect on any specific challenges or privileges you face because or your identity, and learn from the differences in perspectives on race, ethnicity, and nationality from what you are used to at home. One volunteer host explained, "The fact that

263

our volunteers have been multicultural... helped a little to foster a more tolerant attitude in our community."

Differences in perspective on identity go beyond race. Many cultures revere older people, and so while it might surprise you to be called 'old man' or 'grandma,' these terms can be a way of showing respect. And few cultures are as sensitive as the West when it comes to talking about weight. Choch Cho, a tour guide in Cambodia, recounts this experience: "I was driving two foreign ladies around the Angkorian temples all day. One lady was skinny, and the other was overweight. I couldn't remember how to say their names in English, and anyway, it is rare to call someone by their first name in Cambodia, so I called them 'skinny lady' and 'fat lady.' I wasn't trying to be mean, in fact, I was trying to be nice and friendly. At the end of the day, the woman I had been calling 'fat lady' got out of the tuk-tuk and started to cry and her friend yelled at me for being so rude. I felt horrible! Actually, to this day, I cringe when I tell this story. I now realize it is cultural—there are different ways of describing each other and different views on beauty. In Cambodia, being fat is associated with being rich and is therefore considered attractive. I had to learn how to speak to foreigners without being offensive, but my advice to visitors to my country is to try to not take offense if someone says something you think is rude. Like me, they may have had no idea about what they were doing wrong!"

Traveling abroad can open your worldview and your time volunteering may, in turn, challenge and transform stereotypes and assumptions held about people of your race, nationality or other identity. A volunteer who went to Kazakhstan for a year explained, "There were a lot of stereotypes about us based mostly on music videos – for example, that the US is very dangerous and we're all interested in sex and money – and I showed that we could also be kind, hard-working, normal people." Wherever you travel as a volunteer, whatever stereotypes you face, think about how you can live and work in ways that will challenge these beliefs.

Love, dating, and sex
Cultural interpretations of friendship, dating, love, and sexual relations vary greatly. The people we interviewed agreed that

international volunteers should exercise extreme caution when dealing with romance in a cross-cultural context, as there is always the potential for serious miscommunication. Your reasons for being involved in a romantic relationship may be quite different from that of your foreign partner.

In many countries, friendships between men and women are rare. Spending a lot of time with someone of the opposite sex, even if you avoid physical contact, may be misinterpreted by that person (or the community). In some cultures, for example, when a woman lets a man walk her home or meet her outside of work, they are considered to be romantically involved. Claire faced this unfortunate situation in Nepal when a male teacher from the school where she was volunteering invited her for tea every afternoon. She only realized that this had romantic connotations when she overheard other teachers speculating about their marriage! She then had to go through a painful 'breakup' that hurt both herself and her colleague. Jeff Stebbins, who worked at the English Language Institute in Vietnam, said, "Single western men often go crazy over Asian women… but dating does not necessarily exist here. A couple of dates and it is assumed that you have slept together, that you are engaged, and, if the Westerner casually breaks it off, then that woman can be viewed as 'polluted' and unmarriageable."

Mixing work and love can be dangerous in any culture. Before you start dating your organization's staff, consider the implications. If you are living in a small community, your private life might not really be private, so be sure to be very clear about your boundaries.

Sex in a cross-cultural context is also extremely complex. We'll keep it brief: we recommend avoiding sexual relationships while volunteering. If you are tempted to get physically intimate with someone, think through the power dynamics involved, and how the relationship might harm you, the other party, or your organization's reputation.

Homophobia

In many parts of the world homophobia might be expressed in more extreme ways than in the country where you grew up. Even otherwise open-minded and progressive people may not be accepting of LGBTQ volunteers or queer-positive perspectives. In some places, political and religious leaders like to claim homosexuality as a colonial import. Under these conditions, we recommend that the default option for volunteers should be to be very cautious of revealing your sexual orientation and views to others, at least until you can assess the community's openness to discussing and accepting what you are planning to share. In some countries, people can be jailed for same-gender relations, so it's best to understand the local context before putting yourself (and others) in danger. Barry Bem, former Deputy Country Director for Peace Corps in Ecuador, himself an out gay man, cautions that all volunteers "have to make cultural adjustments of all sorts in order to live and work effectively in another culture." For LGBTQ volunteers, he told us, "being much more circumspect about one's sexual orientation is one of the possible adjustments."

Sadly, international volunteers are sometimes the ones fueling homophobia. The award-winning documentary *God Loves Uganda* details how homophobic preachers and volunteers from the US have been fueling anti-gay activism in Uganda. How embarrassing for the volunteer travel movement that such hateful practices are being done in the name of 'volunteering.'

In many countries, even those where homosexuality is frowned upon or criminalized, there are local community organizations and NGOs established to support LGBTQ people and to advocate for their rights, so seek them out and, if appropriate, find ways to support their work.

Perspective: "Asians Can't Read Maps"
By Daniela

I spent about a decade living in Asia. When people would visit from the United States I would often hear them say things like, "Why can't Cambodians read maps?" or "No one in Japan knows how to give directions even in their own town!" I can remember feeling similarly the first time I asked to be taken to a specific street address (and yes, there *was* a time before smartphones when you had to ask human beings when you wanted directions!)

I had been raised to think that the 'correct' way to give directions was something like "turn left at the second street. After four blocks, turn right." This turned out to be just my cultural lens. In the US, where I grew up, we label the streets and give directions using roads names. In Japan, Cambodia, and many other places in the world, directions are not given via the streets but by the names of the areas between the streets. This is how my Cambodian friends might tell each other how to get somewhere. "Go to the place nicknamed 'where the fire happened,' then head towards the famous pagoda." By this time I'd already be lost. In places where it is assumed that you have a shared set of experiences and knowledge, directions (and all communication) take a different form. It's not confusing if you grew up with it, but hard to get your head around if you didn't!

Cross-Cultural Communication

To communicate well in different cultures might mean reconsidering the words you use, what you say in public and private, how much emotion or metaphor you put into your arguments, and a whole lot more. You might not realize that you have a 'preferred communication style,' but rest assured you do. Chances are you have had no reason to become aware of it until you are thrown into a place where most people have a very different style of communicating from your own. Understanding your own preferences and style is key to knowing where you might conflict with others.

Your way of doing things might clash with local customs. Trying on a new way of interacting, in the same way you might try on the local clothing, is the only way to really see how it fits.

Non-verbal communication

Communication is not just about language, but about all the subtle cues and gestures that go along with it. Case McCrea, who volunteered in the Philippines, told us, "A big smile… can get you further than almost anything else." A smile, however, can mean different things in different cultures, so take your cues from local people and learn to be friendly in appropriate ways and at appropriate times. Therese Arkenberg, who volunteered in Ghana for a week, advises, "Learn about the non-verbal communication used in the local area, so you don't use a gesture that may be offensive!" Head nods, pointing and eye contact can also all mean different things, so be sure to augment the spoken language you are learning with non-verbal 'language' learning too!

Polite disagreement

Another cultural nuance to be aware of is how to politely disagree or reject something. In many cultures, a direct 'no' is considered impolite and, therefore, you have to be on the alert for the ways some forms of 'yes' or 'maybe' can actually mean 'no.' Bernard Butkiewicz, who volunteered in Bolivia, explained, "If people say yes to you when they know that they are not going to be able to make it, later they can apologize and the relations are not broken. If they just say no to your face, then relations are broken." Similarly, Claire's experience with Nepalese culture has taught her to see how agreeing with you is simply more polite than pointing out your mistakes. Asking, "Is the village this way?" will always result in an affirmative answer from good-willed passersby, no matter its exact location. Your status as a foreigner may also skew the answers people give to your questions. For example, maybe people will give the answers they think you want to hear or assume you are a donor so give the answer they believe will result in you giving more money. If part of your work is to get community feedback, it may be better to have a supporting or analyzing role rather than being directly present in such interviews. Through studying the language, making friends, and asking questions, you will learn how to distinguish a 'yes' from a 'no'—or, ideally, to frame questions differently to avoid confusion altogether.

Indirect communication

In cultures that prefer direct communication – for example, New York Jewish and Italian American communities – most people think it is 'polite' or 'proper' to speak their mind clearly and honestly. As Daniela notes, "I remember feeling so frustrated when I first worked in Cambodia and I would hear things secondhand, like 'Sophal is upset that he didn't get a raise.' I'd think, 'Well, why didn't

Sophal himself just ask me if that is how he feels?' My cultural lenses were strapped to my head so tightly that I hadn't realized that what I thought was polite (speaking directly to someone) versus impolite (speaking indirectly through someone else) was actually the opposite in Cambodia, where you would never speak directly to someone older than you, or a boss at work. It took me longer than I would like to admit to realize that many of the things I thought were rude were in fact acts of politeness, and even longer to realize that then, hence, many things I was doing that I thought were polite were, in fact, rude! Oops!"

Furthermore, in some cultures, disagreements and debates are encouraged, while in others conflict is avoided at all costs. This can seem frustrating until you can see beneath the surface and understand that ideas can be improved and changed without direct confrontation.

High and low context culture

Most of the current North American and European culture is what can be described as a 'low context culture.' What that means is that there isn't much assumed common knowledge as there would be in 'high context' cultures like much of Asia, for example. Some historians track this back to rice farming, as the systems of growing rice generally require collective action, meaning people needed to work together to irrigate their fields and harvest their food. As such, they spent a lot of time together and had a shared set of norms and experiences. In many Asian cultures even today people live in homes with extended families, in contrast to more individualistic cultures like the US where offspring generally move out and start their own homes, increasingly very far from where they grew up. Petra, a volunteer host from Syria, told us about the importance of knowing the cultural context in conflict resolution. "If there is a problem between two families and you want to know what happened to try and fix it, you need to know the history between them. If they invite you to drink coffee or tea or even have lunch at their house and you refused, it would be more difficult to break the ice. It would be even worse if you accepted the invitation from one of the two families and refused the other. Small details matter."

It can be hard for outsiders to navigate high context cultures, in the way that Daniela couldn't navigate Cambodia using local directions, and vice versa. Emily Braucher, a cross-cultural communication trainer from ReFresh Communications, uses this example. In the US, which supposedly has a higher number of lawyers per capita than anywhere else on the planet, most written contracts assume little shared context. Everything needs to be spelled out explicitly—otherwise someone could say, "Well, that wasn't in my contract!" Chinese contracts, on the other hand, are usually much less detailed, not because they don't expect the same level of compliance in legal partnerships, but because there is an implicit shared understanding of what the partnership means. "That wasn't in the contract!" is not a valid excuse in a high context culture.

If cross-cultural misunderstandings are not identified as such, people from both sides of the disagreement feel they have been treated rudely or unfairly. We leave you with some sage advice from Emily Braucher. "Assume positive intent. If you become jaded from a few negative experiences, you will be hard-pressed to find the type of inspiring connections that will warm your heart and fill your stories for years to come. When you start with a positive assumption (maybe they do just want to invite you to dinner and do not want anything in return) you may find that the ground for cross-cultural connection grows around you."

Dealing With Being a 'Privileged Foreigner'

The first thing that almost everyone you meet will know about you is that you are a foreigner. There will be many assumptions tied to your foreign status, which are different in different countries, but in most places the very fact that you have the ability to have traveled so far implies wealth and privilege. "Everyone assumed I was rich just because I am from the UK," said volunteer Katy Vidler. "Although I recognize that I am wealthy in some ways, I have student loans I need to pay each month and less money in my bank account than many of the local staff!"

Many foreign volunteers, especially those who saved up their own money or took out loans to be able to go abroad, might resonate with Katy's comments, as it can be frustrating when people have expectations of your financial capacity. However, if you look at your opportunities in a different light, you can start to understand how they might be perceived by others. As she recognized, although Katy had fewer financial resources at her immediate disposal than her local peers, her wealth is not just measured by her possessions but also by her contacts and freedoms. Her ability to use her credit card or bank overdraft, her university degree that gives her future earning potential, her access to supportive and relatively wealthy family and friends, all open up opportunities many of her colleagues would not have had. Even her British passport was a major factor in her ability to volunteer overseas in the first place, as it meant she could choose from nearly every country in the world, with little hassle getting a visa.

Merely having the time and resources to travel, and not having to work to meet your family's basic needs, is a luxury some of your local colleagues may never have the opportunity to enjoy. As Rani Deshpande, who volunteered in West Africa, commented, "The very ability to take a few months or years of one's life, usually unpaid, to work supporting social change outside of one's own community must be recognized as a form of privilege."

Volunteers often think this kind of privilege is invisible. But their possessions, food, and clothes, as well as the vacations and short excursions they take, are all part of the 'umbilical cord of privilege,' a term coined by Kelly Reineke, who volunteered in Brazil. Even if you live simply and in a local style you have this umbilical cord, and at a moment's notice can meet your desires for comfort, health care, and entertainment: an option the majority of your local friends and colleagues will not have. This umbilical cord also provides you with an escape route if things get uncomfortable, overwhelming, or dangerous—you can always pull on the cord and bounce back to life at home. A volunteer who spent two years in Kyrgyzstan had this important reminder, "Even as volunteers, we are just long-term tourists. *Do not* lose sight of that. For us, to leave is a significantly different proposition than for the locals."

Recognize that, even though you may be living at a level that would be well below the poverty line at home, you will most likely still be living far above the level of working families in the place where you are volunteering. You may be asked for money by someone you know just because you are a friend, not because he thought you were rich. Such experiences can be disheartening but the wider inequality is a reality that must be faced. In fact, some host organizations see that as a major benefit of volunteer travel. One host told us "It is important for (typically) financially privileged westerners to explore the world in order to better understand the factors contributing to the poor distribution of resources throughout the world."

Volunteers must avoid assuming that a stint as a volunteer learning from and supporting the communities in which they work enables them to truly understand the challenges faced by people in those communities. You may be able to gain awareness, get angry about the root causes of poverty, and cultivate empathy, but that umbilical cord, which acts as a safety net, means you will not be able to experience the effects of such problems in the same way. Andrea Foster, who volunteered in Guyana says, "Our economic background makes it hard for us to understand the degree of financial struggle most people in developing nations endure. Volunteers eventually come to realize how fortunate we are and usually how spoiled we are." The most important advice we have about the umbilical cord of privilege is to be aware it exists and realize others can see it, even when you cannot.

What to do about begging

To give or not give to people who are begging is often one of the most difficult decisions volunteers face while abroad. Depending on where you are based, the extent of begging can vary from omnipresent to nonexistent, just as it probably varies in your home country. Volunteers who come from areas with little begging or who have limited exposure to extreme financial poverty, can find widespread begging very stressful. Consequently, the desire to take immediate action to help can seem like the right thing to do. Giving money directly to people on the streets, however, rarely solves the underlying problems—and in some cases may exacerbate the situation. Rachel Springer, who volunteered in Lebanon, recalls, "A friend of mine really struggled with the number of mothers, babies, and kids she saw on the street, so she started handing out juice boxes and granola bars to people she saw. The thing is, she would get swamped with people asking for food on a daily basis, and she realized that she would just never have enough juice boxes and granola bars for them all." Thankfully, there are other, smarter, things you can do with your money that will help address a root cause.

In many countries, there are complex social bonds and spiritual implications behind offering money to people begging. Your local friends and colleagues may offer something as a matter of course, to certain people (perhaps the elderly), or on special occasions. In some cultures monks and holy people beg for alms and the money offered is in exchange for good karma! Talk to local people about their beliefs and practices, but be aware the connotations may be different when it is a foreigner offering the money.

The decision to give or not to give is a personal one, but the situation is particularly fraught when it comes to child beggars. Chhon Yut, a tour guide in Cambodia, said, "In tourist areas kids can make a lot of money begging on the streets, more than their parents make working. This incentivizes families to keep children out of school. I ask travelers to my country to not give to child beggars as it prevents them from getting an education." In other tourist areas around the world, like in the movie *Slumdog Millionaire*, children living on the streets may be part of organized criminal groups where the ringleaders take most or all of what the children earn. These situations – which prevent children from being in school, put pressure on desperate parents, facilitate child trafficking, or lock vulnerable children into servitude to manipulative adults – are fueled by the good intentions of visiting foreigners. Finding ways to support local organizations countering the root causes of urban poverty through education or employment programs, can help keep kids off the street.

If you decide not to give when someone asks, you can still acknowledge that person's presence, smile, or start a conversation with them. But remember, if you decide not to give because you don't think it addresses a root cause, think about what action you will take that *will* have a more sustainable impact.

Bypassing the system: When to offer direct help to someone in need?

Through volunteering, you can make close connections with your co-workers and local community members. The chances are, at some point, through those friendships, you will identify real or perceived needs within the lives and communities around you, separate from those connected to your volunteer placement. This might be a co-worker whose house is damaged in a storm, a member of the community who needs funds for school supplies, or a beneficiary of your host organization whom you feel needs support above and beyond what the organization is providing.

When you realize that the amount of money involved is small in your home currency, to jump in and offer support can seem like the right thing to do. However, in the same way we advised caution before giving to children begging, think carefully about this situation. We have seen multiple examples of volunteers trying to take a matter into their own hands by making personal donations that led to negative side effects. Although it might seem like a practice of kindness, it is important to remember the wider context and implications of your gestures.

One important consideration is that as a volunteer, you are part of an organization, and your action can have an impact on that organization's long-term ability to work in the community. Imagine you want to help someone by offering a scholarship, but this comes into conflict with your host organization's carefully arranged, fair, and transparent student financial aid scheme. No matter how much you try to make a distinction between your actions and the official program, it will be difficult for outsiders to discern, and your choices, biases, or favoritism will end up reflecting back on your host organization. We have seen cases where volunteers appointed a local person to administer the grant they decided to give and instead fueled corruption, nepotism, and unprofessional behavior, with no monitoring to check where the money was going.

To avoid these problems, make sure not to give any gifts or make any promises without first speaking with the host organization management. They might have policies in place, additional perspectives on the situation, or advice on how to proceed, which will help you put your good intentions to the best use. If you do decide to make a personal grant or donation, consider making it anonymously or through a third party so there is no undue pressure on you or other volunteers to make future grants.

If you encounter a person with a genuine need that is outside the mission or capacity of your organization, consider connecting them to another organization that can help. For example, rather than trying yourself to counsel someone you find out has been abused, or provide medical care to a sick child, or permanently take on responsibility for paying the school fees for a girl not attending school, you can seek out organizations that professionally offer these services. In this way, you will be able to connect them to higher-quality or longer-term care than if you tried to solve the problem on your own. You could also consider making a donation to that organization.

Learning service means reflecting on the message created by your actions and the sustainability of their impact. One outsider generously bestowing a gift might solve one problem for a short time, but a local community group pulling together to tackle an issue might be more empowering and sustainable. Instead of fueling an unequal 'donor-recipient' power relationship, support local institutions to build trust in them to continue to provide long-term solutions.

Getting Perspective

It goes without saying that, at some point, things will go wrong during your time abroad. Not disastrously wrong, but wrong enough that you feel upset or angry. Maybe you even start questioning why you came all this way in the first place—this was meant to be fun, right? Well, as we've explained, a key part of learning service is the understanding that your attitude towards setbacks can make all the difference to how you deal with them.

Fun A vs. Fun B
'Fun A' is the type of fun you have where you are smiling and laughing through it all. It's a water slide, silly movie, riding a wave,

pillow-fight type fun. During the experience you are thinking, "WOOHOO! This is FUN!"

'Fun B,' on the other hand, isn't always fun at the time. It's hiking up a mountain, which seemed like a good idea at first, but then it gets cold, or steep, or long, and you are tired, and hungry, and sore. Then it starts raining. Then you realize you might have taken a wrong turn. Then you meet a herd of angry-looking sheep. You start to think, "Why am I doing this again?" but you keep going, and when you get to the top and sit down to look out at the view, you think, "Wow, that was fun! When can I do it again?" Sometimes it can take a bit more time – hours, a good night's sleep, or even months – for Fun B to eventually feel like it was fun.

A lot of your experience abroad will be Fun B. Fun B is when you say to yourself, "When I get home, and I'm dry, and I've had some food, and the sheep have stopped following me, this will be a really fun memory." Fun B often involves trying something new or something unexpected happening, learning on your feet, and being pushed out of your comfort zone. When you succeed at whatever the challenge was, part of the 'fun' is the pride you have in yourself for getting through it.

Daniela remembers a great 'Fun B' moment. "I was traveling with my friend Peppi in Vietnam. It started with a long day of mix-ups: forgetting one of our passports in the hotel safe, missing our original boat to the mainland, needing to buy new tickets, missing the chance to bike as we had planned, and instead buying express bus tickets to take us to the border, where the ticket officer pocketed the fare difference and instead put us on a cheaper, slower, and cockroach-infested bus. We ended up arriving at the border town late at night, tired and hungry. We rushed to a local hotel, hoping to grab a meal and a room but soon found out there was a festival going on and every hotel room in the entire town and surrounding area was booked. After making lots of phone calls we asked if the hotel would let us sleep on their restaurant floor. Seeing our distraught looks, one of the hotel desk staff offered to have us stay at her family's house. So we biked to the outskirts of town with her, to a one-room house on stilts by the edge of the river. Her whole family, seven people, was sleeping under two mosquito nets, and they moved over to accommodate two more people. Neither Peppi nor I slept more than an hour over the course of the night, but every time we looked at each other, we smiled. What a memorable day! Fun B, but fantastic!"

It's those Fun B memories that usually last far into the future. In Daniela's case, the woman who hosted her and her friend that night eventually got in touch, more than a decade later, via Facebook, and they were able to reconnect about their shared memory of the cross-cultural sleep-over!

What to tell the folks back home

Relaying your experiences through letters home, group emails to friends and loved ones, or by sharing reflections on a blog, can help you to reflect on and process your experiences and allow those who care about you back home to share some of your adventures. The majority of the people you know most likely have not had the chance to spend an extended period of time in the country you have come to know. Most of them will not volunteer abroad and some might have no interest even in traveling outside their home turf. In many ways, you have become an ambassador for the country and culture you are newly experiencing, so be mindful of the impression you give. Offer open and balanced perspectives and be careful to use respectful language. Here are some ideas for how to represent your experience fairly in your communications to people back home.

Don't exaggerate. When everything is new, there can be a tendency to want to play up the differences and play down the similarities. Try to resist the temptation to exoticize your experiences or to go for the shock factor. Instead, try to portray things more roundly, which is essential if you want your audience to truly learn from your narrative.

Don't generalize or fall back on stereotypes. As a volunteer engaging in a deep cultural exchange, you have the opportunity to look past stereotypes and invite others to do so as well. Try not to be condescending in your descriptions or to define others by what (you perceive) they lack. It's fine to use humor, especially if it is self-deprecating and as long as you avoid being derogatory.

A good rule is to avoid sending anything to others you wouldn't mind being translated and read by the people it's about.

Consider how your audience will respond. Writing home while you are going through an intense emotional crisis will cause worry or even panic. Your friends and family back home may have a hard time understanding the context and feel powerless to help. If you need emotional support make sure you are also asking for this from your friend network in your new community, who may be better placed to provide practical advice to ease the situation. One way to make sure you are being realistic in your messages and not causing undue worry about something that might quickly dissipate is to draft an email first, and then leave it a few days before sending it. You may be able to write with more perspective after giving yourself time to see if the intensity of your experience changes.

Be humble. Try to be humble both in your writing style and the topics you choose to write about. One good rule is to write as an observer not a judge, refraining from imposing your opinions or solutions on a situation. Although the people you are writing to will be mainly interested in you, mentioning the efforts and achievements of others around you will help to prevent everyone at home from imagining you are singlehandedly out in the wilderness combating poverty (although trust us, you probably still will have to cope with a few people who walk away with this impression).

Share what you have learned. You can play a role in the development education of your friends and family. If you have learned about the complexities of a particular issue, experienced inspiring grassroots work, or realized the root cause of local challenges is linked to decisions made in your home country, share this through your communications home. Do so sensitively, as you don't want to come across as preachy. Think about what your readers would be interested in and share it in an engaging way. They will, hopefully, learn from your first-hand experiences, and maybe even change their minds.

Immersion into a new culture can be extremely challenging and extremely rewarding. If you regard the challenges as learning opportunities (including the chance to learn about yourself) you will be surprised how quickly the difficulties become less daunting. Eventually, the boundaries of your comfort zone will expand. That's part of the transformational power of this kind of travel.

We'll now turn to another part of the transformation— learning how to offer your skills in a way that will have a positive, sustainable impact on the issues you care about and the people you hope to serve.

ACT

15.
USING YOUR SKILLS APPROPRIATELY & SUSTAINABLY

Perspective: From Placebo to Meaningful Impact

By Lawrence Loh, volunteer in Dominican Republic and Co-Founder of The 53rd Week

It was mid-way through my residency in public health when I finally went abroad on my first volunteer medical trip, providing care to dozens of patients a day in mobile medical clinics. Our focus of work was on providing primary care services to migrant Haitian workers in the *bateyes* (work village) around La Romana, Dominican Republic. As we traveled in a rickety school bus, dressed in scrubs and setting up makeshift clinics in churches and schools, I was skeptical that my work would target the underlying factors that were the root of poor community health. We were providing simple primary care and treating patients, and heavily limited by language and cultural barriers, unavailable tests and treatments, and limited knowledge of the diseases present in the community. Was I really making a difference?

There are myriad reasons why medics go abroad. Some want to improve skills—be it language, cultural sensitivity, or medical skills. Some believe that treating the odd patient, providing temporary relief, is a small success that resonates. Many responded to entreaties from communities abroad that welcomed any help, even if it was temporary and perhaps not in their long-term interest. Such medical volunteers were happy to participate if it reminded the communities that they were not alone; that they are cared for.

To me, however, this simple form of clinically-focused, service-oriented medical experience seemed a form of placebo: the volunteers felt good, the communities felt good, but the underlying causes of poor community health remained largely ignored. While I had face-value competence to treat patients, my desire to conduct community health education and development work remained unfulfilled. Attempts to engage the local hospital to identify broader development priorities were met with polite deference: "Our priorities? They don't matter. You can help us however you like to help. How about you focus on caring for the patients, you are doing a good thing."

Trouble was, I knew my clinical work wasn't having much impact beyond the minimal. Sure, I could provide a salve for their rash, soothe their cough, and give antibiotics for an ear infection. But the big-picture, community health side of me would not rest. How could I increase my volunteering impact beyond just seeing patients? How might I attack the underlying causes of ill health in the community? Different from many medical volunteers, I returned after five days of clinics and hundreds of patients seen with a deeply unsettled feeling, rather than satisfaction at what I had done. I hadn't bought into the placebo.

Together with some friends, we decided that the issue wasn't medical volunteering as a phenomenon that was the problem. Rather, it was the way we were doing it—without local leadership, focused on treating diseases rather than addressing root causes, siloed into one week of care. Our belief soon became: "Go abroad right, or not at all."

From that one trip, we founded a nonprofit that aims to optimize the outcomes and minimize the harms associated with short-term medical volunteering abroad, which has since morphed to answer the bigger questions about volunteering writ large through evaluation, advocacy, and collaboration. Taking on the challenge to make medical and other types of volunteer efforts work more sustainably, we ask: can we match the intentions of volunteers to genuinely positive outcomes for communities? Can we eliminate stand-alone, potentially harmful efforts? Can we turn these efforts into a force for good to address the numerous health and development challenges that we collectively face? I would venture we not only can; we must.

Sustainability and Continuity: Avoiding a Void

"Work with, and not instead of, local people."
-Maggie Cox, who volunteered in
South Africa for three weeks

Working towards a sustainable impact after you leave is probably one of the most important things you can do as a volunteer. One of the most serious challenges to effective development is a lack of continuity. Bearing this in mind will help ensure that the work you do has both a positive short-term effect and a long-lasting legacy for the organization you volunteer with.

If you have the necessary skills and experience, you can be as useful overseas as you can in your home community by just 'doing a job.' A doctor can treat patients, an engineer can design infrastructure, an English teacher can teach English. However, due both to the cross-cultural context in which you are working and the finite nature of your placement, there are reasons why when you go overseas to 'do a job,' a completed task in the short-term may not translate to a positive impact in the long-term.

Here's an example. A doctor volunteering in a rural community where the existing health system is inadequate may do a great deal of good for the patients she sees, even if she is only present for a short time. However, once that volunteer has gone, what might her legacy be?

- The community still does not have access to a quality healthcare system.
- Patients who were seen by the doctor and who need long-term follow-up and care won't have access to it.
- The community may develop distrust towards the existing healthcare providers in the village, as the foreign doctor didn't work with them or show regard for them.
- The community may wait for the next time a western doctor comes to their community to get treatment (because it is perceived as higher quality or lower cost than existing local services.)
- The local government will have an incentive to delay allocating the funds for the community to get their own doctor, as it would make it less likely another volunteer will come.

Now consider an alternative. The doctor came to work in the same community, but instead of working independently she works from the government-provided health post. She works alongside a counterpart healthcare provider, who was one of the only women from the village to complete high school and who went on to qualify in community medicine. Instead of directly treating patients, the doctor devotes her energy to mentoring, training, advising, and supporting the local health worker. She supports programs to mobilize the local community to advocate for their health rights, as well as supporting communication and collaboration between the community and the government. The long-term impacts of this approach may be:

- The community will have access to an improved healthcare system.
- The patients who need longer-term follow-up and care will have access to it.
- The community will be more likely to trust the local health worker as both her skills and reputation will have been bolstered through the support shown by the doctor.
- There will be no incentive to wait for the doctor to return as she never directly treated patients on her own anyway.

- The community will be more active and engaged with the health service and aware of the channels through which to advocate for the local government to allocate more funds for health care. The government will be more likely to be responsive to requests for providing the community with their own doctor.

In the first example, a void was created. Once the volunteer moves on, the organization will need to search for someone else to take on that role who might have to start from the beginning again. Rather than making the system run more efficiently without her, the organization is becoming more dependent on outside support. In the second example, the volunteer focused on building capacity of an individual, community, and institution rather than simply 'doing a job.'

Taking a collaborative approach can be frustrating and it may even feel as though you are wasting your time. (Imagine a doctor who can diagnose and prescribe medicine holding herself back so the less-qualified trainee can figure out what to do.) But, as the previous example illustrates, sharing skills, rather than 'doing a job', often represents a sustainable solution to long-term problems.

A good rule is to ensure you are never working completely independently. If a task is allocated to a team instead of you alone, then your role becomes that of supporting the team to complete the task to the best of everyone's ability. If you have someone working alongside you at all times, you can pool your strengths and work together to ensure both that the job gets done, and that someone in the organization knows how to do it after you leave. Ultimately, with this approach you can avoid creating dependency on outsiders.

Kyla Solinger, who volunteered in Cambodia, said, "In the past, I would design and teach classes to students, and as effective as those might have been, my efforts didn't feel very 'sustainable', as another foreign volunteer was going to have to come and fill my role the next term. In my final volunteer role in Cambodia, I took a position supporting teachers in creating training materials for their teams." She went on to tell us, "This meant that all of the work we were doing together was turned into toolkits for those same teachers to use again and again, and once I left, the system would run better without me."

Ultimately, the way in which you work in your volunteer placement should be collaborative and dynamic, so in addition to passing down your knowledge and transferring your skills you will be offering new perspectives, learning from others, and participating in a vibrant exchange of ideas in order to innovate and create new solutions—all ways to avoid a void. (Yes, pun intended!)

Training and mentoring

If you are an experienced practitioner volunteering in a field you know well, you may find yourself asked to train staff at your host organization or mentor individuals. If you find many of your activities involve mentoring, make sure to allow ample time for those you are mentoring to drive the conversation, ask questions, and point out their areas of interest. This might mean setting aside a time each week or even each day where you and your local counterparts connect to set the agenda about what areas of skill learning or exchange they want to explore.

Keep in mind, *being* a mentor doesn't prevent you from *having* a mentor, so you can and should still seek out a mentor for yourself who will help you learn the cultural and contextual norms, as well as give you feedback and support on any issues you might come across in your work. Maybe you even identify those skills or qualities in your mentee, so you can transform your mentoring role into an exchange.

Training can be a way of formally passing on the knowledge and skills you have. To be a competent trainer, however, you have to both have mastery of a field and effective training techniques, which can be even harder in a cross-cultural context, so if you have one and not the other, work on those skills before taking on a training role. As with any of these ways of supporting individual or organizational growth, make sure the need for the training has been identified and expressed by the local team. It is best if you can co-design the training with someone who better understands the context of the organization and the current capabilities of the staff. Heather Perry, who volunteered in Cambodia providing training for health staff, said "Because I had very little contact with the management, or any information about the long-term aims of the organization, it was hard to tailor my trainings to fit perfectly with the organization's goals."

There are a number of things to consider when designing a training course, such as who the audience will be, how many participants there will be, how long the training will be (which could be anything from a few hours to several days), if there is a budget allocated for equipment and materials, how participants will be expected to apply that knowledge, and who will monitor and follow up from the training. You will need to consider challenges such as language barriers. Will you need a translator? If so, should you pick someone from the team, who knows the group well, or will choosing that person mean they can't participate and fully learn? Or will it possibly create strained power dynamics if they appear to be on the training team and are therefore elevated above their peers? If the topic being discussed is a difficult or sensitive one, you might want to consider bringing in an external translator who does not have as much relationship baggage.

If you are training in English or your own language, consider the speed of your presentation and your vocabulary choices. Keep checking in to make sure the message is being understood and give time for discussion in the local language to ensure everyone is keeping up. Whether or not you have a translator, you will find you need to speak slowly and that the training will take a lot longer, so budget time generously. If you are working through translation and you haven't had previous experience, you will probably need to practice or work with the translator in advance of the session.

Alternatively, you may want to see if there is someone on the team who can administer the training directly with your support, without you taking the lead, or who could work with you as a co-facilitator. That might save a lot of time and help someone else gain valuable training skills. If you are a really experienced trainer, you may want to use a 'Training of Trainer' model, and instead of investing your time training a big group, invest your time and energy training a small group of local trainers who are then able to go out and deliver the message to a wider audience in their local language.

Supporting the development of policies and processes

For many volunteers, their most sustainable impact is helping to document or formalize manuals, toolkits, or processes for the organizations in which they are placed. If you have previous experience in management or human resources, maybe you can use this expertise to document or co-develop training manuals or assessment procedures for the organization. As with other tasks, make sure you have a local counterpart who is working with you to ensure your materials fit the needs and styles of the organization.

Assisting and advising management

Some volunteers, whose skills were specifically matched with the needs of an organization, find their entire role is to assist and advise management. Claire's role through VSO was as an 'Organizational Development Adviser,' and she was encouraged to support and assist local staff rather than lead and take charge. As Claire describes, "I was placed with an organization called Cambodian Rural Development Team (CRDT). Initially, I was given small tasks to do and treated as an extra pair of hands around the office. Eventually I was able to build strong relationships with the management team, and I offered to be used as a sounding board for decisions they were making. Based on my prior experience in managing nonprofits and the ongoing trainings we had through VSO, I was able to support the local leadership team as they created new strategies, reached out to new funding sources, and improved internal structures and systems. My placement was for over two years, which gave me the time I needed to grow into the role and be able to be of value in these areas, and I made sure I always worked alongside whichever permanent staff member had ultimate responsibility for the task."

Remember to be honest if you feel you are being accorded a position of authority you are not comfortable with. Empower local management by reiterating that you are an adviser, not a decision-maker. But by offering a fresh perspective to, or new suggestions for, the everyday issues and challenges of running an organization, you might be able to work with the organization's management team to create innovative solutions.

Advocating for your partner organization

Sometimes the capacity-building role of a foreign volunteer is focused more on the growth of the organization's reach and brand than on developing any one person's skills. Perhaps one of your greatest assets to the team is your global network and professional connections to other organizations working on similar issues. If that is the case, putting your name as a supporter of their work, making introductions to potential partners or funders, and helping the local team understand and manage the potential relationships can be a way for you to provide the group support that continues long after you leave.

What to Do About a Difficult or Corrupt Organization

No one should expect your host organization to be perfect at what they do. The organization may be facing huge challenges that you are unaware of, learning as they are going. They may have made some decisions that from your perspective are the wrong ones. However, if you feel the organization is not learning from its mistakes, is not transparent, is not making decisions in the interests of the beneficiaries, or if you suspect outright corruption, here are some factors to consider:

First seek to understand

As an outsider with only limited knowledge of the context, you may be leaping to conclusions, not fully understanding the situation, or simply seeing something from your own cultural perspective. For example, in Nairobi, Zahara met a supervisor at a program for street children who almost fired a volunteer medical student because the volunteer thought the petty cash system the staff used for taking taxis (based on trust and not receipts) did not comply with proper accounting standards, and he repeatedly tried to force the organization to change their accounting systems. Take time to ask questions both internally within the organization but also of experts and long-term residents in the area. Look for a local governing body or advisory service or speak with someone who has worked in the field for much longer who might be able to shed light on the organization or situation you are dealing with.

Examine who makes decisions and how

Try to understand the motivations of the organization's management. Whose voice and influence is directing the work? Is the organization tightly controlled from the top, or do beneficiaries and employees participate in decisions? Do the managers seem more interested in the impact of their work, or the profits they are making from fee-paying volunteers and other services? Are the failings you have seen a result of the natural trial and error that comes with the challenges of aid and development, or is there a lack of critical thinking going into the planning? Is the management willing to engage in this discussion and work towards more positive change, or do they have valid reasons why they are choosing to operate in their current way?

Offer feedback and support

Ask the organization's management if they would be open to answering some questions and hearing your feedback. You can offer a reciprocal session in which they can give you suggestions for improvement as well. Prepare for the meeting, and ensure that you articulate specific problems instead of offering general concerns and refrain from being accusatory or confrontational without offering space to respond. Be open to hearing the views of others, admitting your own mistakes, or accepting an alternative perspective in case there was a miscommunication.

Set your own boundaries

Some issues are just viewed differently in different cultures, and you ultimately will have to set your own boundaries with regards to what you don't like but will accept, and what you need to take a stand against. In some cultures, corporal punishment in the classroom is an acceptable form of discipline, not 'child abuse.' Arranged marriage may not be seen as a 'human rights violation.' Even if you have strong feelings about each of these things, through discussion you may realize that these things are not going to change during your volunteer placement and you may have to work with them and agree to disagree. Kara Filbey, who volunteered in India for over three months said, "The most negative part of my experience was seeing corruption that I didn't have the confidence to question or challenge and knowing that I couldn't do much to change it." If the practices you have uncovered are beyond your baseline limits and not something you can work with, and the organization is adamant about refusing to change, you might want to expedite your departure so you do not get too wrapped up in work that is fundamentally misaligned with your values.

Look past 'confirmation bias'

If you suspect that the organization you are working with is corrupt or otherwise having a negative impact, it can be very difficult to admit to yourself or to friends and family back home that you have been pouring your time and energy, and often money, into such an organization. In fact, psychologists have a term for this: *confirmation bias*. Volunteers have been known to turn a blind eye or refuse to heed warnings from others, and only select the information that confirms their choice to continue volunteering. Daniela has firsthand experience of this from her time in Cambodia. "Many times I would try to warn visiting donors or volunteers about the transparency issues or corruption myself or other volunteers had uncovered, but most refused to listen, just like I had at first. We are our own worst enemy: if we let our assumptions and egos lead, we miss out on opportunities to notice our own mistakes and reallocate our funds and time to worthwhile and ethical causes." Be fair to overseas organizations and allow them to make mistakes, but be sure that you are not lying to yourself and defending a person or institution to the detriment of the impact you want to have.

Spread the word

If you have uncovered facts that led to you leaving a corrupt organization, you owe it to the project beneficiaries, future donors, and volunteers to let others know. You do not need to be unnecessarily inflammatory, blame individuals, or make personal judgments—just recount the details of your experiences. You may want to inform local authorities, the volunteer-sending organization you worked with, or other local organizations or experts, or in some cases, share your story more widely using the media.

> **Confirmation bias**
>
> In psychology, *confirmation bias* is when people subconsciously select or interpret information based on what they want to hear. Facts that reaffirm deeply-held assumptions are noticed or believed more in order to confirm what the person already thinks is 'true.' Information that runs counter to this 'perceived truth' is rejected or ignored. Volunteers working in corrupt or harmful organizations have been known to fall prey to confirmation bias because they want to believe that their work has been for a good cause and, therefore, will ignore red flags instead of investigating issues further.

Leaving Your Placement Early

As we have explored, all volunteers go through significant ups and downs during their service. It is not uncommon, especially if you are on a long-term placement, to consider giving up and returning home during one of your lows. While many volunteers successfully wait out and learn from these low periods, some realize volunteering abroad just isn't for them. Others discover the project they are working on is in conflict with their values. Even if your volunteer program is a good match for you—illness, a traumatic experience, conflict, or an emergency back home could cut your time abroad short.

While each case will be different, we can make a few general suggestions. Don't be rash. Ask yourself if you have really given the volunteer experience a chance or if there are ways to change your mindset towards the experience (or even aspects of your role) to make it a better fit. Make a list of the things that you are finding overwhelmingly challenging and what steps you can take to make them more manageable. Do you need to have a meeting with your manager to discuss concerns? Do you need a better work-life balance? Do you need to change your living arrangements? Find someone to talk with and consider your options.

Remember, if you do decide to leave early for whatever reason, it does not mean you are a failure. There are many valid reasons to leave a placement, and even once you leave, there are many things you can do in the future to ensure you are connected to global issues and making a positive contribution. Reflect on what you have experienced and learned during your time abroad, even if you didn't stay as long as you expected. Blogger Rachel said in her popular blog, *Why a Bad Travel Experience Isn't the End,* "Sometimes it takes more courage to give up than to go on. Early on, one of the girls in our group decided she'd had enough and went home. Some people in the group were quite harsh about it, but honestly, I think she was incredibly brave. I didn't have the courage to stand up and say, 'You know what? I'm not enjoying this either.'… And I spent three months not only being miserable with my surroundings, but actually hating myself for being so grumpy, for complaining all the time, for bringing other people down with me. Carrying on with that program wasn't brave of me. It was cowardly, because I couldn't face going home and admitting that I had failed. Knowing yourself well enough to know when to call it quits is an important skill to have. Sometimes going back on your words and your plans is the best – and the bravest – thing you can do."

Transitioning Out: Preparing to go Home

It's common to overlook the importance of properly preparing to go home. Time might have flown by, and you'll be too caught up in the projects you are doing to think about your impending departure. Or, you may be enjoying the work so much that you don't want to think about having to leave all your new friends and colleagues behind. However, taking adequate time to prepare to leave will not only help you to meet the challenges of the transition, but perhaps more importantly, will help to ensure that you leave a meaningful and lasting legacy with your host organization.

Reflect on your impact and learning
As you prepare to leave, reflecting on your impact can be useful both to you and to the organization as they consider if or how to engage future volunteers or staff on similar projects. Your impact may be hard to measure, and might not come to fruition until long after you leave. If you trained a team in fundraising and later a big grant is secured, perhaps a small part of that achievement

is due to your efforts. If you made some spreadsheets for a data collection project that went on to influence government policy, you share in that success. If you did the filing for an organization that has decreased urban poverty, everything you did supported that wider mission.

The most important long-term impact of your work may, in fact, be breaking down barriers, challenging cultural stereotypes, or offering solidarity and inspiration—and these are not small things! By considering your impact as relational to those you are working with, perhaps success looks like a colleague who is now confident enough to stand up in front of her team and lead a training that, until you arrived, she felt she needed to rely on a foreigner to do. Helping make that happen is something to be proud of!

We interviewed a number of host organizations and community members who enjoyed working with volunteers because they brought new energy or a fresh perspective. Mr. Sok Sim from the Koh Pdao community in Cambodia often recounts a story about his first interactions with international volunteers. "I watched one of the foreigners open a bottle of water. They removed the plastic seal and carefully put it in their pocket. I was with my friends at the time and we all fell about laughing when we saw that. 'That bit of plastic is so worthless that we just throw it on the floor!' we laughed. 'And here these rich foreigners think it is so precious they want to keep it!' It was only much later that I realized why that volunteer behaved in that way. We had so little awareness of the environment in those days, all our plastic was just dropped on the ground. Now I am involved in cleanup programs, and I will always remember that one volunteer who didn't want to pollute our island."

When reflecting on your impact, don't forget to think about the most important aspect—the impact on yourself! The new things you have learned about can help you change your lifestyle and future actions, which over time can add up to having a larger impact than anything you can achieve in a volunteer placement.

Make a transition plan

Try not to take on too much in your final few weeks, but be sure to tie up loose ends. There is nothing worse than leaving half-finished tasks for others to untangle after you leave. Consider how you can hand over any work you have been a part of to your colleagues. Imagine how frustrating it would be if they remember that you worked on a project, but they can't find the files. Even worse: if you don't do an effective handover, everything you worked so hard on could go unused. Don't leave your team searching for your documents or re-doing the tasks you completed. When asked about the challenges of hosting international volunteers, one hosting organization said, "They leave. This is undoubtedly the biggest challenge. They leave and if there is no well-developed framework to translate their knowledge to the local community, then it is lost."

The best way to go about this is to make a clear plan of transition for your work from the start. Get into the habit of documenting the files you create, and recording where they are stored. Giving regular updates to your team or counterpart on this process may be one of the most useful things you can do during your time. Maybe you have found that people who filled your role in the past have each had to make up their own way of doing things, and this inconsistency has caused problems or repeated work—or maybe you can see this happening in the future unless you document what you have done. You can do this by making a folder of documents saved on a shared drive or computer, or by making a hardcopy binder. Make sure your files are organized clearly and that when you leave more than one person on the team knows where any information you were managing is now kept. If you have a plan or some ideas for the next steps in your project, make sure they are included in your transition plan and that you have talked them through with whoever is taking on your role.

Provide and request feedback

Offer feedback to the organization you have been placed with, or the managers and team members you have been working with, and ask for it in return. Hopefully, you will have found ways throughout your placement to give (and receive!) feedback, so nothing should come as a huge surprise at this point. Saving up criticisms of the program for the end is a cheap parting shot and is disempowering for those who receive it, as they have no chance to explain or rectify the issues you bring up. A formal feedback session at the end of your placement can be a nice way for both you and the organization to get closure and to look towards growth in the future.

If you traveled abroad with a volunteer sending organization or used an online platform, make sure to give feedback to them as well. Don't be afraid to share negative feedback if you have identified areas for real concern, or just have ideas for ways to improve their offerings and make the service more responsible. If your sending organization was great – you feel they made responsible choices and provided you and your hosts with the support you needed – tell them and the world! If, on the other hand, you felt the sending organization lacked in fundamental areas, such as not vetting or preparing the hosting organizations or not providing training or support for volunteers, explain your dissatisfaction to them. If you uncover open corruption in your sending organization, don't stay quiet about it and let bogus or profiteering companies continue recruiting unsuspecting new supporters.

Give yourself enough time

As you come to the end of your time abroad, don't rush the work you are doing to fit into your timeline. The prime time to make mistakes or cause harm is when you hurry an activity that requires a longer timeline to be successful. Tom Benevento, who volunteered in Guatemala suggests that you "focus on the process rather than the successes, and try not to do too much." If you've spent months working on a collaborative process where people feel like they are working together to achieve a goal, your hard work can be unraveled if you press on solo and force an action just to be able to tick it off within your personal timeframe.

It may sound obvious, but not rushing also means leaving enough time to say goodbye to everyone who has been a part of your experience. This may mean starting on your farewell tour long before your final day. Find a way to celebrate the people who have given their time to make you feel welcomed. That might be through making them a card, cooking them a meal, or just stopping by to say thank you and goodbye. Telling someone how much their support meant to you can be one of the kindest gifts you can leave them with.

Don't make promises you can't keep

Leaving a project and community can be emotional. Maybe you feel an urge to repay the kindness you have been shown through future actions, such as fundraising for your host organization, or offering to help your homestay brother get a visa to study in your country. We caution against making promises of things you will do when you get home, as you do not want the main legacy of your time volunteering to be a disappointment if you realize you were being impractical. Although you might be very serious about these commitments, we suggest telling your local friends and host organization you will email them two weeks after getting home, when you will have a more realistic idea of your availability and priorities.

Keep learning and processing

It is important that you take some time out to process your experience while you are still in the country because it is likely that everything will feel different when you land back at home. Ideally, schedule reflection in as part of your regular routine, but if you find yourself coming to the end of your placement and you haven't yet had some time out to reflect on what this experience has meant to you and what you have learned, you certainly won't regret setting aside time for that before you leave. Such reflection can help you clarify goals for your future life. Perhaps you can even write a 'letter to self,' covering the important things about who you are now and what you don't want to forget or lose, to be opened in six months' time when you are back at home in the daily grind.

The End?

You might feel sad, exhausted or excited to be leaving your placement and heading home—or all of the above. Take the time to reflect, rest, and build up your energy for all of the learning, action, and adventures that you have ahead of you. The work has only just begun! You still have the rest of your life to work towards making a positive impact on the world.

ACT

PART SIX:

ACTION RETURNING HOME & THE REST OF YOUR LIFE

"I'm having a little bit of trouble dealing with the wealth that surrounds my community, and having even more trouble imparting my feelings onto others. Peru really opened my eyes to what the majority of the world is about, and thankfully, just when I think I'm falling back into the swing of things at home and might be forgetting some of what I've learned, I see an article about coca and get really excited (enough to ignore the weird looks from my family and realize that there is absolutely no way Peru is ever going to leave me)."

–Nora, who spent six weeks in Peru on a learning
trip with Where There Be Dragons

Coming home from a trip abroad can seem like the closing of a book. A transformative, unique, challenging, and exhilarating experience that lands with a crash into the real world as soon as the airplane touches down. Normal life resumes, and all you have left are dream-like memories.

In fact, the 'normal life' that you may have been anticipating with excitement or dread might not even exist anymore. If you traveled using the learning service philosophy, you will have gained a new cultural lens and different perspectives, which may result in you never seeing the world the same way again. This is an unsettling feeling, but it is also a powerful one. There are ways to channel this experience positively and ensure that you take a learning service approach to the rest of your life. As trite as it may sound, coming home, in many ways, is not the end, but the beginning.

This is, therefore, the most important section of this book. Learning service is a lifelong philosophy, and the beauty is that it can start any time. There are no shortcuts when it comes to solving some of the big issues that our world faces today, but we still passionately believe that each person can make a difference. We dedicate this final section of the book to exploring the things you can do throughout your life, both big and small, that will add up to a powerful positive impact.

16.
TRANSITIONING HOME

Perspective: What I learned About Reverse Culture Shock

By Emily Braucher, ReFresh Communications

Coming home is the inverse of going abroad. When you go abroad, everything outside of you is different: the smell of food, the public transportation system, the clothes that are considered appropriate, the pace of a day. It is all brand new. This calls for a certain arc of adjustment. Typically, coming home is initially exciting, then overwhelming, then eventually it is just daily life. You learn new ways to speak and make friends, new ways to center yourself, and new ways to understand what is happening around you.

But here is what they don't tell you when you are about to return home: when you come home the environment is familiar, but you are now the stranger. A new way of seeing the world has been absorbed into your internal reality, leaving you with a fresh, yet disorienting perspective on this 'familiar place.' Your friends look the same, but they cannot relate to the experiences you just had. Your room looks the same, but now you see the excessiveness of your material possessions. You use the same language, but words like 'poverty,' 'privilege' and 'community' hold different meanings for you.

Another thing that might not be immediately apparent: the experience you just had adjusting to a new culture abroad has perfectly prepared you to adjust to being back at home. You only need to be fully aware of what just happened in order to apply the same lessons going forward. The cultural adjustment (commonly called culture shock) you went through when you traveled abroad is emotionally identical to the transition of coming home (commonly called reverse culture shock). In both cases, you are initially flooded with the excitement of novelty. When you come home, it is truly wonderful to see friends and family again. The homemade pasta your mom makes? Yes, it does taste amazing. Your bed is absurdly comfortable. But like the initial thrill of being in an unfamiliar place, this wears off as the reality of needing to navigate new terrain sets in— and it can be a challenge to every level of your being. During this deep adjustment, you may experience a slump, irritability, aggressiveness, depression, or even rage. It will probably kick in two to three weeks after you have been home. It is normal. More than that—it is predictable.

After years of international travel, I found it comforting to learn the neurological basis for this deep slump. It turns out that these prevalent negative emotions are a side effect of your brain working overtime to understand a new reality. When you adjust to a new environment, whether it is external or internal, you lay down new neural pathways to meet your needs. Your brain is creating new networks to cope with your changing conditions. This complex endeavor leaves less energy available to manage your emotions and your reactions, thus you may experience a period of feeling out of control.

But if you stayed overseas despite facing various challenges, you probably learned two things: firstly, a set of useful coping strategies to help you transition, and secondly, that it was well worth the challenge. In fact, wouldn't you say the challenge is what made the experience so rich? Learning to support yourself in cultural transition is a life-skill that will serve you repeatedly. Life is a string of transitions. The more you work to support yourself consciously in the cultural adjustment process, the more resources you will have on hand in all of life's changes.

Reverse Culture Shock

Re-entry is an important time, and preparing for it is just as important as preparing for your time abroad. You are likely to have confusing, conflicting feelings upon returning home. You may cycle between elation at being back to your 'normal' life among your friends, and depression as you realize a life experience you had been excited about for so long is now over. One moment you may be bouncing off the walls with excess energy, the next you may feel drained and fatigued. Among feelings of helplessness and being overwhelmed may arise a sense of purpose. As intense as these emotional peaks and troughs are, they usually don't last, although you may cycle through them a few times before you begin to feel more settled.

Commonly experienced emotions include boredom, a sense of alienation from your surroundings, and homesickness for your life overseas, even (or especially) if your time abroad was also a difficult experience. It is common upon returning to feel guilt or disgust at the consumer culture, the media, or lavish lifestyles. Many long for the perceived simplicity of life overseas. Guilt can be directed at your own actions and lifestyle before you went overseas, or maybe at the speed at which you settle back in, seemingly forgetting the things you learned abroad. You may even find yourself being critical or quick to judge others for having one-sided views or seeming shallow. Or, you may find that spending time out of your normal context helped you to understand yourself and your values more clearly, and helped crystallize what is truly important to you.

Claire describes experiencing this roller-coaster of thoughts and emotions the first time she came home from Nepal. "I remember getting on the train from the airport to my hometown, marveling at how clean the platforms were, how no one spoke to each other or even made eye contact, and how cold my feet were in the flip-flops I was still wearing. My mom came to meet me at the train station, excited to tell me all the news from the past three months that I had been away. A family friend had bought his wife an expensive watch, but then she lost it and was so upset that he bought her another watch for twice the price. The neighbor's cat was messing up our backyard. I could feel a panic rising up in me—I didn't know how to relate or respond to these stories. What did I do previously? Did these things matter before?

"Things got worse when we stopped at a supermarket on the way home. My mom suggested I get some bread while she got a few other things, and then we'd meet at the checkout. I hadn't been into such an enormous building in three months. It took me several minutes to even find a place that was likely to have bread in it, and when I got there I saw that there was an entire aisle full of different types of packaged bread, as well as a bakery churning out fresh bread. In Nepal, 'bread' was what you made out of flour over the fire. What was the difference between all the different types of bread? Why did we need all this bread? What did my mom even mean when she said 'get some bread?' Which one? How do you choose?

"I found myself standing in the supermarket sobbing, tears dripping onto my freezing, uncovered feet. Was I that incapable of re-navigating my own culture and fulfilling a task that was so simple and normal? I felt despair, but there was also another tiny voice speaking to me at the back of my head, saying, 'You know that you don't need this. This way of living is not a luxury but a burden. You have seen different ways to live; you can make different choices.'

"It wasn't about the cat or the bread or the expensive watch or the way people interacted on the train, it was simply the realization that I could choose whether these things were important in my life or not. I stopped crying, grabbed the nearest loaf of bread and suddenly felt clearer and freer than I had in a long time."

Although we can anticipate reverse culture shock, it doesn't make the feelings less real. Our best advice is to be aware that this may happen, be prepared for them, and try not to be too hard on yourself or others. Don't disregard these emotional reactions as something to 'just get over'—explore them, work through them, find people you can talk about them with, and channel them productively.

Your body may also need time to adjust. Beat jet-lag by getting back into a normal sleeping pattern as soon as possible. Even though you may have been craving fast food for months, eat rich foods in moderation and make an effort to eat healthily. If you have spent a significant period of time abroad, your stomach can have trouble adjusting to the food you are returning to. Volunteer Morgan Canup said, "After being in Namibia for three months, I had a hard time digesting and keeping food down. I was used to chemical-free and unprocessed food. But almost everything in America is processed or has some type of chemical to preserve freshness or enhance taste. The first two weeks were the worst and I actually lost weight." If you continue to feel unwell, you may want to visit a doctor. For instance, Zahara discovered upon coming home from Uganda that she still had malaria, despite having been treated for it.

Two extremes: Settling back in too easily vs. not being able to cope

Having had many experiences with re-entry ourselves, facilitating groups of students through it, and interviewing hundreds of returned volunteers about it, we can extrapolate commonalities and lessons. However, in the same way that people experience moving and adjusting to a new culture differently, people experience re-entry differently too. This is okay. Claire had a breakdown in a supermarket, Daniela was confused at how reliant everyone was on GPS to get around, and Zahara spent a whole year moving from place to place as she processed her five-month experience in Zambia. Don't hold yourself to any expectations or judge your reactions too harshly, but if you find your reactions are extreme or don't fade with time, you may want to ask for more help.

One extreme is to seemingly not experience any reverse culture shock at all and just slip back in to your old life right where you left off. In some ways, it is great that you can settle in easily and be comfortable with yourself in different settings. Maybe this shows how well you have developed cultural adjustment skills. On the other hand, some people embrace everything back home in an attempt to reject difficult learning experiences abroad. If your placement was challenging and you are just glad to be home, you may be actively or subconsciously avoiding thoughts about your life overseas. A risk here is that you are just repressing the reverse culture shock for a later date, or ignoring important learning from your time away. If you find yourself completely settling back in to your old self and old habits and compartmentalizing your experience abroad as something irrelevant to your life at home, look again through a learning service lens. Take some time out to address and process your time abroad, and ask yourself:

- How was my life abroad different from my life at home? How was I different?
- What did I find most surprising, challenging or rewarding about my time abroad? And what is now surprising, challenging or rewarding at home?
- What are the most important things that I learned? Are there any changes in me that have stayed since I got home?
- Are there any further changes in the way I live that I want to incorporate into my life?

Hopefully, you will be able to identify something from your experience that you want to bring forward and apply positively to your future life, while not undermining the great way you are reintegrating. You might find it helpful to write about your experiences, especially if you didn't do this as you went along, as this may help you to process your time abroad and remember it more clearly in the future.

At the other extreme, you might find reintegrating is an exceptionally difficult process. Maybe you are someone who dislikes change and who found transitioning into life abroad problematic too. In this case, it may simply take some extra time for you to adapt to the disruption of your routine. Maybe you feel guilty about leaving or miss the work you were doing overseas. Maybe your experience abroad brought about gradual and imperceptible changes that you see and appreciate only when you are back in your 'normal' context. Some people return from overseas feeling as though they have changed so much that they can never fit back in to their own society. Maybe you feel alienated, unable to relate to anyone or anything, and think the solution is to move back overseas permanently. Or maybe you feel a strong sense of empowerment and determination, and want to reject all aspects of your previous life, for example, by deciding to drop out of school, quit your job, or end a relationship.

These are all understandable reactions and are not unusual, but instead of making rash decisions, take some time to let your emotions settle before making a move. Don't fixate on needing to make one big change, but focus on small changes, such as continuing the yoga practice you learned abroad, or reconnecting with friends you missed. Although it is possible that the big life change you have identified is what you need, there *is* a danger that it is providing a false promise of freedom from difficult emotions that are not so easily quieted. It may be helpful to reach out to others about what you are feeling—talk to friends or family who can offer an external perspective, or to other returned volunteers. You might be surprised how many others find your experience familiar.

Strong emotions upon re-entry are entirely normal and there are often ways to channel them positively. However, if your return home is followed by severe depression, mood swings, or altered perception for several weeks, we advise you to seek professional support.

Thinking and Talking About Your Experiences

It takes time to digest a powerful experience and work out the implications and meaning for your future. Even thinking about your experience abroad might therefore be confusing for some time. Talking about your experience may be even harder. Taylor Huffman, who went on a learning trip with Where There Be Dragons to Thailand and Cambodia, reflected, "It seems to be a common theme that all of us are having trouble conveying our experience to others. I have faced the same problem, but I've realized that I can be content with just holding onto it myself. If they don't understand, then that's fine. Human articulation and linguistic prowess doesn't have the range to explain particular and complex emotions and experiences." Continuing to process your experience is an important part of learning service, so that you can apply what you've learned abroad to your future life.

Reflecting on what you have done and achieved

It may feel hard to reflect on your time abroad, but the worst thing you can do is to box up your experience and stash it in some mental closet. People process things differently, so figure out what works best for you. Some people need time on their own whereas others need to talk it out. Some ideas for this include:

- Writing a reflective journal (or continuing the one you started while you were away)
- Staying in touch with those you knew overseas
- Calling up another volunteer from your time abroad.

We are aware that these are simple tips, but we also know from experience and from the stories of other returned volunteers that if you don't take active steps to continue reflecting on the experience you'll lose the opportunities to extract learning from it. Take stock on how far you have come and celebrate what you have achieved.

Mark Dunn, who volunteered in China, offered this advice, "I would recommend sitting down one day to just write. Get all of your emotions and memories out on paper. Do nothing else that day, except think about how you are feeling and what you have just gone through. I did that and felt much better afterwards… Bask in the enjoyment of returning home for a few days to let your mind settle. Then sit down to write."

If you don't feel like writing, you could make a list or brainstorm of your experiences and observations, the learning you want to record, and the feelings you wish to capture. It doesn't have to be eloquent and no one else needs to read it, but it will help you to process your experience, and you might appreciate the notes later to jog your memory.

Judging and feeling judged

Your time volunteering abroad may have been a powerful learning experience, and you may feel that you have changed for the better because of it. We talked to volunteers who had radically changed their political beliefs or future career plans. It may take a while for friends and family to adjust to the changes they see. Maybe you feel that people you talk to jump to the wrong conclusions or seem to trivialize points that to you are deeply significant. It can be frustrating when everyone around you assumes that you will soon be back to your 'old self.' Try not to see yourself in terms of an old or new self, but as a work in progress that will continue to change throughout your life.

What you have learned abroad might make you question some key tenets of your life at home. Maybe thoughts such as these seem familiar to you, "No one walks here. The store is less than a mile away, and yet we drive. In other parts of the world, people wouldn't be as lazy as we are." Or, "We buy too many things, and everything is wrapped in plastic. Our consumption and greed is causing harm in the world and no one seems to even care!" These expressions may be genuine and heartfelt observations on society, but depending on how you express it and to whom, others might feel that your judgments are directed at them. Check yourself: remember that the world did not stop spinning while you were gone and that your friends and family back home were living their lives and learning things as well. Think carefully about how you present the feelings you are experiencing.

You may also find you have a strong reaction when people say things like, "Oh, you are so lucky! I wish I could do that too!" and be tempted to counter by explaining all the preparation, work, research and money-saving that went into your trip. Although that is certainly true, we would encourage you to look with humility at what makes you lucky in this situation. Think about the ease with which your passport allowed you to cross the borders you needed to cross to arrive at your placement. Or think about the availability of funds (even if you had to save for months) for purchasing an airline ticket, and compare your experiences with those of the people you interacted with abroad. Also, think about the friends and family members who would have loved to travel abroad, but couldn't because of their perceived barriers, or the myriad of reasons that crop up in life – caring duties, financial restrictions – and interfere. If anything, this could be an excellent opportunity for self-reflection and discussion of these issues. If you find the right way to frame the conversation, you might help a friend find that they too can create an opportunity for them to learn and contribute if they put in the work and planning to make it happen.

The bottom line is to be thoughtful about how you present new ideas and perspectives so that others can see you are not trying to act superior, but instead, sincerely grappling with how to mesh your new world views with your previous lifestyle. Try to refrain from 'culture-bashing' (denigrating every aspect of your home culture) and instead make a conscious decision to channel these feelings into constructive action. Take a learning service approach towards your interactions with friends, holding back judgment and being willing to learn from differences of opinion. Above all, be patient with both yourself and others.

Hero worship

Be warned that some people in your circles may start to treat you as a returned hero when you come back from volunteering abroad. Friends and relatives will feel happy to have you back and maybe proud of your courage and the choices you have made. Some may only see the altruistic side of your trip, and they might describe it in ways that make you feel uncomfortable. We call this the 'Mother Teresa complex'—when people put you on a pedestal, talk about the sacrifices you have made, or act like everything you were involved in overseas was your singlehanded achievement. Friends or professional connections may assume that just because you have recently been in a place, or been involved with a cause, that you are now an expert on it. We have met volunteers who were asked to make presentations about the place or issue they were working in for fundraising or education events, or were interviewed on local radio, when they had only spent a few weeks volunteering.

An integral part of learning service is helping people see the more rounded reality. Share what you feel you learned, and by highlighting the roles of other people in the work you did overseas – perhaps an inspirational manager or community leader – you can show others the larger processes that go on without you. If you are honest about what you feel you are still learning, and convey that you have more questions than answers, you can help others see the complexity of development issues. Letting others know that you are not an expert keeps you (and them!) open and motivated to continue exploring.

Sharing your experience

It is crucial to think about *how* to share what you experienced with those around you. Learning service involves educating others to also ask questions and add nuance to their perspectives. This could be just in how you tell stories in casual conversation over dinner, as well as more formally to wider audiences.

Think about concise and meaningful ways to answer the question, "How was your trip?" Be prepared for some people being uninterested in the details and just wanting to know that you had a safe and positive experience. Remember that people at home will not have the same frames of reference as you. See if you can give an answer you are happy with in a few sentences, for example, "I worked with an organization that supports street children in Brazil. It is an extremely complex issue but I learned a lot." Different people will ask different questions and then you can choose how deep you want to take the conversation based on their interests.

You may have a message you want to share with a wider audience. Presenting what you have learned to others can help you further reflect on and solidify your own learning. Furthermore, giving a talk or writing an article can help educate others, which can be a crucial part of your continued service. You could give a presentation at a local community group or festival, develop a workshop for schools, or write for an online publication or blog.

When you are planning to share with a new group, keep in mind the audience you are addressing and make sure the format you choose is appropriate for their needs. Show, not tell. For example, choose an anecdote that exemplifies a meaningful issue or a poignant personal moment from your experience. This can give people a glimpse of your life abroad and even share a lesson without you making the teaching explicit. Ask yourself how to make your presentation accessible, engaging, and interactive. Maybe you want to present some controversial material and then facilitate a discussion, or create a role play where people can represent different interest groups in a scenario. This style of learning can be a lot more powerful and also more fun than a traditional lecture. Additionally, think about what you hope to inspire your audience to do. For example, you can ask them to join a campaign, donate to a cause, or change a behavior in their daily life, such as reducing waste. If you suggest clear next steps, you will be more likely to get people to act on your story, rather than just enjoy it.

Continuing Engagement: Staying Connected With People and Organizations Abroad

Some people find that after spending a period of time abroad they have to establish a balance between building a life in their own country and nurturing links to their 'other home.' Although it is important to stay present in whichever place you are in, it is also healthy to keep those other relationships alive, along with the connections to the interests and passions you acquired. Frankie Rushton volunteered in India for five months with Development in Action, and on her return got actively involved in running the organization in the UK as the committee co-chair. When asked what some of the most positive aspects of her volunteer placement were, she said, "The opportunity to stay involved on my return to the UK allowed for my experience not to simply be a five-month internship but a stepping stone for further professional development, as well as the chance to impact change from the UK."

You may assume, due to distance and the pressures of everyday life, you will naturally lose your connection to people and organizations abroad over time. We have found examples, however, of people who still have close connections to a place decades after they left. All relationships require effort, and there are proactive ways you can stay engaged. Here are some tips for how to do this effectively.

Be realistic
When you first get home from overseas it may seem like nothing is as important to you as the relationships you made or the cause you volunteered for. You may feel like your time at home stretches out before you, endless and empty, and that you will easily be able to prioritize staying involved with your volunteer project. However, you will soon find your life filling up with friends, work, study and other commitments. Some volunteers end up

losing all contact with friends and organizations abroad because they couldn't live up to their own unrealistic expectations.

Continue to monitor and follow up

Learning service emphasizes the importance of thorough research at every stage of your volunteer experience, and this is still important after you have left, especially if you intend to stay involved. Express your interest in receiving updates on the project you were involved in, or receiving evaluation reports and strategic plans. If you volunteered for just a short time it will have been difficult to see the real impact of the organization whilst you were abroad, so receiving updates will give you a sense of progress in the longer-term.

Organizations change, so even if you had a good experience when you volunteered, don't let your confirmation bias get in the way of your assessment of the organization's future work. Stay in touch with at least two different people from the organization so you can be sure you have a more balanced perspective. Try not to burden your ex-colleagues with too many extra tasks—perhaps there is already a donor newsletter or other ways to keep in touch? Or maybe someone would be happy to give you a call occasionally so that you can keep up-to-date on the organization's progress and perhaps find ways to help from abroad.

Continue to volunteer from home

There are several ways you could continue to be involved with your organization from home. If your organization overseas regularly hosts volunteers, being available to answer questions to let potential volunteers know what to expect is one of the most valuable roles that you can play. Tell the organization that you would be happy to be put in touch with potential future volunteers. If you know others who are looking to volunteer, you could even reach out to them directly and recommend your organization. However, don't let your recommendation replace their own process of research—remember that a placement that was a perfect fit for you may not be appropriate for somebody else.

Since you are already familiar with the organization's philosophy and operations, other tasks that you can do from afar might include proofreading documents, fundraising, keeping the website updated, connecting the organization with other marketing, legal, or advisory groups with whom you are already in touch, or improving the organization's social media strategy. Do not take on a role like this lightly, however. Remember that all the pointers from previous sections on volunteering still apply. For example, make sure that you are not taking on more than you can effectively deliver and avoid taking the lead on something that would be more effectively or sustainably led by someone in that country.

Instead of doing it alone, you could work with alumni who have had a similar or shared experience volunteering, by coordinating roles for each of you to take with the organization. Some strong alumni networks even decide to formalize this by creating a 'friends of' organization—although think carefully before setting this up yourself as it is a significant ongoing commitment.

Ruth Taylor, who volunteered in Ghana, reflected on the benefits of sustained involvement, "I remained involved with KickStart back in the UK, by supporting them with publicity and recruitment. It was a way for me to remain attached to that first experience in Ghana that had so inspired me and work alongside people that I felt truly 'got it.'"

Fundraise

Raising funds for the organization you volunteered with overseas is a way that you can have a direct and immediate impact from afar. Many international organizations that take volunteers are dependent on support from outside donations, and you may have much-needed language skills or connections to potential overseas donors. A volunteer who spent three weeks in Cambodia told us, "I now work in international development and have raised thousands of pounds to support an NGO in Cambodia as a result of my volunteering experiences."

A learning service placement abroad is a great opportunity to experience and evaluate work being done on the ground overseas in a way that most of your contacts cannot. A founder of a small children's charity in Nepal commented, "Volunteers often returned to their parent countries and became great supporters of the charity, and without that kind of input this small charity's funding would be severely lacking."

Donating money effectively requires as much research and planning as donating time, if not more—as when there is money involved, the risk of corruption is always higher. Even if you know an organization well, be aware that it may change policies or direction, or that you may find another organization that has a mission that you support even more. Keep up with your research, avoid stubborn loyalty, and ensure that to the best of your knowledge the money you give or help raise is being spent in a way that aligns with what you learned about development best practices.

Remember personal friends

Many volunteers find that they are treated with unparalleled kindness when they are overseas, and if that was your experience, return that kindness when you are back home. One of the easiest forms of service we can do for another person is to show they are not forgotten. Emails, phone calls, letters—whatever you prefer and whatever is most accessible for the receiver. Perhaps you can make a note of the birthdays of all the people you want to stay in contact with, so that at the very least you can send them a special note once a year. Shelia Hu, who volunteered in Vietnam, Morocco and Bolivia, said, "Even after more than two years, the friends I made abroad remain some of my closest."

We cautioned against making promises to your community overseas, but if you did make some, even small ones such as sending back photographs, do what you can to keep them. If there is a problem with keeping the promise, at least acknowledge it and apologize.

The transition home can be a time of great learning and growth, comparable to your time overseas. Although it can be intense, you'll likely feel calmer settle and back into a routine within a short time. On the other hand, you may have only just begun unpacking what the long term impacts of your time abroad could be. The last chapter in this book looks at how you can use what you learned in your time abroad for lifelong learning service.

17.
USING LEARNING SERVICE TO MAKE A LASTING CHANGE

Perspective: It Made Me an Activist

By Gina Colligen, who volunteered in Bolivia for two years

Bolivia is a country that in any given moment is marked by numerous blockades and protests. As a US citizen volunteering abroad, I found these political manifestations to be confusing, inspiring, frustrating, dumb, unfounded, or admirable, depending on the cause (and my current state of mind). Bolivia is also a country inhabited by people who believe in organizing. Living in a small *pueblo*, I became involved in teachers' meetings, community meetings, government meetings, and just plain local gossip about the goings on at the mayor's office. I sat through what felt like endless days sitting in hot offices as people spoke in a language I was still struggling to understand, confused as to my role there and what I might be learning from the experience.

When I returned to the US, I celebrated a return to my old sense of communication and efficiency. However, I quickly realized that I felt a lack. My time in Bolivia taught me more about the importance of citizen participation, and more about democracy and direct action, than anything that I had experienced in the US. In a country where voting is a legal responsibility and voter turnout is almost 100 percent, Bolivia taught me that voting is not enough.

While I might not start blockades in my home country, my time abroad deconstructed the divide that I had always felt between my government and myself. I now push myself to understand government policies more deeply and push to involve myself in local politics. I seek out community organizations and I look for places for my voice to be heard. I know that I am an essential part of my country's democratic processes because of what I experienced as an overwhelmed volunteer abroad trying to make my way through political protests that, at the time, I could barely understand.

Translating to Action

"I really discourage against isolating your volunteer experience to a certain 'event' that happened one time and that was it... I believe that education should not be isolated, and neither should service, but both should be integrated to see how our impact on the world does not just arise from service work, but from all our actions we do in this world."

–A volunteer who went to the Philippines, Costa Rica, and Peru

The vast majority of those returning from an immersion abroad do so feeling inspired and determined to take further action. We encourage you to do this and consider it an integral part of your learning service experience. You may want to shake up your big life decisions or identify small lifestyle changes, either to make you happier or to have a stronger impact on the world (or most likely both, as these are so intertwined!) Maybe you start to see the issues in your own community and the role you can play in them in a new light. Zahara, after volunteering in Zambia for five months, said, "I left Zambia feeling that instead of Americans helping Zambians to develop, Zambia should send people to the United States to help us develop our humanity—a more polite and civilized way of relating to each other as individuals, a more evolved concept of the extended family, and a higher level of integration of spiritual beliefs with day-to-day action."

We spoke to a number of returned volunteers who said that they felt transformed, but who were also nervous about whether they would follow through with their intentions. In the words of one volunteer we interviewed, "I feel like this experience changed me, although I fear for its longevity." Let's start, therefore, by looking at how to translate your intentions into meaningful changes that you can stick to.

Identifying Your Goals

On returning home from a powerful experience, you may feel as if your life will never be the same again. Though strong, these feelings can feel fuzzy and undefined—'something' has changed that makes you want to behave 'differently.' It can be hard to get to the bottom of exactly what this means for your future decisions, quickly leading to frustration.

Many returned volunteers recognize that their current direction isn't leading them towards their future goals. If you realized abroad that you want a career working with young people, your current qualifications in accounting may not be enough. Or maybe you now see more clearly that your stressful high-powered job isn't giving you enough time to connect to family and community. When the dust has settled from your initial return home, if you still want to make some changes, identify ways to integrate new goals on top of your current path. Maybe you can add different courses to your studies, or take on a volunteer position as a mentor outside of work, or cut down on the number of hours you work a week.

Part of the learning service model is to transform these intentions into tangible goals for your future life that you can act on and hold yourself to. Here are some questions you can ask yourself to pinpoint what you learned overseas and apply this to your life going forward.

What did you find impressive about the culture abroad?

Try to identify aspects of your life abroad that you admire and want to emulate. If you were impressed by a tendency to reuse and mend items rather than discarding them, or by cooking your meals from fresh, local ingredients—consider how you can integrate these aspects into your daily life at home. Maybe there is something more symbolic you want to do, such as starting your day with a ten-minute meditation to remind you to live mindfully. A volunteer who went to Japan for over three weeks said, "[The experience] definitely changed me. There were so many ways, but one specific one that stayed with me was seeing how Japanese people put the good of the community before their personal well-being... I was humbled to realize that I've slowly and unwittingly succumbed to the 'me-first' culture. it was a little painful to realise, but it's made me alter my lifestyle." Consider taking some time to make some active commitments to yourself in the first few days after you return, write them down and share them with others to hold you accountable.

What aspects of your home life did you miss when you were away?

If, while you were abroad, there were things you missed, like being around for family events, visiting your local coffee shop, or hiking in the hills near your home, try to find ways to keep that appreciation alive when you get back. Let people know they were missed, go out and experience the places you love, and find ways to remind yourself how privileged you are to be connected to them. That might be continuing to keep a gratitude journal when you are at home that you can refer back to when your routine settles down and life seems more 'boring.' Or maybe you need to set goals for yourself to get out into the hills each month, call your grandmother each week, or write that coffee shop owner a thank-you note.

What parts of your home culture do you want to embrace further, and which ones do you want to break away from?

Spending an extended period of time abroad can give you an appreciation for how transient or changeable aspects of your life at home are, which you might have previously considered as static. Recognizing your culture and traditions as learned behaviors rather than fixed norms gives you the opportunity to examine them more closely. You have a choice—you can keep the ones you love and try to detach yourself from the ones you don't. Do you see a binge-drinking culture at home that you want to challenge? Are there negative attitudes that you used to thrive on that you now view as time wasters? Did you used to have opinions of people or groups that were actually harmful stereotypes that you now want to re-examine? Are there freedoms you enjoy or rights you can exercise that you know others do not have and that you want to celebrate? Make a list and think about how to act on these feelings. Try to capture how you feel now, and why you want to make a change so that you can refresh your memory later.

Sticking to Your Goals

While considering these questions, you might have come up with a list of changes that you want to make to your lifestyle. This is a good start, but as you no doubt have learned by now, good intentions don't lead to good results without some hard work in between! Whether you identified large or small actions you want to take, make a real commitment and ensure you follow through. Here are some tips and tools for sticking to and achieving your goals.

- Write them down. This might seem obvious, but it's worth taking the time to write down the goals that are in your head.
- Make sure your goals are realistic. By asking yourself questions like "How can I make this goal more specific?" or "Does the timing for this goal make sense?" you can create a more realistic path to success. A common framework is to make your goals SMART: Specific, Measurable, Achievable, Relevant (or Realistic) and Time-bound.
- Break down bigger goals into smaller, more achievable parts. If one of your goals is: "Volunteering locally for a cause I believe in," your goal for the week could be

ACT

something like, "Identify at least three organizations in the area that are seeking volunteers." The next week you might set a goal to, "Contact two of the places on the list and ask them to connect me to two current or previous volunteers so I can ask about their experience and impressions of the organization."

- Set yourself a 'North Star.' Your North Star might be a mantra you want to live by or a vision of your life in the future you want to work towards, as a kind of umbrella for your goals. You might want to write it up on your wall and look at it each morning.

- Build a goal-setting club. This is a great way to get external support to hold yourself to your goals. Daniela and Claire were part of a 'Monthly Resolution Club' where each member informed the group of a resolution they had made that month. You might find that sharing your goals with your peers is motivation enough to help you adhere to your commitments.

Staying Engaged as a Life-Long Learner

When you are overseas, everything is new and stimulating so it is easy to see learning opportunities everywhere you turn. The great thing about learning service is that the learning never stops, even when you are back home. However, keeping up that commitment and even recognizing the opportunities to learn once you are back in your daily routine can be difficult. To commit to continued learning, you could keep up with current affairs by watching documentaries or reading newspapers from around the world, or find books that critique development and explore global issues. Alternatively you could sign up for public lectures or conferences, or take an online course. Or you could just explore opportunities that take you out of your comfort zone without leaving your local area, such as going to different cultural events, meeting new people or learning a new skill.

Take a learning service approach to your travels

Traveling can be addictive. Each new trip opens you up to further new places you want to experience and learn about. By traveling with a learning service approach, you can continue to develop skills you need to contribute as an active global citizen throughout your life. You can even adopt these learning tactics when traveling to different areas of your own city. We know of some teachers who organize learning trips right on their students' doorsteps. For example, Professor Darren Grosch organized 'community connecting' trips, taking students to parts of Los Angeles with large immigrant communities. Students were hosted by local Korean and Mexican families to learn about the issues they cared about such as job security and immigration laws.

Anna Lee White, who went on a learning trip in Nepal for three months, found a way to deepen her learning after returning to the US. She explains, "After returning home, I wanted to find a way to continue learning about Nepal and the surrounding Himalayan region. When looking for summer internship opportunities, I found out about a refugee resettlement organization located nearby. I looked at the job descriptions and saw that Nepali language skills were desired for the internship. I soon found out that there was a significant population of refugees from Bhutan living in New Hampshire. I was able to practice my Nepali language skills with the refugees, and I found that my experience traveling in Nepal gave me insight (although to a very different extent) into the culture shock that they underwent upon arrival in the United States."

If, like many who set out on the path of learning service, your trip abroad has motivated you to learn more about the world and how to contribute to it, you may already be considering re-volunteering. Many people ask us if we think it is best to go back to the same country or to try something new. Ultimately, as with all learning, we advise you to follow your passion and interests. If you have been to a place or learned about an issue that touched or excited you, then why not keep up your connections? If you want to broaden your horizons, discover a new place on another learning service journey.

ACT

Daily Choices: Changing the Way You Consume

One of the most commonly-expressed views in our interviews with returned volunteers was that the time they spent overseas resulted in a heightened awareness of how they and others consume back home. Maybe you see people consuming things that are unhealthy for them or just consuming too much. Perhaps when you were abroad you witnessed the effect of some industries on the environment, like extractive mining, or on the people working in them, such as sweatshop labor. Maybe you feel strongly about the huge disparity of wealth in the world. It can be empowering to realize that the choices that you make and encourage others to make every day have an impact on these issues.

One of the fundamental messages of learning service is that small actions count. You do not have to dedicate your life to charity work to make a difference as long as you remain aware of the wider implications of your daily choices and commit to acting mindfully. Many consumers are now taking a more considered approach to the choices they make about the food they eat and the products they buy, as a way of lessening the harmful impacts of a consumer society.

In the same way that we were unable to tell you where to volunteer, we are unable to give you an exhaustive list of brands to buy or avoid. You always have to do research to be sure that your choices align with your values. However, here are some ideas of actions for you to research and consider.

Buy Fair Trade

Fair Trade is an approach that empowers producers to have more of a say in the process of buying and selling, aiming to have lasting impacts on families and communities. Products sourced through Fair Trade processes are not as susceptible to the fluctuations of the worldwide commodity markets, and farmers or factory workers are meant to be paid at a rate that enables them to have a reasonable standard of living. These products are sometimes a little more expensive, but people choose them in an effort to push more of their money further down the supply chain.

With all certification processes, there are complications, so a product doesn't needs to be certified 'Fair Trade' to be ethically sourced, but these types of certifications might help you consider your options when you have a range of unfamiliar products to choose from, so an easy course of action is to look for the Fair Trade label when you are shopping.

You can also delve deeper by finding out about the reputations of the companies you buy from, where the product comes from, and whether those producing it are being treated fairly. Online reports, such as Oxfam's *Behind the Brand* report, can help you compare and contrast producers. There is also a growing range of plugins and apps that help you research and compare brands as you shop.

Eat local or organic produce

Increasing numbers of stores, markets and restaurants are becoming environmentally conscious. Food produced organically can be healthier for both you and fragile ecosystems. Similarly, eating local produce sourced within a limited radius of your home reduces the amount of fuel used from farm to table, and often the amount of packaging involved too. Find out where the food you buy comes from and explore how you can reduce both the pesticide usage and the distances your food has traveled. Maybe there's a farmers' association that delivers vegetable boxes to your door. Alternatively, organic farmers' markets can make shopping a more enjoyable experience, as you can connect to producers and to your community while getting your food for the week. In fact, you may find the experience similar to what you were used to when you were overseas.

Recycle and reduce packaging

Buying items that use recyclable materials or that have minimal packaging is another way to reduce your impact on the environment. Refusing plastic bags, avoiding cosmetics with plastic microbeads and refilling reusable containers all reduce plastic waste. Alternatively, look for products that are in fact recycled themselves—such as when you buy something secondhand in a thrift store.

ACT

There are other considerations that might be important to you, such as whether a product is tested on animals, whether it contains chemicals that can leak into and disrupt ecosystems, or whether it contains rare earth elements that are difficult both to mine and to dispose of. Consider which issues are most important to you and how you might adjust your habits to contribute to that cause.

This ethical approach to consumption is not always straightforward. As with everything in this book, we urge you to apply a learning service approach to your shopping and spend time doing research and make considered choices. If you want to be sure of the impact of every item that you buy, it can cause paralysis, as there are often tensions between the choices you have to make. For example, do you buy the Fair Trade grapes that have been shipped from Chile, or the organic grapes from your own country that have a lot of packaging? The more mainstream 'ethical shopping' has become, the more that clever marketers have realized which words and concepts sell. It may be difficult to see past their 'green wash.'

Questions to ask to research a product

If, upon returning from volunteering, you want to change your consumption patterns and make sure that your money is not supporting practices that go against your values, you can ask questions like:

- Which company makes this product? Sometimes the brand on the packet is a subsidiary of a larger conglomerate that is involved in questionable practices.
- Where has this product been manufactured, and by whom? Manufacturing products may be extremely expensive in your home country, perhaps due to minimum wages or strong legal protection for workers. Many companies exploit the fact that this is not the case overseas and have employees working in unsafe conditions, for long hours, on low pay. Other companies proudly enforce much higher ethical standards and make that part of their brand. Rachel Faller, Founder of Tonlé, a brand committed to ethical clothing production

says, "Buying from responsible brands makes a statement to the industry that we need to value the materials and the labor that went into them."

- What impact does this product have on the environment? You can think about what the product is made from, what processes or chemicals were used to make it, where it was transported from, how much packaging it has, and what happens to that packaging once you dispose of it.
- What alternatives are out there? Sometimes there are ethically-produced versions of the same product. Other times it may be that you would have to alter your habits slightly, for example, by shopping in a different store, not eating fruits out of season, or choosing to pay more for 'green' dry cleaning (or perhaps giving up dry-clean-only clothing altogether).

If this list looks daunting, remember that you don't have to completely transform your habits overnight. Maybe you can set yourself one or two goals such as buying only Fair Trade coffee, not eating meat on Tuesdays, going to the farmer's market every weekend, or finding out which supermarket in your local area has the best track record in supporting human rights and the environment, and see how you get on. These can feel like tiny changes that don't have a large impact, but remember that consumer demand shapes supply. In fact, the only reason corporations have a lot of power is because consumers give it to them, and if we want them to change their practices, we collectively hold that power with our purse strings.

As a final word of consideration, keep in mind that just because something is ethical, doesn't mean you should buy it. The paradox of ethical shopping is the new marketing cry, "Buy this and save the world!" However, what the world (or you yourself) needs most is probably not another tee-shirt or jumbo pack of chocolate-chip cookies, however fairly produced. The most ethical kind of shopping will not just include consuming differently, it will include consuming less. Asking yourself if you *need* something before you buy it could be the most important question you ask.

ACT

Activism and Volunteering

"The anti-apartheid movement in the US and Canada accomplished much more to help the South African people than did any North American volunteering in South Africa. As South Africa rebuilds in the post-apartheid era, we will still need this type of international advocacy. If ten volunteers return home and work to limit the power of the World Bank and World Trade Organization, they will help more South Africans in the long run than a hundred volunteers doing direct service in South Africa."

–Dennis Brutus, former political prisoner, South Africa

Many people's interest in international volunteering is motivated by a desire to create change. Maybe your trip overseas was sparked by an increasing awareness of injustice or poverty, or maybe you only started to delve into these issues when you were overseas. In analyzing the root causes of any issue, you can find links, influences, or stakeholders back in your own country. Maybe a company from your country is involved in mining or deforestation in the place you volunteered, or international trade rules have created an imbalance you feel is unjust. Continuing your learning service after you come home involves exploring these connections, and looking into what action you can take. We are inspired by the words of Jason Hickel, who wrote, "What if the 2.5 million young people that leave Britain's shores each year used their energy and money (billions of pounds, remember) to tackle the ultimate causes of global poverty? To challenge the pathologies of power and imagine new ways of organizing international economics? Another world might be possible after all."

There are many issues affecting the world to get angry about, many causes to get behind, and many new ideas to feel passionate about. There are also many forces in our world with an interest in maintaining the status quo. Global corporations, national governments, and powerful individuals are often benefiting from processes that are exploiting people and the environment. Those with the most power to change things often have the most to lose, and therefore the least motivation to make the changes our world might need. But there is power in numbers, and if there are things you don't like in the world that you want to challenge, or things you do like and want to promote, there are ways to spread these ideas. To make large changes, you usually need a lot of people with you, but don't underestimate the influence that one person can have, particularly by motivating and mobilizing others.

When considering your options, the most obvious solutions (or the ones with the loudest marketing campaigns) may not be the ones with the biggest or best impact. Apply the learning service approach to how you engage in action at home and find groups that are working on the issues in a way that align with your values.

There are a wide range of actions you can take to work toward a change on an issue you care about. Here we offer just a few ideas to get you started.

Campaigning

Campaigns are a way of mobilizing the public to make a change. They generally have two fundamental components: raising awareness about an issue and getting the audience to take an action. An example is Move Your Money, a movement helping consumers understand the ethical implications of how banks invest their money—which can range from the arms trade, to animal testing, to genetically-modified food. Move Your Money has a clear two-part agenda: firstly, to raise awareness about how different banks use your money, and secondly, to get people to move their money to the most ethical options.

Remember to apply the principles of learning service: first do your own research about any campaign you might get involved in. Who has decided which issues it will focus on? Is the campaign based on a nuanced understanding of the situation, of what change is needed, and of how to create that change? Are the people the intervention aims to benefit involved in planning and making decisions about the direction of the campaign, and do they have a platform to make their voices heard?

Lobbying

Lobbying is advocating for a specific change at the government level and raising your voice in the political system. In many democracies, your elected representatives are obligated to listen to you and respond to your questions. Many of the big lobbyists work for large corporations with a lot of money backing them, but when many individuals are mobilized to demand a change, it becomes difficult for politicians to ignore you. After all, elected officials need votes to stay in power. Keep an eye on political developments and what bills or laws are being debated or voted on. You can influence government decisions by signing or starting an online petition, emailing your elected representative and asking them to vote in a certain way, or writing an open letter to be published in a newspaper.

If the issue is more in the domain of governments overseas, you can still take similar action. Although you do not vote for politicians in other countries, they are likely to still be extremely concerned about their international public image. You could also lobby your own government to raise the issue with the government in question through diplomatic channels.

Alternatively, if there is a party in your country that you feel represents your views (and you might have to do research to find that out), get involved! Go to a meeting, help with the campaign, or give your input to help steer the direction of the party. Politics needs people who have a genuine commitment to doing good in the world, who can listen, learn, and show humility, not just those with an interest in gaining power. Maybe you even want to set a goal to run for election one day!

Boycott or carrotmob

A boycott is when you avoid buying products from a certain company or country to create pressure for change. You may have had firsthand exposure to how a certain international company is causing harm in a country you visited. Returned volunteers have voiced concern related to large agricultural businesses displacing local farmers, companies causing pollution or dumping waste in impoverished areas, or factories paying unfair wages and subduing local protests through violence. There are ongoing boycotts organized by different activist groups that you can find out about or you can work to start one.

Alternatively, a carrotmob flips the notion of a boycott on its head. Instead of protesting bad behavior, it rewards and incentivizes positive behavior—for example a decision to not source products from the rainforest, or a ban on plastic bags. The 'carrot' incentive is the 'mob' of people who purchase something at one set time and therefore boost sales. Carrotmob organizers might work with a local business to encourage them to change a certain policy and incentivize them to do so by organizing a mob of shoppers to make purchases on the day of the new policy's launch.

Protest and direct action

If you feel that your voice hasn't been or won't be heard through other channels, you can join or start a protest. Usually this takes the form of a demonstration in a public place, drawing attention to an issue, or showing solidarity for a cause. The location is usually chosen to have a maximum impact on the people you want to listen to you—for example, in front of government buildings or a certain country's embassy, or outside a business conference. Mobilizing a lot of people, and retaining a calm and peaceful atmosphere can help you gain support and be listened to.

Taking direct action means physically trying to prevent something from happening that you don't think is good for the world. This is usually the last resort, either when everything else has failed or when time has run out. People who have resorted to these efforts have taken actions that range from creating a human blockade or occupying a building, to acts of sabotage. A strategic use of social media can bring your cause into the spotlight. Many forms of direct action are illegal, so be extremely careful when considering getting involved—know your issue, your rights, and the probable consequences. Rather than attempting it alone, you might want to consider joining a well-funded and respected activist group with good legal protection, such as Greenpeace.

ACT

Volunteer locally

If learning service is in your blood, you may feel that you want to bring the volunteer spirit with you into your future life. When volunteering in your local area, you are less likely to have problems with cross-cultural communication, and it is usually easier to see your impact and follow up. As well as full-time volunteer opportunities, volunteering close to home can allow you to offer a few hours a week around a full-time job, study program, or other life commitment. You can even volunteer from your own home, through online platforms that connect skilled volunteers with micro tasks or longer-term commitments. Furthermore, many organizations have training programs or continuous learning opportunities for volunteers while they serve.

Education

Education is an important tactic in getting more people to understand an issue, but it differs from most of the examples here in that it is about providing more information, but doesn't promote a specific action or change. It may leave the audience with more questions than answers and allow them make up their own minds. In the long run, this can be the most powerful form of social transformation, as once individuals have had access to all the information they need to reach their own conclusions, they are likely to feel more strongly about an issue than if they had been told how to feel. This option fits much better with the philosophy of learning service. It is, however, much slower than other options and therefore can feel frustrating for people who want to be given a simple answer!

You may be interested in finding a way to get involved with global citizenship education. This is about helping people to learn about the world around them and particularly about issues of poverty and injustice, in a nuanced way. Some organizations will train you to deliver workshops in schools or communities or to engage the public on these issues in other ways.

Career Choices

"As a result of this trip I have pursued postgraduate studies in occupational therapy back in my home country (Canada). It is now my dream to return to Cambodia and help adults with upper extremity injuries or children with disabilities by enabling them to become engaged in occupations they find meaningful such as activities of self-care, leisure and productivity."

—Volunteer who went on a learning trip to Cambodia

If you have been inspired by your learning service experience, you may decide that 'doing good in the world' will be less of a hobby and more a full-time occupation. Getting involved in long-term action may sound exciting and invigorating to some of you, and daunting and stressful to others. But, as with overseas volunteering, you do not need to be directly saving the lives of sick children in order to be doing something needed and useful. If you are committed to living in a way that will be of benefit both to yourself and others, you can plan your big and small life decisions around that—including your career.

Many returnees say that one of the biggest impacts of their overseas experience is that it has crystallized, influenced, or altered their future career paths. Laura Wedeen, who volunteered in Haiti for three weeks, reflects, "My experience abroad gave me life direction and pointed me towards a career that's offered tremendous fulfillment and a sense of purpose for over 25 years."

Some volunteers realize that they would like to work in international development. Heidi Machnee, who volunteered in Bangladesh for five months, reports, "It's made me consider making aid work a consistent part of my life. I've applied to work with the Canadian Red Cross, am learning French, and have begun reading a list of books that help one make informed choices when choosing an organization to work with." Alternatively, you may have dreamed about working in international development for years, but after a few months volunteering, decide it is not for you. Thankfully, learning what you don't want to do in the future is an important step in identifying what you do want to do!

ACT

Sometimes experiencing areas that lack basic services, such as hospitals or schools, brings a new-found appreciation for these professions in your own country, and some volunteers return home to study teaching or medicine. Simply having time and space away from the pressures and expectations of normal life can enable new seeds of career ideas to be planted and provide ripe conditions for them to flourish. We talked to a student who went abroad to learn about organic farming and decided his life calling was to work with children, and someone who went to Myanmar to support an engineering project and returned home to become a teacher of Buddhism.

If, when you were abroad, you decided that you wanted to have a career that is both fulfilling for you and has a positive impact on the world, there are many paths to look into. We urge you to take a learning service approach to these decisions—just like with volunteer travel, certain careers paths or job roles might market their social impact, but don't take those claims at face value. Here are some areas you might want to consider and research further if they appeal to you.

Follow your passions

"My friends and family in the US sometimes have a hard time with the changes in my perspective; they think I'm 'floundering' or 'unsatisfied' because I have been in so many countries volunteering or working for low-paying NGO jobs, instead of starting a long-term career on Wall Street. But I love what I do, I met a man that I want to spend the rest of my life with, and making a lot of money just isn't a priority for me. I'd say I'm much more successful than I ever thought I'd be in school (I always figured I could make money but never thought my life could possibly be this interesting), but my standards for success are very different than they were before."

–A volunteer who went to Haiti, Indonesia and India

Almost any skill, qualification, or interest can be used for a positive impact career. There is no point in working for a nonprofit, becoming a doctor, or going into teaching because this is what you think you 'should' do. The last thing any of these professions need are people who are martyr-like, uncommitted, or resentful because they always wanted to be a chef but felt they 'should' work in development. The fact is the world is made up of diverse people doing diverse things, and that diversity is both valuable and necessary. If you have a commitment to do good in the world, work out how your passions can help you achieve that.

Working abroad vs. working at home

Many people going overseas for the first time are shocked by the poverty or human rights violations that they see and compare it unfavorably to the relative affluence and freedom at home. Although you recognize that there are problems at home, in your mind they pale in comparison to the magnitudes of the problems you see elsewhere. Alternatively, your time abroad might have given you the perspective that there are many ways to rank which problems are 'worse' than others and, on returning home, you might be shocked to notice the problems of institutional care for the elderly, over-consumption, high divorce rates, the prevalence of mental health issues, teenage pregnancy, drug addiction, firearm ownership, or binge-drinking and realize that those issues might seem 'worse' to a subsistence farmer living with his extended family.

If there is a particular issue that motivates you, invest time learning about the landscape of current solutions and what changes are still needed to address the issue. In her report *Tackling Heropreneurship*, Daniela released a tool called the Impact Gaps Canvas, which provides guiding questions to help you do just that: map out and understand a problem, the landscape of current solutions, and the gaps that need to be filled in order to create greater change. By using a tool like that, you can consider what is missing—which might be the direct delivery of a service, a change in government policy, a change in attitudes or behaviors across a population, or a combination of these or other interventions. You can then see how you might plug into that ecosystem of change. Even for issues that mainly affect communities overseas, you can probably find several organizations in your home country looking for people to work in awareness-raising, fundraising, or advocacy for those issues.

This work can have an impact in countries and communities around the world that you have never visited.

In fact, as you probably learned from time spent volunteering overseas, the impact that you can have working in a foreign culture can seem frustratingly tiny. Although you can certainly find important roles to fill in any country, the power you have to leverage change may actually be in your networks at home, your access to voters, consumers, and marketing channels, and your ability to use your qualifications and experience to get an influential job.

As with volunteering, asking questions (such as where your skills fit best, what you are most interested in learning about, and what your passions are) might help you decide on whether you are better off working at home or abroad. A vital consideration is where you would likely be most happy, and therefore most able to contribute effectively.

Working for NGOs at home and abroad

Working for an NGO is a career choice that is commonly explored by returned volunteers, especially those who learned more about development work during their time abroad. NGOs vary in mission, size, levels of professionalism, levels of impact, and methods through which they seek to create change, so as with all aspects of learning service, you need to do your research so you can be sure what they do aligns with your values and skills.

If volunteering abroad lit your fire, you may be inspired to do similar work in the same or other countries in your future career. Just like in an unpaid volunteer role, a paid job overseas is equally at risk of creating dependency or shifting power dynamics, so ask the organization for a clear case as to why they want a foreigner in that role. Many paid roles for foreign nationals are office-based and may include tasks such as fundraising, strategic management, and monitoring and evaluation. If these kinds of roles sound interesting, you have the relevant skills and experience, and you want to commit to an extended period overseas, this could be an option for you. If the organization is doing good work on the ground, your role could be vital support for achieving their development goals.

Alternatively, you may be drawn to social impact work in your own country. Nonprofits may work on local or global issues, directly provide a service or work in advocacy or education, and have positions available that span almost every skillset imaginable, from accountant to professional dancer. That said, office roles, such as fundraising, are still more common.

"My initial reaction was to return to my home country and help tackle UK poverty issues, rather than trying to 'intervene' in somebody else's country", says Katie Boswell, who volunteered in India for five months. "I moved to London and worked on policy and research issues for a few years. More recently, I ended up moving to California and found an international development organization that is much more aligned with my values of respecting local people's knowledge and supporting community-led initiatives, so I have moved back into the international development sector."

Working for a social enterprise
Social enterprises can also offer a chance to do an interesting job for a cause you believe in. You can find roles with organizations ranging from tiny grassroots start-ups to large international businesses. If you have an idea for your own social enterprise, there may be research grants, loans and investments, and free training available. You can solve a problem, do something you love, do it in a way that is good for people and the planet, and have self-generating income (which is more sustainable than a nonprofit relying on fundraising) However, the same rules apply: if you plan for your work to be of benefit to a certain group, you still need to involve them and do careful monitoring, as you would for a nonprofit.

Working for large aid agencies or philanthropic foundations
Aid agencies include government bodies (such as USAID or the UK's DFID), multilateral organizations like the European Commission, UN subsidiaries, and even international institutions such as the World Bank. Large philanthropic foundations include the Bill and Melinda Gates Foundation or the Chan Zuckerberg Initiative. These bodies often fund the work of local and international NGOs, and have offices and programs throughout

the world. Work with these organizations is high-level and usually requires considerable qualifications and experience. It is not an option that is for everyone, with many people questioning the political motivations of how aid is given. Before you devote the next few years building up your résumé with an aim to get this kind of position, read up about the agency, the work they do, their successes and failures, criticisms, and long-term impact. Some of the policies of these agencies may have effects that by your definition are unhelpful or damaging. You also might want to examine your own motivations for wanting this kind of job and be sure it fits with your values and requirements. On the other hand, your experience volunteering overseas may have influenced your perspectives and built empathy for people on the ground that people with desk jobs in those agencies may be sorely lacking.

Rachel Cooke, who volunteered in Thailand for over a year, found that volunteering with the Peace Corps, "opened opportunities for federal government employment, and free graduate school credit. So after going to grad school, I worked at the EPA, NASA and finally the State Department, where I'm now a Foreign Service Officer—working on big-picture policy and with regular people around the world every day."

A career that helps people
Volunteering abroad motivates some people to change or re-focus their careers towards a role they believe in—becoming doctors, lawyers, engineers, architects, or other specialist professionals. Some are motivated to cultivate a skill that can be put to good use everywhere in the world. After volunteering for a year in Cambodia, Rachael Wölffel said, "I have now changed my career plan to become a primary school teacher."

Doctors are needed in refugee camps, engineers can help to solve water problems, and lawyers can combat human rights violations and, unfortunately, these issues are prevalent around the world. Having a professional skill can give you flexibility in terms of where you live and how you contribute, but you have to be truly sure that it is a job that you want to do and will be happy doing, as you have to dedicate years of your life to gaining the qualifications you need.

Something else you could consider is gaining a language teaching qualification, as in our globalized world English is a sought-after skill in almost every community and country. There is also a demand for other languages such as French and Spanish, and now increasingly Arabic and Chinese. Make sure you do research about whom and where you will be teaching and think through whether you will be contributing to a change that you want to see.

Remember that learning service is about making choices that impact positively on others and also fit with your values, so staying in your home area and taking on a role such as teacher, nurse, or caregiver is just as (or more) valuable than anything you choose to take on overseas. These careers are always in need of people who can bring enthusiasm and dedication to the role. Although not necessarily accorded high status or large monetary rewards, they are deeply-valued societal roles. Don't underestimate the profound impact you can have. You might remember an inspiring teacher who made you look differently at the world or a healthcare professional who calmed your fears and made you smile when you were sick. Some people worry that in a direct service position they are not having a great enough impact on enough people the world, but the strong ripple effect of a role model can provide inspiration to thousands and help motivate others.

Making change from the inside

If you are committed to making the world a better place, one option is to join any kind of profession or company and commit to changing it for the better. Large institutions, governments, and corporations have a lot of power, and a small change in policy can therefore have a large impact. This technique is sometimes referred to as *intrapreneurship,* and there are an increasing number of training courses and programs specifically designed to help people who want to create change from within existing organizations. As Nicko Gladstone, who volunteered in Guatemala, India, and Argentina, says, "I had thought I wanted to become an activist, but after finally hitting on the obvious point that activists can only try to persuade power, I've decided that holding the levers of government policy is a more potent tool to create change."

On the other hand, keep in mind that working in a large organization with a lot of entrenched ways of doing things requires patience if you want to create change. You may have to accept that much of your job will *not* be creating change (as this may get you fired!) but will instead be toeing the line. It may take you a long time before you gain the trust and influence required to shake things up. As with many career paths, there is a danger of becoming jaded and losing your idealism, so if you choose such a long-haul option be sure that your motivation to create change has staying power!

Starting Your Own Organization

It's not uncommon for a visionary volunteer who had a successful experience overseas to want to continue doing similar work by starting their own nonprofit. Either abroad or at home, if you see a need in a community you may want to start something new to fill that need. For example, a volunteer teacher in a remote area overseas may see that many children were not going to school and know that his friends at home would happily donate money for the cause. Or perhaps he gets offered a management role in the school and takes on responsibility for raising money, training, and supervising staff. Taking matters into your own hands and starting an organization might seem like a simple next step, but unfortunately, it's not that simple.

Randy Bollig, who volunteered in Nepal for three weeks, reflects, "Based on my initial volunteer experience, I started a project to help children in Nepal. I feel it would not be possible to turn back now, and feel we are doing some good, and basically headed in the right direction. But feel too, that I went in with somewhat reckless enthusiasm, and am becoming increasingly aware of the need to first learn more about the country, culture, situation, and people, before actually going in and trying to do anything to help." Anna McKeon, who volunteered in Kenya for over a month, also shared, "My volunteer experience made me realize that I had been very naïve, short-sighted, and irresponsible in how I chose to undertake a move into the nonprofit sector. It taught me how not to run an organization."

All the authors of this book have had experience starting organizations, and after experiencing many of the challenges and making many mistakes, our strong advice is not to jump in. The learning service approach can also be a helpful framework to apply to this context. Especially if you are not from the place where you want to work, do not speak the local language fluently, or do not have the necessary qualifications or experience, take the time to investigate and question before taking action that is reflective and humble. Here are several questions to ask yourself if you are considering starting or taking over an organization:

What is the need to be filled?

Take some time to work out where the problem stems from and the gaps in current approaches to a solution. Does the solution you propose address a root cause, so that eventually the services of the organization will no longer be needed? Is the gap you are trying to fill one that is traditionally expected to be filled by governments, and would advocacy to enhance government service provision and accountability to citizens be a more sustainable option? Being clear about what the need is can help you see if a new organization is necessary.

What else has been done to address this issue?

There are very few new social problems, which someone hasn't already tried to ameliorate in some other location or some other way. Perhaps something similar to your idea was tried in the past. See if you can find out what has worked, what hasn't, and what holes others can find in your plans. As you will know from your experiences volunteering, what seem to be the simplest or most obvious solutions may not be have the desired impact or be sustainable. For example, in Cambodia, the authors have seen firsthand instances where well-meaning foreigners are so moved by the plight of street children that they have taken them into their house, and without any learning or planning, they 'accidentally' founded a new orphanage.

Who else is involved?

List all the stakeholders of the proposed project, everyone from local government, to the intended beneficiaries, to other organizations working on the same issue. Have you talked with them? What are other informed people's perspectives on the issue and the reasons it is not already being addressed? No problem is usually solved by any one organization, so understanding the landscape of change that already exists can help you understand where the levers of change lie. Find out if there are other organizations filling a similar need that you could support or learn from. Have you already learned about their growth plans and found out that they do not plan to meet the needs you want to address? Have you explored if there is an opportunity to team up, to utilize their experience in the issue, rather than head out on your own?

From our experience, many foreign volunteers that start their own organization walk away after just a few years, which often results in the organization collapsing. The amount of time and money that was used, and the expectations that were created by that person often could have been put to much better use if the founder had been willing to partner with, or work for, an existing organization rather than splitting resources and creating another structure that competes for funds and influence.

How much time do you have?

Most social problems are not solvable in any short amount of time, and most fledging organizations cannot survive without heavy input from the founder for many years. Are you prepared to commit the next decade of your life to supporting this project? Think carefully about the other dreams and plans would you have to give up or put on hold. All of us authors have started organizations and, years down the line, found ourselves tied to work we had never initially intended to be involved in for so long. While the creating part might seem exciting, sustaining an organization to create a lasting impact is a stage most founders never reach.

Are you the best person to run the organization?

Think about how your ego may be playing into your decision to found something new. Organizations don't just need visionary leaders. They need accountants to keep their finances in check. They need monitoring and evaluation experts to help enterprises keep true to their social impact goals. They need skilled agriculturalists, community mobilizers, teachers, and other technical experts to deliver programs. They need marketing teams, human resource managers, and web designers. Some people who love teaching, nursing, or training think they would love running a school, hospital, or organization. But running an organization requires a very different skillset, and starting an organization of any kind in any place takes a full-time concerted effort. If everyone tried to be an entrepreneur, we'd have a lot of egos running around with billboards about their ideas, but little impact on the ground to show for it. Before deciding if you want to be an entrepreneur, go work for one, or for a more established organization, and build a better understanding of where your skills, risk tolerance, and experience might fit in an organization.

Even if you are entrepreneurial, a skilled leader, and knowledgeable in the subject matter, you still need to ask if *you* are the best person to lead this initiative. This question is especially relevant if the organization is in a foreign country where you don't intend to spend the rest of your life. All too often NGOs are started by affluent and well-connected foreigners as they are the ones who have the most access to resources. Instead of starting something and then needing to find someone to carry out *your* vision, why not find a local person who has their *own* vision for the future of their community, and offer your resources and contacts to make their vision a reality? Of course, many of these same questions apply to a local founder too, so make sure they have enough time to commit to the cause, and that they have the knowledge and experience to make informed decisions before offering your support.

Is this the best place for this organization?

Many organizations are products of chance—if you are familiar with a place and experience certain problems there, you may want to start an organization to address the need you see. But what if that issue is more pressing in another community that foreigners rarely visit? In Nepal, villages situated along trekking routes tend to have more development projects, as their needs are more visible. Do assessments and try to separate your plans for a project from your personal relationships with a community.

Do you understand the technicalities and legal context?

There is nothing like paperwork and bureaucracy to make otherwise well-laid plans grind to a halt. The legalities of starting an organization in any country are on a sliding scale between straightforward to near impossible! Starting a new organization can attract a great deal of attention, some of it unwanted, as officials and authority figures can start looking into creaming off some of the money they are sure is on its way. Research the process first, as there are restrictions on what kind of organizations can be established and how they are allowed to function—especially if you are a foreigner.

Being an entrepreneur is not for everyone, despite the media frenzy around 'heropreneurship' that places those who start their own initiatives on a pedestal, overlooking those who build on what already exists. Not everyone should or can be an entrepreneur, and especially not in a foreign culture where naïve but well-intentioned entrepreneurial efforts can seem more like a playground for NGO experimentation than structured development planning. Daniela's reflection at the beginning of this book is an example of that: her advice to herself, if she went back in time, would be to not have jumped in to start an organization but first to have worked for another organization to gain experience.

The Learning Service Approach to Life

Many volunteers find that their experience abroad was a springboard onto a new path that they could never have foreseen. Hopefully, you now can see that the philosophy of learning service is not only applicable to volunteer travel, but to many other decisions you make in your life. We have ended by describing some common ways that volunteers go on to take future action; but to know if that decision is right for you, is to apply the learning service loop of learning and action. Everything from your future career path to interacting with others on a daily basis can be part of the continued impact you have on the world, and your actions are part of a larger ecosystem of millions of inspiring people working towards – and achieving – positive change.

ACT

PARTING WORDS

"You get a strange feeling when you're about to leave a place, I told him, like you'll not only miss the people you love but you'll miss the person you are now at this time and place, because you'll never be this way ever again."
— Azar Nafisi, *Reading Lolita in Tehran*

At the close of this book, we wish to take you back to the beginning, imitating the loop of the vajra itself. The vajra is a symbol of the eternal cycle and balance between learning and action. Learning comes *first* but doesn't stop. Once you have learned all you can about a problem at a given time, you can create meaning by putting that learning into action. Humble, mindful, self-reflective action is the best way to continue learning, to peel back the next layer of the onion, and find out what you want to learn next, which will in turn lead to more thoughtful action.

We offer learning service not just as an approach to volunteer travel, but as an approach to life. Embracing learning service requires a paradigm shift, from short-term quick fixes to learning how to contribute to real and lasting change. Whether through volunteer travel or any other path, contributing to positive change is complex, and hardly ever clear-cut. In providing a philosophy instead of a step-by-step guide, we hope this tool will help you navigate the messy reality of our world. In that sense, we have never claimed to have all the answers. However, by starting these conversations and creating a movement of informed critical thinkers we trust that you all will uncover more of them. We want to continue these discussions, to widen them to include your voice, and to continue to improve them based on our collective experience.

We end with our final call to action for all thoughtful readers of this book: stay engaged. We're excited to send you off on your journey into making a better world, and can't wait to see how you shape the world through learning service! We will update our website and social media sites with extra tools and further reflections, and encourage you to learn and share with us to drive the conversation forward. We hope to provide a forum for all our readers to:

- Embrace challenges as opportunities, and find a way to learn and grow through each one
- Be honest in our failures so as not to repeat them, and humble in success so others can build on learning
- Talk with and involve others—especially those you aim to help serve.

As a volunteer you will realize it is only by weaving together many individual journeys that a vision of change can emerge. Thank you for joining the international community of people making the world a better place through learning and service.

FURTHER READING

The vast majority of volunteer travel opportunities operate within the broad field of international development; that is, volunteers from 'richer' or 'developed' nations providing assistance to the 'poorer' or 'underdeveloped.'

If you are interested in exploring this vast topic further, there is no shortage of books on the matter. In fact, it is so hotly debated that it is difficult to find two development theorists who agree with each other about either the nature of the problem to be tackled or the potential solutions. To truly explore all these arguments would take another book – or ten! – and we still wouldn't be close to finding satisfactory answers. We strongly recommend, however, that anyone considering international volunteering should start thinking critically about development. Take the time to locate yourself, your values, and your actions within this broader theory and context. Here are some popular and controversial books that look at this topic in detail and depth (in order of publication date).

Rural Development: Putting the Last First (Robert Chambers, 1983)
Based on the author's experiences of grassroots development all over the world, this book introduces the concept of 'participation': how to involve the beneficiaries of aid programs in the decision-making process rather than treat them as passive recipients.

The Anti-Politics Machine: 'Development,' Depoliticization and Bureaucratic Power in Lesotho (James Ferguson, 1990)
A accessible academic work on a rural development program in Lesotho in the late 70s and early 80s. One of the first sustained attempts to unpick the idea of 'development', it shows how development projects that have failed to meet their original objectives are often redefined as 'successes' anyway. In this process, 'development' becomes a way of expanding bureaucratic influence, to the detriment of other, more important, development needs.

The Development Dictionary: A Guide to Knowledge as Power (Ed. Wolfgang Sachs, 1991)

This is a collection of essays defining, contextualizing and often destroying many of the terms and concepts commonly used by development theorists, such as 'aid,' 'helping,' and 'markets.'

Encountering Development: The Making and Unmaking of the Third World (Arturo Escobar, 1995)

A seminal work in development studies and hugely influential since its original publication. Escobar argues that the post-WW2 shift to 'development' actually just recreated the systems of control that had existed in the colonial era and did little to tackle the underlying problems of poverty and inequality. A revised edition was published in 2011.

Guns, Germs and Steel: The Fates of Human Societies (Jared Diamond, 1999)

This book looks back into prehistory for the roots of current development inequality and disparity, exploring how agriculture spread through continents. It looks at how established agricultural societies were able to stockpile resources and power and eventually use these to overthrow other forms of society.

Development as Freedom (Amartya Sen, 2000)

This book argues that the key element to ensuring a minimum standard of living is freedom. The current world, Sen argues, denies basic freedoms to a large portion of society, which if it were granted, would allow a greater sense of social accountability.

The White Man's Burden: Why the West's Efforts to Aid the Rest Have Done So Much Ill and So Little Good (William Easterly, 2006)

This book outlines the failures of current models of international aid. It argues that whilst grandiose top-down plans sound appealing, they often fail to have the impact intended. Instead of 'planning' solutions from the top down (increasing supply), he suggests 'searching' for them from the bottom up (increasing demand).

The Bottom Billion: Why the Poorest Countries are Failing and What Can Be Done About It (Paul Collier, 2007)

This book identifies a group of small nations, collectively home to a billion people, which are experiencing decline instead of progress. Collier argues that corrupt leadership, civil war and an over-dependence on natural resources are all contributing factors; that traditional models of aid do not work; and that more far-reaching plans are necessary.

From Poverty to Power: How Active Citizens and Effective States Can Change the World (Duncan Green, 2008)

Green argues that the current generation has both a great responsibility and a great opportunity to radically redistribute power, opportunities and assets in order to address the great tragedies of poverty and inequality, in the wake of a changing climate. It calls for action from individuals, groups and governments.

Dead Aid: Why Aid is Not Working and How There is a Better Way for Africa (Dambisa Moyo 2009)

As an African author, Moyo writes about how the billions of dollars sent in aid to her continent have not achieved the results intended. Instead of decreasing poverty and suffering, international aid can be linked to a growth of corruption, increased dependency on outside support and escalating poverty rates. She calls for a new model of economic growth in Africa.

Poor Economics: A Radical Rethinking of the Way to Fight Global Poverty (Abhijit Banerjee & Esther Duflo, 2009)

Drawn to the great ideological differences in the thinking of development economists, the authors use randomized control trials in a range of countries to test out theory in practice. They focus on the priorities and behavior of 'the poor' and conclude that answers are rarely as neat as economist's models predict.

World Hunger: Ten Myths (Updated) (Frances Moore Lappé and Joseph Collins, 2015)

Driven by the question, "Why hunger despite an abundance of food?" the authors refute the myths that prevent us from addressing the root causes of hunger across the globe. This book draws on extensive new research to offer fresh insights about tough questions, from climate change and population growth to genetically-modified organisms and the role of US foreign aid.

ENDNOTES

Introduction

"Resham phiriri, resham phiriri..."
A folk song that translates as "silk scarf blowing in the breeze."

The number of visitors to Cambodia
Ministry of Tourism, *Tourism Statistics Report*, April 2014, www.tourismcambodia.com/ftp/Cambodia_Tourism_Statistic_Apr_2014.pdf.

According to a study commissioned by the United Nations
Ministry of Social Affairs, Veterans, and Youth Rehabilitation, *With the Best Intentions: A Study of Attitudes Towards Residential Care in Cambodia*, Phnom Penh, 2011.

More than three quarters of the children
Ministry of Social Affairs, Veterans and Youth Rehabilitation, *Alternative Care Report*, 2007, www.unicef.org/eapro/OVC_Situation_Assess_June_2008.pdf.

Despite the growing movement
Go Overseas, *2014 Official Volunteer Abroad Trends Report*, www.gooverseas.com/industry-trends/annual-volunteer-abroad-report.

Then an actual movie was made
Daniela Kon, *Changing the World on Vacation*, 2009.

Mickey, who awed our trip participants
"Karaoke Videos Teach Safe Water Techniques," January 2009 www.npr.org/templates/story/story.php?storyId=99898898
"Meeting Mickey," 21 July 2012; www.youtube.com/watch?v=jZBcr8sCGWc.

I also teamed up with some experienced childcare experts
Orphanges.no, www.orphanages.no.

The original plan was to publish an updated version
Joseph Collins, Stefano DeZerega, Zahara Heckscher, *How to Live Your Dream of Volunteering Overseas*, 2002, New York: Penguin Books.

One study found that 55 percent...
Lark Gould, "Travel as the New Philanthropy," Travel-Intel Newsletter, 1 October 2015, www.tours.com/travel-intel/travel-as-philanthropy.

As many as 10 million volunteers a year are spending up to...
Gabriel Popham, "Boom in 'Voluntourism' Sparks Concerns over whether the Industry Is Doing Good," *Reuters News*, 29 June 2015, www.reuters.com/article/us-travel-volunteers-charities-idUSKCN0P91AX20150629.

Claire's article in The Guardian
Claire Bennett, "Don't Rush to Nepal to Help. Read This First," *The Guardian*, 27 April 2015, www.theguardian.com/commentisfree/2015/apr/27/earthquake-nepal-dont-rush-help-volunteers-aid.

'Gap yah' entered popular lexicon
VMProductions, "Gap Yah," YouTube, 24 February 2010, www.youtube.com/watch?v=eKFjWR7X5dU.

A spoof of the popular program
SAIH Norway, "Who Wants to Be a Volunteer," YouTube, 7 November 2014, www.youtube.com/watch?v=ymcflrj_rRc.

J.K. Rowling, of Harry Potter fame
Lisette Mejia, "In 13 Epic Tweets, J.K. Rowling Shut Down People Who Think 'Voluntourism' Is a Good Thing" *POPSugar*, 22 August, 2016, www.popsugar.com/news/JK-Rowling-Talks-About-Why-Voluntourism-Bad-Twitter-4226249.

In addition, we had access to studies...
Erin Barnhardt, "Engaging Global Service: Organizational Motivations for and Perceived Benefits of Hosting International Volunteer," Portland State University Dissertations, 2012, pdxscholar.library.pdx.edu/open_access_etds/372/. In her research, Erin Barnhardt made the names of the respondents anonymous to enhance the likelihood of honest responses and decrease the possibility that anyone would suffer retribution for sharing their perspectives. Our own surveys also offered people the option to share anonymously. When we have names and permission, we use them.

We call this 'learning service.'
Daniela and her team first coined and defined the term 'learning service' to redefine their work at PEPY Tours. When we conducted research, we found an important prior reference to the term, with a different focus than ours: In a 2006 article, Boyle-Baise *et al* used the term but focused their definition of learning service on teaching civic engagement at the university level. That is an important concept, but different from the way we use learning service in this book. "Learning Service or Service Learning: Enabling the Civic" Marilynne Boyle-Baise et al, *International Journal of Teaching and Learning in Higher Education*, 2006, Vol. 18, No. 1, 17-26.

Chapter 1

She told me the volunteers always gossiped
World Travel Guide, 'Does Voluntourism do More Harm than Good?' 30 March 2016. www.worldtravelguide.net/features/feature/does-voluntourism-do-more-harm-than-good/.

People want to come and feel like they 'make a difference'
Erin Barnhardt, "Engaging Global Service: Organizational Motivations for and Perceived Benefits of Hosting International Volunteers," 2012.

Chapter 2

International volunteers have certain expectations
Erin Barnhardt, "Engaging Global Service: Organizational Motivations for and Perceived Benefits of Hosting International Volunteers," 2012

...has a positive impact on the world
Karl Moore, "Millennials Work For Purpose, Not Paycheck," *Forbes*, 2 Oct 2014, www.forbes.com/sites/karlmoore/2014/10/02/ millennials-work-for-purpose-not-paycheck/#3f493e485a22.
Adam Miller, "3 Things Millennials Want In a Career (Hint: It's not more money)," *Fortune*, 26 March 2015, fortune.com/2015/03/26/3-things-millennials-want-in-a-career-hint-its-not-more-money.
Ariel Schwartz, "Millennials Want to Work at Organizations that Focus on Purpose, Not Profit," 2 May 2015, www.fastcoexist.com/3041738/ change-generation/millennials-want-to-work-at-organizations-that-focus-on-purpose-not-just-p.

In a presentation recorded at Stanford University
Randy Komisar, "How Do You Find Your Passion and How Do You Pursue It?" *Stanford eCorner*, 28 April 2004, ecorner.stanford.edu/videos/1000/ How-Do-You-Find-Your-Passion-and-How-Do-You-Pursue-It.

Peter Buffet, son of the famous investor and philanthropist
Peter Buffet, "The Charitable Industrial Complex", *New York Times*, 26 July 2013, www.nytimes.com/2013/07/27/opinion/ the-charitable-industrial-complex.

Chapter 3

Not long before, angry crowds had hurled eggs
"Vice President Richard M. Nixon's Trip to South America, April 27 – May 15, 1958," *Foreign Relations of The United States, 1958-1960, American Republics, Volume V*, United States Government Printing Office, 1991, images.library.wisc.edu/FRUS/EFacs/1958-60v05/reference/frus. frus195860v05.i0010.pdf.

Once we used to send gunboats and diplomats
Quoted in Robert Phillipson, *Linguistic Imperialism*, Oxford University Press 1992.

Christopher Columbus, letter to King Ferdinand
Christopher Columbus, "Letter to King Ferdinand of Spain, Describing the Result of the First Voyage," 1493, xroads.virginia.edu/~hyper/hns/ garden/columbus.html.

The Taino population of Hispaniola
Robert M. Poole, "What Became of the Taíno?" *Smithsonian Magazine*, October 2011, www.smithsonianmag.com/people-places/ what-became-of-the-taino-73824867/#6TpWbAK3VICXDVsQ.99.

...his mixed legacy also included promoting immigration
David Orique, "Bartolome De Las Casa: a Brief Outline of His Life and Labor," www.lascasas.org/manissues.htm.

The latest posterity... will wonder
Quoted in Richard Drayton, *Nature's Government: Science, Imperial Britain, and the 'Improvement' of the World*, Yale University Press 2000.

...international volunteering can be traced to the Thomasites
"Education: Thomasite Troubles," Time. *Time Inc.*, 12 April 1937, content. time.com/time/magazine/article/0,9171,788034,00.html.

A Filipino uprising
LaFeber Walter, "Anti-Imperialism in the United States," *PBS*, PBS, www.pbs.org/wgbh/amex/1900/filmmore/reference/interview/ lafeber_antiimperialism.html.

...the US government was eager to put a positive spin
Francisco Luzviminda, "The First Vietnam: The U.S.-Philippine War of 1899," *The First Vietnam: The U.S.-Philippine War of 1899*, N.p., 1973, www.historyisaweapon.com/defcon1/franciscofirstvietnam.html.

Sending educators abroad also seemed like a good strategy
Roma-Sianturi Dinah, "Pedagogic Invasion: The Thomasites in Occupied Philippines," *Kritika Kultura*, Département of English at the Ateneo de Manila University, 2009, journals.ateneo.edu/ojs/kk/article/ download/1487/1512.

The Thomasite program lasted until the 1930s
"A Comparative Study of the Thomasites and the Oyatoi Gaikokujin: Foreign Teachers and Their Language Teaching," www.bit.ly/2JylCP8.

...the positive legacy of the Thomasites includes a high rate of literacy
"Education," *Country Studies*, U.S. Library of Congress, 1991, countrystudies.us/philippines/53.htm.

Smiley-face propaganda
Stanley Karnow, *In Our Image: America's Empire in the Philippines*, Ballantine Books, 3 March 1990.
Dinah Roma Sianturi, "Pedagogic Invasion: The Thomasites in Occupied Philippines," *Kritika Kultura*, 2009, journals.ateneo.edu/ojs/kk/article/ viewFile/1487/1512.

The Thomasites left their mark, not only on the Philippines
"To Preserve and to Learn," *Peace Corps Writers*, 2008, www. peacecorpswriters.org/pages/1999/9911/911pchist.html.

Pierre Ceresole and the other founders
"Nobody Lift Out!" Senior Volunteers Exchange Network, 5 April 2007,www.seven-network.eu/site/files/Nobody%20lift%20out!.pdf.

Because of the domestic upheavals of the 1950s and 1960s
Paul Rutherford, *Endless Propaganda: The Advertising of Public Goods* (pp.34-38), Toronto University Press, 3 May 2000.

The mission of the Peace Corps to "promote world peace and friendship"
www.peacecorps.gov/about.

...its programs fell short in recruiting highly skilled volunteers
P. David Searles, *The Peace Corps Experience: Challenge and Change* (pp.1-29), University Press of Kentucky, 1997.
Ryan Cooper, "Good News First, Bad News Never," *Washington Monthly*, March/April 2012, washingtonmonthly.com/magazine/marchapril-2012/good-news-first-bad-news-never.
Stanley Meisler, *When the World Calls: The Inside Story of The Peace Corps and its First Fifty Years*, Beacon Press, 22 February 2011.

In the UK at around the same time, Voluntary Service Overseas (VSO) was founded
Sarah Bell, "The first VSO volunteer," *BBC News*, 15 May 2008, news.bbc.co.uk/2/hi/uk_news/magazine/7401326.stm.
"Our History," VSO International, www.vsointernational.org/about-us/our-history.

...a powerful speech in 1968 to a group of young US volunteers
Ivan Illich, "To Hell With Good Intentions," 20 April 1968, www.swaraj.org/shikshantar/illich_hell.htm.

A Norman Rockwell painting of Peace Corps volunteers
"Peace Corps Ethiopia and Norman Rockwell," *Peace Corps Worldwide*, October 2009, peacecorpsworldwide.org/peace-corps-ethiopia.

Expanding volunteer programs in Central America during the Contra war
Reed Karaim, "Peace Corps Challenges", 11 January 2013, *CQ Researcher*, www.library.cqpress.com/cqresearcher/document.php?id=cqresrre2013011100.

A recent study found that nearly half of those ... who volunteer abroad do so for two weeks
Benjamin L. Lough, "A Decade of International Volunteering from the United States, 2004 to 2014," Center for Social Development, George Warren Brown School of Social Work, March 2015.

Researcher Jason Hickel found
Jason Hickel, "The Real Experience Industry: Student Development Project and the Depoliticization of Poverty," *Learning and Teaching: The International Journal of Higher Education in the Social Sciences*, 11 March 2013.

A survey of 240 companies
Michael Stroik, "Giving in Numbers," *Committee Encouraging Corporate Philanthropy*, 2013.

In Bhutan, the government rejected Gross National Product
Raymond Zhong, "In Bhutan, Gross National Happiness trumps Gross National Product," *The Wall Street Journal*, 16 December 2015, www.wsj.com/articles/in-bhutan-gross-national-happiness-trumps-gross-national-product-1450318359.

The tool looks at fifty-four indicators
Social Progress Imperative, www.socialprogressimperative.org.

The World Bank estimates that 58 percent of the population lives on less than $3.10 a day
"Poverty headcount ratio at $3.10 a day (2011 PPP) (% of population)," The World Bank, data.worldbank.org/indicator/SI.POV.2DAY.

Poverty has a deep existential impact
Duncan Green, *From Poverty to Power: How Active Citizens and Effective States Can Change the World* (pp.7), Oxfam Publishing, 11 July 2008.

Shifting the balance can also mean working with advocacy networks
Global Justice Now, www.globaljustice.org.uk; Survival International, www.survivalinternational.org; LICADHO, www.licadho-cambodia.org.

Chapter 4

And although they could have read...
"Briton on Child Sex Abuse Charge in Cambodia Orphanage," *BBC News*, 22 October 2010, www.bbc.com/news/uk-wales-11605876.

This work has a tendency to attract people...
Erin Barnhardt, "Engaging Global Service: Organizational Motivations for and Perceived Benefits of Hosting International Volunteer," Portland State University Dissertations, 2012.

Our staff do not have the time
Erin Barnhardt, "Engaging Global Service: Organizational Motivations for and Perceived Benefits of Hosting International Volunteer," Portland State University Dissertations, 2012.

One volunteer host said
Erin Barnhardt, "Engaging Global Service: Organizational Motivations for and Perceived Benefits of Hosting International Volunteer," Portland State University Dissertations, 2012.

However, when they are on a clinical placement abroad
S. J. J. Radstone, "Practising on the Poor? Healthcare Workers' Beliefs about the Role of Medical Students during Their Elective," *Journal of Medical Ethics*, The BMJ, 5 February 2004, jme.bmj.com/content/31/2/109.full.

Julian Sheather, Ethics Manager for the British Medical Association
Julian Sheather, "Electives: Laying the Ghosts of Empire?" British Medical Association Live and Learn Blog, 12 November 2012, www.bma.org.uk/news-views-analysis/live-and-learn/2012/november/electives-laying-the-ghosts-of-empire.

One volunteer host said...
Erin Barnhardt, "Engaging Global Service: Organizational Motivations for and Perceived Benefits of Hosting International Volunteer," Portland State University Dissertations, 2012.

By Elizabeth Becker, author of bestseller...
Elizabeth Becker, *Overbooked: The Exploding Business of Travel and Tourism*, Simon & Schuster, 16 April 2013.

Although data indicates that the majority of children
Anna Bawden, "Save the Children Claims Most 'Orphans' Have Living Parent," *The Guardian*, 23 November 2009, www.theguardian.com/society/2009/nov/24/save-the-children-orphans-report.

A large body of research shows that institutionalized care...
There are over 2000 articles on this topic here: www.bettercarenetwork.org/bcn-in-action/better-volunteering-better-care.

The reasons to avoid supporting orphanages
Corinna Csaky, "Keeping Children out of Harmful Institutions: Why We Should Be Investing in Family-Based Care," Save the Children, 2009, www.savethechildren.org.uk/sites/default/files/docs/Keeping_Children_Out_of_Harmful_Institutions_Final_20.11.09_1.pdf.

These problems don't just exist
"Ending the Institutionalization of Children: A Summary of Progress in Changing Systems of Care and Protection for Children in Moldova, the Czech Republic and Bulgaria," Lumos Foundation, 2014, www.wearelumos.org/sites/default/files/Ending%20Institutionalisation%20of%20Children.pdf.

This evidence includes recent exposures
Ireland's Historical Institutional Abuse Inquiry, www.hiainquiry.org.

Use of institutional care to promote cultural genocide
Final Report of the Truth and Reconciliation Commission of Canada, Truth and Reconciliation Commission of Canada, 2015.

In Nepal, reports estimate that around 85% of children
"Adopting the Rights of the Child," UNICEF and Terre des hommes Foundation, 2008, www.childtrafficking.com/Docs/adopting_rights_child_unicef29_08.pdf.

The UN Convention on the Rights of the Child enshrines
"Convention on the Rights of the Child," 2 September 1990, UN Human Rights Office, www.ohchr.org/Documents/ProfessionalInterest/crc.pdf.

This increase occurred despite the number...
"With the Best Intentions... A Study of Attitudes towards Residential Care in Cambodia," UNICEF, 2011, www.unicef.org/eapro/Study_Attitudes_towards_RC.pdf.

Rebecca Smith, an advisor with Save the Children
Rebecca Smith, "Why We Don't Support Orphanage Volunteering," May 24, 2016, www.blogs.savethechildren.org.uk/2016/05/why-we-dont-support-orphanage-volunteering.

Extensive research from around the world
Kristen Cheney & Karen Smith Rotabi, "Addicted to Orphans: How the Global Orphan Industrial Complex Jeopardizes Local

Child Protection Systems," 9 December 2015, link.springer.com/referenceworkentry/10.1007%2F978-981-4585-98-9_3-1.

The advocacy group *Better Volunteering Better Care*
See the large collection of articles and research papers from countries all over the world on the Better Volunteering Better Care website. www.bettercarenetwork.org/bcn-in-action/key-initiatives/better-volunteering-better-care/research-and-articles.

In an article discussing the phenomenon of for-profit orphanages
Jennifer Morgan, "For Profit Orphanages Keep Haitian Families Apart," *Huffington Post*, 21 March 2011, www.huffingtonpost.com/jennifer-morgan/forprofit-orphanages-keep_b_838206.html.

Philip Holmes, the former CEO
Neesha Bremner, "Fake Orphanages Profit from Western Volunteers," *New Matilda*, 3 March 2014 newmatilda.com/2014/03/03/fake-orphanages-profit-western-volunteers.

This negative impact was recognized in a seminal study
James Bowlby, "Maternal Care and Mental Health," Bulletin of the World Health Organization, March 1951.

More recent research has consistently confirmed
Kevin Browne, "The Risk of Harm to Young Children in Institutional Care," Save the Children, 2009, www.savethechildren.org.uk/sites/default/files/docs/The_Risk_of_Harm_1.pdf.

Children who grow up without stable primary caregivers
European Commission Daphne Programme Directorate-General Justice and Home Affairs et al, De-Institutionalizing and Transforming Children's Services – A Guide to Good Practice, University of Birmingham Press, July 2007, www.crin.org/en/docs/Deinstitutionaliation_Manual_-_Daphne_Prog_et_al.pdf.

Kirjit, a youth from Nepal
Martin Punaks and Katie Feit, "The Paradox of Orphanage Volunteering," 2014, www.nextgenerationnepal.org/File/The-Paradox-of-Orphanage-Volunteering.pdf. For another perspective from a careleaver, see www.rethinkorphanages.org/growingupinanorphanage.

There are cases of children being abused
"Adopting the Rights of the Child," UNICEF and Terre des hommes Foundation, 2008, www.childtrafficking.com/Docs/adopting_rights_child_unicef29_08.pdf.

By Julie Rausenberger, author of Please Mind the Gap!
Julie Rausenberger, "Please Mind the Gap!" www.bit.ly/2KnMWAT.

"Arriving in the slums of Nairobi..."
Leila Chambers, "Voluntourism: We Have to Stop Making This about Your Niece," Huffington Post, 16 July 2012, www.huffingtonpost.com/leila-de-bruyne/volunteer-africa-program_b_1676091.html.

Organizations overseas that receive and host volunteers
Erin Barnhardt, "Engaging Global Service: Organizational Motivations for and Perceived Benefits of Hosting International Volunteer," Portland State University Dissertations, 2012.

When choosing a placement, volunteers usually
Victoria Louise Smith & Xavier Font, "Volunteer Tourism, Greenwashing and Understanding Responsible Marketing Using Market Signally Theory," 2014, *Journal of Sustainable Tourism*, 22:6, 942-963.

"My philosophy is that everything is more complicated…"
Kwame Anthony Appiah, *Experiments in Ethics*, Harvard University Press, 30 March 2010. Cited in Richard Slimbach, "Balancing the Benefit: Strengthening the Community Good Through Education Abroad." Azusa Pacific University, December 2013.

Chapter 5

Erin Barnhardt's survey of 248 volunteer hosting organizations
Erin Barnhardt, "Engaging Global Service: Organizational Motivations for and Perceived Benefits of Hosting International Volunteers," 2012.

My NGO is based in a poor postwar area
Erin Barnhardt, "Engaging Global Service: Organizational Motivations for and Perceived Benefits of Hosting International Volunteers," 2012.

As much as this year might be advertised as a 'service-based' program
Quote provided by Where There Be Dragons, www.wheretherebedragons.com.

…an increase in diaspora … and South-South volunteering
Jenny Lei Revelo, "South-south volunteering: From one developing country to another," Devex, 12 September 2014, www.devex.com/news/south-south-volunteering-from-one-developing-country-to-another-84320.

Chapter 6

a trip specifically designed around learning outcomes
Each co-author has spent time working for organizations that offer educational travel programs, including PEPY Tours (pepytours.com); Food First (foodfirst.org); Global Exchange (www.globalexchange.org); Where There Be Dragons (www.wheretherebedragons.com).

There are programs that combine any number of learning goals
Daniela Papi, "Where should I study abroad?" *The Huffington Post*, 3 Nov 2014, www.huffingtonpost.com/daniela-papi/where-should-i-study-abro_b_6071594.html.

…circumnavigating the world on a boat
Semester at Sea, www.semesteratsea.org.

Chapter 7

research shows that children suffer disproportionately from the brutal effects of extreme poverty
"Nearly 385 million children living in extreme poverty, says joint World Bank Group – UNICEF study," The World Bank, 3 Oct 2016, www.worldbank.org/en/news/press-release/2016/10/03/nearly-385-million-children-living-extreme-poverty-joint-world-bank-group-unicef-study.

When a visiting medical team arrives
"The significant harm of worst practices," Unite for Sight, www.uniteforsight.org/global-health-course/module8.

the wonderful book, Where There Is No Doctor
David B. Werner, J. Maxwell, Carol L. Thuman, Jane Maxwell, "Where there is no doctor: A village health care handbook," The Hesperian Foundation, May 2013.

World Wide Opportunities on Organic Farms
World Wide Opportunities on Organic Farms, www.wwoof.net.

deeply troubling instances of unwitting volunteers helping to hand rear wild animals
Oliver Smith, "Blood Lions warns against the dark side of African voluntourism," *The Telegraph*, 1 Dec 2015, www.telegraph.co.uk/travel/safaris-and-wildlife/Blood-Lions-warns-against-the-dark-side-of-African-voluntourism.

...tourist and volunteering destinations have been linked to the illegal trading of endangered animals
Sharon Guynup, "Exclusive: Tiger Temple accused of supplying black market," *National Geographic*, 21 Jan 2016, news.nationalgeographic.com/2016/01/160121-tiger-temple-thailand-trafficking-laos0.

...reports of teams of doctors that were unable to feed themselves
JoNel Aleccia, "Disaster do-gooders can actually hinder help," *NBC News*, 23 Jan 2010, www.nbcnews.com/id/34958965/ns/world_news-haiti/t/disaster-do-gooders-can-actually-hinder-help/#.VTwkwJMQjm4.

causing some humanitarian groups to dub them "the second disaster."
Pam Fessler, "The 'second disaster': Making well-intentioned donations useful," *NPR*, 12 Jan 2013, www.npr.org/2013/01/12/169198037/the-second-disaster-making-good-intentions-useful.

there were also far too many voluntourists
Jessica Alexander, "Don't go to Nepal to help. Stay home and send money instead," *Slate*, 27 April 2015, www.slate.com/articles/news_and_politics/foreigners/2015/04/how_to_help_nepal_s_survivors_stay_home_and_send_money_to_aid_organizations.html?wpsrc=sh_all_dt_fb_top.

Chapter 8

Initially volunteers didn't have to pay anything
Erin Barnhardt, "Engaging Global Service: Organizational Motivations for and Perceived Benefits of Hosting International Volunteers," 2012.

Chapter 9

Institute for Cooperation and Development (IICD)
IICD's website still exists, but it has recently changed its name to One World Center.

a long history of allegations of economic misdeeds and cultural insensitivity
There are many exposés of this ring of organizations:
Anna Meisel, Simon Cox "Teachers Group: The cult-like group linked to a charity that gets UK aid" *BBC News*, 2 Aug 2016. www.bbc.com/news/magazine-36940384.
Tisha Thompson, Matt Smith, Amy Walters, Rick Yarborough, Steve Jones, Jeff Piper, "Behind the bins: What did Planet Aid do with your taxpayer dollars?" *NBC Washington*, 23 May 2016, www.nbcwashington.com/investigations/Behind-the-Bins-What-Did-Planet-Aid-Do-With-Your-Taxpayer-Dollars-380333921.
Matt Smith, Amy Walters, Kandani Ngwira, "US taxpayers are financing alleged cult through African aid charities," *Reveal News*, 23 May 2016, www.revealnews.org/article/us-taxpayers-are-financing-alleged-cult-through-african-aid-charities.
Matt Smith, Amy Walters, "Planet Aid's ubiquitous clothing donation boxes aren't so charitable", 23 May 2016, www.revealnews.org/article/planet-aids-ubiquitous-clothing-donation-boxes-arent-so-charitable.
This website links all these charities together: www.tvindalert.com/the-ten-charities.

…volunteer companies that have a vested interest in their own opportunities appearing first
Sebastian Drobner, "IVHQ Reviews: The voluntourism industry & its connections to review websites," Responsible Volunteering, 1 Sept 2016, www.responsible-volunteering.com/2016/09/connections-review-websites-ivhq-reviews.

One study of volunteer travel marketing explored volunteers' reactions
Victoria Smith and Xavier Font, "Volunteer tourism, greenwashing and understanding responsible marketing using market signaling theory," *Journal of Sustainable Tourism*, 14 Jan 2014.

Kibera needs land/tenancy rights
"Kiberia Facts & Information," www.kibera.org.uk/facts-info.

Due to lack of support and education around disability awareness in Kenya
"Volunteer in Kenya," International Volunteer HQ, www.volunteerhq.org/volunteer-in-kenya.

[The children's home] has approximately 10 children
"Childcare Volunteer," Volunteer Basecamp, www.volunteerbasecamp.
com/Volunteer-Abroad-Placements/Orphanage-Childcare-
Volunteer/Nepal/Om-Disable-Child-Care-Home/Kathmandu/797.

Such imagery often relies on a simplistic view of poverty
Videos such as "Let's Save Africa!—Gone Wrong," and "Radi-Aid—Africa
for Norway," satirize this kind of approach.

The highlight of the trip is certainly the smiles of families
Real Gap Experience, www.realgap.co.uk.

**Whether you're interested in developing resources in one of the most
deprived areas of Thailand**
"Building Projects," Real Gap Experience, www.realgap.co.uk/
building-projects.

We were in an area where nobody needed us
Why a Bad Travel Experience Isn't the End, rachelrtw.wordpress.
com/2012/05/09/what-i-learnt-in-nepal-why-a-bad-travel-
experience-isnt-the-end/, now password protected.

As a volunteer in Nepal, you can ride on the backs of elephants
"Volunteer in Nepal —It Will Change You Forever..." Helping Abroad, www.
helpingabroad.org/volunteer-in-nepal.

When can I start? Whenever you want to
"FAQs on Volunteering, Interning or Studying Overseas," Travellers
Worldwide, www.travellersworldwide.com/peripherals/faqs.

Compile a list of questions
A full list of suggested questions are found on the Learning Service
website: www.learningservice.info.

Chapter 10

"You are responsible for the energy you bring into a space."
"Jill Bolte Taylor's Stroke of Insight," Oprah.com, www.oprah.com/
oprahs-lifeclass/jill-bolte-taylors-stroke-of-insight-video.

...a list of qualities he wanted to embody
"Thirteen Virtues," www.thirteenvirtues.com.

A more recent example can be seen in the work of Bill Drayton
"How can we teach the world empathy? Bill Drayton says he knows
how," Ashoka.org, 26 April 2013, www.ashoka.org/en/node/4274.

Writer Brené Brown speaks about empathy through her work as a coach
"The Power of Vulnerability—Brené Brown," The RSA, 15 Aug 2013, www.
youtube.com/watch?v=sXSjc-pbXk4.

In the book Lean In, Sheryl Sandberg...
Sheryl Sandberg, *Lean In: Women, Work and the Will to Lead*, Knopf
Doubleday Publishing Group, 2013.

Chapter 11

the stereotype of the international volunteer
Matt Lacey, "Gap Yah," VM Productions and The Unexpected Items, 24 Feb 2010, www.youtube.com/watch?v=eKFjWR7X5dU.

A number of programs and volunteer-matching portals
"International Citizen Service," www.volunteerics.org.

There are also funds and foundations
Go Overseas Volunteer Abroad Scholarship: www.gooverseas.com
The LIVFund Scholarship: www.livfund.org
The Samuel Huntington Public Service Award: www9.nationalgridus.com/huntington.asp.
Allianz Global Assistance ScholarTrips: www.scholartrips.org.
Explore the World Travel Scholarships: www.hiusa.org/programs/travel-scholarships/explore-the-world.

you can apply to a fully-funded skilled volunteering program
Peace Corps: www.peacecorps.gov.
Voluntary Service Overseas: www.vsointernational.org.
Australian Volunteers International: www.avi.org.au.

Chapter 12

"When in doubt, leave it out."
Quoted in Joseph Collins, Stefano DeZerega, Zahara Heckscher, *How to Live Your Dream of Volunteering Overseas*, 2002, New York: Penguin Books.

One excellent tip from Global Exchange...
Quoted in Joseph Collins, Stefano DeZerega, Zahara Heckscher, *How to Live Your Dream of Volunteering Overseas*, 2002, New York: Penguin.

Chapter 13

In his famous speech in 1968 ... Ivan Illich
Ivan Illich, "To Hell With Good Intentions," 20 April 1968, www.swaraj.org/shikshantar/illich_hell.htm.

In the words of a host organization in Tanzania
"The Impact of International Volunteering on Host Organizations: A Summary of Research Conducted in India and Tanzania," Comhlámh and FRONTERA, September 2013, comhlamh.org/wp-content/uploads/2013/09/Impact-of-International-Volunteering-on-Host-Organisations.pdf

Chapter 14

When we had women volunteers
Erin Barnhardt, "Engaging Global Service: Organizational Motivations for and Perceived Benefits of Hosting International Volunteers," 2012.

The fact that our volunteers have been multicultural
Erin Barnhardt, "Engaging Global Service: Organizational Motivations for and Perceived Benefits of Hosting International Volunteers," 2012.

Some historians track this back to rice farming
T.M. Luhrmann, "Wheat People vs. Rice People: Why Are Some Cultures More Individualistic Than Others?" *The New York Times*, 3 December 2014, www.nytimes.com/2014/12/04/opinion/why-are-some-cultures-more-individualistic-than-others.html?_r=1.
David Robson, "How East and West Think in Profoundly Different Ways" *BBC*, 14 January 2017, www.bbc.com/future/story/20170118-how-east-and-west-think-in-profoundly-different-ways.

Emily Braucher, a cross-cultural communication trainer
ReFresh Communications, www.refreshcommunication.com.

It is important for (typically) financially privileged
Erin Barnhardt, "Engaging Global Service: Organizational Motivations for and Perceived Benefits of Hosting International Volunteers," 2012.

like in the movie Slumdog Millionaire
"Slumdog Millionaire," Fox Searchlight Pictures, 2008.

Chapter 15

The 53rd Week
The 53rd Week, www.53rdweek.org.

Blogger Rachel said in her popular blog, Why a Bad Travel Experience Isn't the End
This blog isn't available online anymore, but is described here: haroldgoodwin.info/rachels-volunteering-experience-in-nepal-was-bad-very-bad.

I'm having a little bit of trouble dealing with the wealth
Quote provided by Where There Be Dragons, www.wheretherebedragons.com.

Chapter 16

ReFresh Communications
ReFresh Communications, www.refreshcommunication.com.

It seems to be a common theme that all of us are having trouble
Quote provided by Where There Be Dragons, www.wheretherebedragons.com.

Chapter 17

a growing range of plugins and apps to research and compare brands
"Behind the Brands: Food Justice and the 'Big 10' Food and Beverage Companies," Oxfam, 26 Feb 2013, www.behindthebrands.org/en//~/media/Download-files/bp166-behind-brands-260213-en
"9 Ethical Shopping Apps & Plug-Ins," *Ethica*, 10 Sept 2012, www.shopethica.com/features/ethical-shopping-apps.

a farmers' association that delivers vegetable boxes to your door
Community Farm Alliance: cfaky.org.
Farm Fresh To You: www.farmfreshtoyou.com.
Farmbox Direct: www.farmboxdirect.com.
Rustic Roots: rusticrootsdelivery.com.

Other companies proudly enforce much higher ethical standards
Good Guide: Goodguide.com.
The Good Shopping Guide: www.thegoodshoppingguide.com.
Project Just: projectjust.com.
The Good Trade: thegoodtrade.com.

The anti-apartheid movement in the US and Canada accomplished much more
Quoted in Joseph Collins, Stefano DeZerega, Zahara Heckscher, *How to Live Your Dream of Volunteering Overseas*, 2002, New York: Penguin.

The words of Jason Hickel
Jason Hickel, "The Real Experience Industry: Student Development Project and the Depoliticization of Poverty," *Learning and Teaching: The International Journal of Higher Education in the Social Sciences*, 11 March 2013.

Move Your Money
Move Your Money Project, moveyourmoneyproject.org.

online platforms that connect skilled volunteers
Skills for Change: skillsforchange.com.
UN Volunteers: www.onlinevolunteering.org/en.

In her report Tackling Heropreneurship, Daniela...
Daniela Papi-Thornton, "Tackling Heropreneurship," 2016, tacklingheropreneurship.com.

LEARN MORE

Your learning service doesn't end here! Visit our website for more information:

www.learningservice.info

There, you'll find videos, toolkits, an online library, and other useful resources for anyone considering, undertaking, or returning from volunteer travel—or for educators who want to help students critically consider their overseas travel options.

You can also drop us an email using the site's contact page. We would love to hear from you, arrange to speak at your upcoming event, or hear your feedback on the book.

ACKNOWLEDGMENTS

This book has been a long time in the making. Through the inevitable ups and downs of the journey we have been supported, encouraged, and sometimes dragged kicking and screaming by an array of remarkable people.

First, we wish to thank the contributors to this book—the volunteers, local hosts, students and travel experts who have offered their voices throughout these pages. Even those not directly quoted here have influenced our ideas. Without these voices, there would be no book.

Thank you to our invaluable editors, Andrew Loveland, Alice Robinson and Richard Foot. They all put in countless hours of work to critique and shape the words on these pages. We are indebted to Erin Barnhardt who gave us full access to her doctoral research with volunteer hosts, thereby immeasurably enriching this book. Gratitude also goes to Stefano DeZerega, co-author of Joe and Zahara's previous book on volunteering abroad. Countless others reviewed sections of the manuscript and gave valued encouragement and critical feedback. Thank you.

Dozens of interns in the US, Cambodia and elsewhere helped with research and editing. With Zahara's passing we cannot be sure of the names of everyone we worked with, so please forgive us for not mentioning you individually. You know who you are and how much you have contributed, and we are deeply grateful. We also extend our heartfelt appreciation to the Learning Service Ambassadors—a team of young people helping us spread the concepts of this book across the globe.

Many of our friends and future readers expressed faith in our mission by offering financial support. Special recognition goes to Suzanne LaFetra whose family's foundation provided us with two all-important grants. Over a hundred people supported our initial crowdfunding campaign, many of them pre-purchasing a book that was yet to be written. There are some supporters we promised to give a special shout out to, they are: Denise Marika,

Maggie Durant, Clark Durant, Thomas Holdo Hansen, Adam Vaught, Adrian Chiew, David Schneider, Daniela Kon, Adam Edwards, Rakesh Mehta, Christine Becksted and Ellen Roberts.

We would like to thank Katherine Knotts and the entire team at Red Press for turning our manuscript into a book. Thanks also to our agent Annie Bomke for believing in us.

Finally, we thank our families and friends. Through their love, forgiveness and encouragement we found the energy to keep this book going whenever other things got in the way. Zahara specifically requested that our book offer gratitude to the people who started her journey into learning service: the Mendoza Family from Colonia Ruben Jaramillo in Morelos, Mexico, especially her adopted mother, Nicolasa Arellano Mendoza.

We close by honoring again the person to whom this book is dedicated: Zahara, who believed in this book from the beginning and who was so eager to get this into the hands of those who could benefit from it. Thank you.

ABOUT THE AUTHORS

Claire Bennett

Claire first volunteered overseas as a teenager in Nepal, where she now lives. Driven by an insatiable desire to change the world, she helped to found a rural development organization, PHASE. Confronted with the complexities of the aid world but determined not to become jaded, she shifted her focus towards what she believes to be the root causes of global injustice: the lack of awareness about development issues in the world. She was the UK coordinator of youth organization Development in Action, supported young people to take action on global issues with Global Youth Action, and coordinated a DFID strategy to embed a global dimension in classroom education. After volunteering with VSO in Cambodia, where she met Daniela, Claire now owns a training company in Nepal, works for US-based global citizenship education company Where There Be Dragons, and freelances as a development education consultant.

Joseph Collins

Joe's teenage experiences volunteering in Latin America and the Philippines led to a lifetime of learning, writing, and lecturing about the impact of US policies on the lives of the world's impoverished majority. He is co-founder of the Institute for Food and Development Policy (Food First); a Guggenheim Fellow recognized for his work on issues of inequitable development; and a Distinguished Visiting Lecturer at the University of California Santa Cruz. His books include *Food First; World Hunger: 10 Myths; Chile's Free-Market Miracle: A Second Look; No Free Lunch; Philippines: Fire on the Rim*; and *Aid as Obstacle*. Collins has been a consultant in Africa, Asia and Latin America to UN and international non-governmental organizations. He lives and surfs in Santa Cruz, California.

Zahara Heckscher

Zahara lived a life dedicated to social justice, tirelessly campaigning on a wide range of social issues from ending apartheid in South Africa to ensuring cancer patients in the US have access to life-saving medicines. Her career as a writer and social justice organizer was grounded in her work overseas: volunteering to plant fruit trees in rural Zambia and helping to build a medical clinic in Nicaragua. With Joe, she was a co-author of *How to Live Your Dream of Volunteering Overseas* and she was a contributing editor and regular columnist at Transitions Abroad. Her articles have been published in *Community Jobs* magazine and in the book *Global Backlash: Citizen Initiatives for a Just World Economy*. She had an MA in International Development from American University. After nearly a decade of battling with cancer, Zahara passed away as this book was being readied for publication. She has left many legacies to this world that will continue to have an impact for generations; we hope this book will be one of them.

Daniela Papi-Thornton

Daniela's interest in volunteer travel began with her work in Cambodia as the founder of PEPY Tours (an education travel company) and PEPY (a youth leadership organization). During her six years in Cambodia, Daniela shifted PEPY's work away from a focus on service to a focus on development education. She became an international advocate for a learning-first approach to service, and became active in the anti-orphanage tourism movement. She went on to do her MBA at Oxford's Said Business School through the Skoll Scholarship and subsequently began working for the Skoll Center for Social Entrepreneurship. As the Deputy Director of the Center, Daniela designed new leadership programming for students interested in social impact careers and created educational curricula on systems-led approaches to social change. Her report and accompanying SSIR article, *Tackling Heropreneurship*, have been widely read, and her Impact Gaps Canvas — a tool to help people consider the systems in which they work — is used in many universities around the world. Daniela now lives in sunny Boulder, Colorado with her husband and young son.